[

2

THE VARNISHED UNTRUTH

What would happen if one woman told the truth about her life? The world would split open.

Muriel Rukeyser, American poet

THE VARNISHED UNTRUTH

MY STORY

Pamela Stephenson

**SIMON &
SCHUSTER**

London · New York · Sydney · Toronto · New Delhi

A CBS COMPANY

First published in Great Britain by Simon & Schuster UK Ltd, 2012
A CBS COMPANY

Simon & Schuster UK Ltd
1st Floor
222 Gray's Inn Road
London
WC1X 8HB

www.simonandschuster.co.uk

Simon & Schuster Australia, Sydney
Simon & Schuster India, New Delhi

A CIP catalogue record for this book is available from the British Library

HB ISBN: 978-1-84983-921-1
TPB ISBN: 978-1-84983-922-8

Typeset by Hewer Text UK Ltd, Edinburgh
Printed and bound in Great Britain by CPI Group (UK) Ltd, Croydon, CR0 4YY

For Sharon

CONTENTS

INTRODUCTION

I don't really know how anyone can have the gall to write a memoir. To do so implies an assumption that people will be interested to read it and, right from the start, doesn't that single fact make you a prize ass? Isn't there always a dirty little secret lurking at the back of the writer's mind, an agenda along the lines of: 'When you're finished this, you're gonna love me. You're gonna laugh with me, cry with me, get to know me, and then you're going to buy one for everyone in your family for Christmas and you'll write inside "Hope she inspires you too! XXX"'? Now, I know being this honest doesn't make me loveable, and that being loveable sells memoirs, but I really can't lie about where I am on the endearment scale: I'm not simply 'a lovely person', 'purely a delight to know' or any of that B.S. I definitely have an edgy side, and I can't even fake it for fifteen minutes; sooner rather than later I'm going to say something a bit raw, mention the unmentionable, or be betrayed by my wicked laugh.

And, anyway, I'm always suspicious whenever I hear someone being described as 'a lovely person' – especially when they're in show business. I always think, 'How clever, to have been able to present "graciousness" so consistently . . . What a sneaky, undesirable talent!' Yes, I don't like a person's apparent 'loveliness', and I certainly don't trust it. I much prefer the dark side. When a chink appears and out flies a second or two of sheer brutality, meanness, envy, savagery or fury, that's when I smile inwardly and think, 'Now I can like you; I know a bit about who you really are.'

We're all multi-faceted. I like to think I can truly accept whatever a person despises in himself. It's usually the thing that makes us close – the core of intimacy. My acceptance of someone's 'dark side' is also something that helps me in my work as a psychologist; I try hard to avoid being judgmental of anyone for anything they might have done. We're all just frail human animals and, given the right circumstances, we might all make similar choices. Being capable of a 'warts and all' relationship has meant that I have had some pretty interesting encounters with all sorts of extraordinary people. Some of those encounters have imbued me with inspiration, some have made me gasp with envy. Others have left me feeling uplifted, thrilled, protective, sad, mortified, furious, conspiratorial, confused, and even downright terrified – and that's just outside my therapy office.

Along with my own personal story, I'm going to write down a few things about people who have touched me one way or another – things that may amuse you (or even take you down some other emotional path) – and I'll let you in on a few so-far-unrevealed aspects of my life. I'll try to leave out the boring bits. And I'm going to name-drop a lot because you want me to. Oh, don't start . . . you DO SO!

But don't be thinking this is easy for me. I'm darn good at getting under other people's skin, but opening up about my own life is quite a different matter. And since I truly hate to be misunderstood, how am I going to communicate the gestalt of who I am? People who have come to public attention are portrayed in fragments, and I would be quite afraid to discover which particular aspect of me you had already gleaned. Was it 'the woman in the American Express sketch'? Or 'Billy Connolly's missus'? Or simply 'wacky, zany Pam'? Being reduced to a three-word phrase turns one into a one-dimensional being and the impression that's created is very hard to shift. So how shall I portray myself? There are choices, you know. Wife, mother, psychologist, writer, comedian, actor, dancer, diver, gypsy, dreamer, rich girl, poor girl, beggar girl, thief . . . I am all of those and more. Tell you what, YOU decide. You decide exactly what I am.

American poet Muriel Rukeyser once mused, 'What would happen if one woman told the truth about her life? The world would split apart.' No one's personal story is ever the whole truth. One's history is reflected through the filter of years of self-forgiveness – and necessarily so. It's just too painful to carry the rawness of all one's faults and mistakes from decade to decade. But self-forgiveness can be elusive; I still wince when I think of stupid, unkind or embarrass-ing things I've done many years ago, last year, and even yesterday. The most terrifying thing is, I'm still capable of being a complete idiot. Some people think psychologists are wise beings who never put a foot wrong themselves but, in reality, even the best of us can be wonderfully helpful to others yet, occasionally, utterly imprudent in our own lives. Or maybe that's just me . . .

It may be partly due to my sense of shame about certain things that I've chosen to write this book in a similar manner to the way I get to know someone. When I meet you, I might say something rather bold to get your attention and make you think I'm that confi-dent, articulate, slightly outrageous person from the telly, but if you hang around for a bit you'll see me pulling back and getting quieter and more reserved. I'll put the focus on you instead, draw you out. Eventually it might dawn on you that I'm really rather shy, fairly quiet and extremely private about my life. If I trust you enough to meet you again I might be chattier, but I'll choose subjects you probably already know a bit about – my husband, *Strictly Come Dancing*, *Not The Nine O'Clock News*, books I've written. As we get to know each other more, I might begin to reveal more in stages, natter about my family, perhaps, but always being quite wary – and I'll watch carefully for any small sign that you can't be trusted (and if I see one, I'll snap shut like a spring-box). But if you can tolerate my prickliness, you may eventually get to know who I really am, and then – if I feel you accept me, warts and all – you'll be my friend for life.

I suppose I'm a bit of an anomaly. Human beings go through different stages and at my current age I should probably be taking it easy and reflecting on the past. To a certain extent I can manage the latter, but there's no way I'm ever going to settle gently and gracefully into my final decades. You're about to learn just how vigorously I'm railing against natural physical decline but, actually, I'm ambivalent about the challenge of facing the years ahead. In many ways, growing old gives us licence to be who we really are and, in the past, I suppose I have often felt I needed to hide parts of myself for fear of not being accepted, or in order to try to impress. But there's just no point in pretending any more. And there have been many instances when I've been presented to the world by others, in whatever way they saw me – even times when I had to live meekly with blatant untruths – and that has left me with a magnitude of shame that I would like to assuage. I have also lived through other people from time to time and, although this often goes with the territory of being a wife and mother, it's not necessarily something I intend doing forever. Yes, I wrote my husband's biography and a follow-up book about him, which took the best part of two years of my life, but it's high time I told my own story. Discovering who I really am now – and being unafraid to let it be known – is a daunting but delicious task.

The one thing I know about myself for sure is that I am

ridiculous. My husband and children know it, and you will, too. I think I am also passionate and brave (judge for yourself), although apparent fearlessness usually hides deep-seated, abject terror. I'm also a compulsive caretaker, and I'm not proud of that because it's unhealthy (I've been working on it for twenty years but it's still well entrenched). I am hopelessly optimistic, yet, paradoxically, way too serious about certain things, and I have a very low threshold of boredom. So adrenaline is my drug of choice – which leads me to seek adventure wherever I can find it, whether that's diving with tiger sharks, sailing round the world, or hanging out with people who dance with crocodiles (yes, really). No, I'm not your usual bearer of a bus pass – you may even think I've lost a few marbles here and there. If so, I thank you for the compliment. I've been flirting with crazy my whole life; one day I might just achieve it.

Chapter One

VICODIN, VALIUM AND VEUVE CLICQUOT

Just before last Christmas, I broke a tit. It's not the same as breaking a fingernail (if only it were that simple). Far from a quick trip to the manicurist, reparation involves surgery, cash and some hard-core narcotics. The tragedy occurred in a jive club near Madison Square Garden in New York. I love swing – one of my favourite dance styles (I've continued to enjoy social dancing since doing *Strictly Come Dancing*). Anyway, my wonderfully optimistic partner led me into a crazy lift – the 'Death Drop'. This involved me being swung in between his legs, suddenly plummeting towards the floor face down with my arms crossed, then being revolved 180 degrees to face upwards, before leaping back on to my feet. I slightly miscalculated the first part of the action (my fault entirely) and my right breast hit the deck at speed. I felt no pain and was unaware of the deflation until the next morning when I looked in the mirror and realized I had one melon and one fried egg.

Terrible timing, really, because if you're going to turn up at holiday parties wearing low-cut dresses, a minimum of two proud mounds is required. I love showing off my breasts (oh, shut up! They are mine – I bought them!). Could I make it through the holiday season in such a state? Probably not. Now, mine had been water-filled so, thankfully, I didn't have to worry about silicone leakage but, even so, this was an aesthetic emergency. Since this is a memoir, i.e. about memories, and getting a flat tyre is currently one of my most striking, recent memories, I'll tell you what I did about it.

See, this chapter is really still part of my introduction. I'm being deliberately provocative as a distraction – for myself, as well as for you – because I'm really nervous about telling you certain more serious things about me. There are things in my past that still produce strong feelings in the wee small hours, and I'll get to them soon but, for now, I'm just going to be a bit of a loose cannon and talk about my breasts. Believe me, body modification is the easy stuff. You'll find out some seriously dodgy things about me but I do think you ought to know right away that one of the ugliest things about me is my refusal to age gracefully. I'm as vain as vain can be and would totally sell my soul to the devil to be a babe forever. Thank God for Botox, lipo and the surgeon's knife. However, I must point out that this is not just all about pleasing myself or getting wolf whistles. Since I inflict my image on others via TV and other media, I'm actually being thoughtful. Be grateful, people; I tweak myself cosmetically as a public service.

So now I've opened my big mouth about having had surgery (as if you hadn't already noticed!), I might as well tell you about the latest: I needed re-inflation, but finding the right nip'n'tuck merchant wasn't easy. The surgeon who worked on me in the past has now retired, so Dr Bev Hills was my knight in shining armour – and also my harshest critic. 'Well, I can perk up that right puppy but, in any case, you're about due for a bit more tweaking, aren't you? And you lost weight too quickly on that dance programme – your skin's sagging. Shall we take care of everything at once?' Now, to put this in perspective, I was fairly fresh from the *Strictly* tour, during which I was expected to share a dressing room with the unbelievably gorgeous pro dancers. Ola Jordan, for example, the adorable siren married to my temporary dance paramour, James. And Kristina, the Russian diva, and that lanky Aussie bombshell whose name I've forgotten . . . oh, that's right, Natalie. Sensational! Of course, they're all half my age, but in my mind that doesn't count. Why can't I just give myself a free pass to accept that a teensy bit of gravity-induced sagging is hardly a crime? Anyway, those goddesses thrust their perfect, naked bodies into my line of vision for hours on end, and it was excruciatingly humiliating to have to sneak into a corner to try to change without displaying my own fleshly inferiority. Thankfully, salvation was at hand in the form of Dr Bev. He would give me back my bodily pride, my pertness, my youth. To hell with the risks. 'Do you take American Express?' I panted.

Please try not to judge me – although, at some level I do judge myself for such madness. And I certainly admire and envy the many self-confident women who've never bothered with any anti-ageing procedure beyond elegantly draping their bingo wings. Fortunately, in my younger days I avoided saying, 'I'll never resort to plastic surgery.' Youthful women sometimes make that mistake and, when those first saggy bits appear, they panic and have to backtrack. But, in my view, if a person really wants to stop the clock, she should give it her best shot. Mother Nature is a two-faced bitch, isn't she? So provided people fully understand why they're doing it – and what the risks are – I think they should redesign themselves in whatever way makes them happy. Well, unless that involves altering their bodies to resemble any kind of domestic pet.

Oh, I know I'm extremely lucky to have the means even to contemplate a major make over. And, if you catch yourself being a bit harsh about all this, please bear in mind that it's all very well to criticize a person for attempting to improve on nature, but taking radical steps in the beauty department is not without risks, pain and frustration.

On my first visit to Dr Bev's rooms I was granted only limited access. 'I had rather hoped I'd meet Dr Bev in person,' I complained to his office manager. Hayley pouted snootily at me from behind her cluttered desk, but I stood my ground. 'I mean, it would be normal to have a face-to-face discussion . . .' She cut me off. 'Dr Bev is very, very busy,' she said, 'and I'm not sure we could schedule you at all. But what are you interested in having done?' 'Generally improved gorgeousness,' I replied. I was promptly marched to a photography room where I suffered the humiliation of standing naked against a white glaring background while some nurses took pictures of every tiny 'imperfection' on my body and face. OK, I know, like beauty, 'imperfection' lies purely in the eyes of the beholder, but unfortunately my eyes can't stand some of the saggy, flabby aspects of ageing. 'Look,' I rationalized to myself, 'right now I'm really healthy and fit and, thanks to *Strictly*, my weight is low – good time to undergo a surgical procedure. Am I goting to wait another ten years? What's the point of looking good when you're drooling and incoherent?' 'But your husband, and anyone else close to your age, has become short-sighted anyway,' argued my Voice of Reason, 'so, surely, they'll overlook your wrinkles?' 'It's not them I'm worried about,' I replied. 'Have you SEEN yourself on HD? Mamma mia! And you regularly dance tango, lambada and salsa in close embrace with twenty-year-olds – those boys have twenty/twenty vision. They can spot a chin hair at twenty paces!' 'OK,' my Voice of Reason conceded. 'You win.'

When I finally met with Dr Bev – after a whole month of attempted scheduling – I was rather underwhelmed. 'Oh, no!' I said to myself. 'Is that a toupee?' Then I had to chastise myself for being judgmental about his attempts at self-beautification considering I was planning a far more permanent and comprehensive make over myself. He was very direct. 'When I look at you, what I notice most is your jowls and saggy neck. What I'd rather be drawn to is your eyes.' Excellent selling point. I showed him my tummy. 'Three large babies and rapid weight loss – wouldn't mind being able to dance in one of those dresses with the midriff missing, like Flavia Cacace . . .'

Dr Bev had clearly never heard of the tango goddess. 'OK,' he said curtly, 'but a tummy tuck is not an easy procedure. Look, sit down.' His large, hairy hands grabbed a couple of handfuls of saggy tummy skin and hung on firmly. 'Now try and stand up!' he ordered. I felt the searing pain as my skin was stretched like hide across a native drum. 'What you'd have to do for a good result with minimal scarring,' he explained, 'is stay hunched over for a full ten days after the operation. No standing upright or lying flat – you'll have to use a walker.' 'That's OK,' I nodded, thinking that at least I could sit and work on my computer – probably get a lot of writing done. Of course, I hadn't factored in the fact that I'd be shit-faced on Vicodin and nothing I'd write would make any sense, or that since I opted to have my double chin and under-eye bags removed at the same time, I'd also have to keep my head up towards the ceiling while seated. Kind of a racing driver position, which meant I could do nothing post-operatively but crouch beneath a wall-mounted TV, watching *Keeping Up with the Kardashians*. After that fortnight I was brain-dead. I was calling friends saying, 'I'm really worried about how Kourtney's treating Rob . . . doesn't she understand the fragility of the male ego?'

Dr Bev was definitely of a similar ilk to other top-notch surgeons I'd met – strong, opinionated and obsessive – exactly what you need in a plastic surgeon, and I'm not kidding. His narcissism wouldn't allow him to risk ruining his reputation with any mistakes, and his obsessive nature means he pays great attention to detail, but a bedside manner is something he entirely lacks. In fact, I suppose that's something that drew me to him – after all, wouldn't you rather place your trust in someone who doesn't feel the need to butter you up? With the queues of women and men at his door trying to get him to shape-shift them, I can assure you he doesn't need my business. And it's his scheduler Hayley's job to filter those he should accommodate and those he should avoid. 'He's truly the most wonderful doctor,' she gushed, with tears forming in her large cow eyes. 'He's doing my own face next month . . .' The second time I saw the elusive Dr Bev was on the morning of my surgery. Starving and dehydrated from my mandated colon cleansing the day before, I signed all the forms that relinquished him, the clinic, the President, God, and anyone connected with them, from any responsibility for screwing up. I've come to the conclusion that it's better not to read such documents – 'Could lead to severe complications including death' is not my preferred thought as I'm about to go under the knife. I was stripped of clothing, jewellery, dignity and dressed in paper booties, shower cap and an open-backed hospital gown with my arse peeking out. Nice look. And why, exactly? Was Dr Bev going to throw in a surprise butt lift? One could only hope.

A middle-aged nurse came into my waiting room to check my vitals and make sure I hadn't forgotten my name. 'Yeah, I'd love to have a tummy tuck myself,' she said, 'but I'm way too scared.' Now, if my best friend Sharon hadn't been with me I might have bolted after that, but luckily we caught each other's eye and had a good chuckle.

But when Dr Bev arrived, Sharon, who is normally warm and delightful, allowed her concern for my safety to turn her into a harridan. 'Do you know who she is? You better not make any mistakes . . .' Dr Bev was rightly incensed. 'I treat all my patients with exactly the same care,' he replied, getting very shirty with her. I sat there watching in horror as their dislike of each other escalated. 'OMG,' I said to her after he flounced out. 'That man is just about to mess around with my innards and you've thoroughly pissed him off! In a couple of hours I'll look like Rumpelstiltskin!'

A ridiculously fresh-faced anaesthetist arrived. 'What, did you graduate when you were twelve?' I inquired. Then I realized – of course! With this being a plastic surgery facility, I was surrounded by Dorian Grays. 'Got any particular concerns?' he asked. 'I'd like to avoid puking if possible,' I pleaded. 'Usually seems to happen to me post-operatively . . .' 'I'll see what I can do,' he replied. 'You allergic to anything?' he inquired. 'People who say you should dress your age,' I replied, 'but if you guys work your magic, I should graduate as lamb dressed as lamb. Oh, and try to keep cats out of the surgery room.' I noticed I was picking at my skin, something I do when I become very anxious (yes, if the truth be told, I was extremely frightened. Didn't that woman . . . the mother of that guy who played Rocky . . . Damn! I've met him but I can't remember his name – didn't she nearly die of complications after a tummy tuck?). 'And, er, it's 8am and so far no Valium in sight . . .' I said pointedly. 'Coming right up,' he replied, sticking me in the arm with something tingly, warm and woozy-making. 'Can you give her a truth drug?' asked Sharon. 'I'd love to know if she really did sleep with Kevin Costner . . .'

Well, maybe I did. I have definitely put it about a bit. When it comes to boyfriends, I barely remember the difference between fact and fiction. But the one-night stand was never my thing. In fact, 'going all the way' for me tended to be synonymous with 'moving in for a few years'. When I first met my husband Billy Connolly we shared our sexual histories and he found mine very funny. 'What, did you turn up for every first date with a van containing your furniture?' he asked unkindly. Billy wasn't too happy about the surgery. He thought it was unnecessary and, except for the boob renovation, he's right. But Billy has a different view of ageing from me. He embraces it in a very healthy way. He just loves his bushy eyebrows, his long white hair and being a grandpa. He's still sexy, but when I met him he was a dark-haired crazy man with an unintelligible Glaswegian accent. I remember him in skinny jeans over strong, muscular legs and buttocks (he still has those), and a satin bomber jacket (well, it was the eighties). I was in leggings and an over-sized man's jacket from a charity shop, and I'd never heard of Scottish comedian Billy Connolly.

That was an era when intelligent men were cottoning on to the idea that if they espoused feminist platitudes bright women would jump into bed with them. It was the new chat-up formula and it worked – except for me. I didn't get it. See, I'd been battling my inner nerd for many years and was actually happy to be appreciated for my looks – looks I'd worked on in a most dedicated manner. The fact that I had my bosoms enlarged at twenty-one should give you a clue. Looking back on it, I wish I hadn't, but my own were slightly asymmetrical (I've since discovered that is quite normal) and, more importantly, it was the height of the Playboy era; witnessing the cleavage clout wielded by my more buxom, airbrushed 'sisters', I naturally (or rather, artificially) wanted my share. I could go on to expound the feminist view and decry the tyranny of the male obsession with the C cup, but that would only bore both of us.

Fact is, in my young life I had learned that intellectual prowess alone did not necessarily translate to a happy life; my own mother (who did not relish her femininity) was a brilliant scientist but she struggled with anxiety, stress and sadness. Ergo, in my twenty-one-year-old imaginings, acquiring a curvier body held the promise of a wonderfully happy, glamorous life – a bit like Elizabeth Taylor's. Well, in those days, we believed her publicity.

I'm going to tell you all about my childhood in the chapters ahead but, right now, I might as well put it out there that it was far from idyllic. Unhappy parents usually produce unhappy kids, and my impression of my parents was that they struggled in many ways. At home, things could get pretty tense. For most of my childhood I was anxious, over-serious and unpopular; as a teenager I was pilloried for my freckles, my mousy hair and my flat chest.

Oh, please don't feel sorry for me – at any point in this book – even if you're a big softy and stories like mine always get you going. See, I've more than made up for it. For example, I'm told I eventually got to be a sex symbol. I never really understood what that meant – and still don't – but apparently I was one. The papers said so. Of course, that was thirty years ago (nowadays I'm only one by default, when someone mistakenly calls me Pamela Anderson – and, to be honest, I'm not quite sure whether to consider myself insulted or flattered). But, back then, the label confused me. Did it mean I represented sex in some odd way? Surely not. I certainly didn't consider myself to be in the same category as other women labelled sex symbols – Raquel Welch, Ursula Andress, Marilyn Monroe, Joan Collins and Bo Derek. I knew I was small fry. Anyway, wasn't being a female sex symbol a terrible curse? Once labelled, you had a ridiculously short sell-by date. As opposed to, say, Sean Connery, Warren Beatty, James Garner, Tom Jones, Mick Jagger, Cliff Richard and Burt Reynolds, who could keep their sexual puissance alive long after their fortieth birthdays. One rule for boys, another for girls – not fair. Men still come up to me and say, 'Oh boy, I used to fancy you on *Not The Nine O'Clock News*.' Yes, a backhanded compliment, but I've learned not to take it as an insult. I simply smile and say, 'I'm surprised your parents let you stay up that late . . .'

I'll be telling you a lot more about *Not The Nine O'Clock News* later on, too, but, since we're talking about bodily attributes, it seems right to mention nudity. I am aware that many viewers were . . . titillated . . . by a couple of outrageous sketches I performed on the show that involved upper-body nudity. For example, there was a spoof ad for 'Jacques Cousteau bath salts' in which I was attacked in my bubble bath by a scaly sea-monster. Due to a wardrobe malfunction, producer Sean Hardie had to spend hours in the edit room trying to preserve my honour on that one.

Our 'American Express' sketch caused quite a stir, too; I played a car rental salesperson who replied to a customer's question 'American Express?' with the answer 'That will do nicely, sir, and would you like to rub my tits, too?' I unbuttoned my blouse invitingly and revealed my cleavage (courtesy of Wonderbra). Cue voiceover: 'Put your head in between them and go bbl bbl bbl with American Express.' I never quite understood why at the time, but the *NTNON* boys hooted at that like stuck pigs. I suppose they'd never imagined a girl would actually agree to it. Well, you wouldn't have caught, say, Emma Thompson doing that kind of thing now, would you? But I didn't think anything of it. It wasn't like I'd be letting the side down or anything (did I even have a side?). No, I'd do anything for a laugh.

Ironically, the one fully naked Bristol seen on *NTNON* was not mine. It was displayed in a sketch called 'Baby on the bus', which opened with a woman walking down the road apparently unaware that she had one large naked bosom emerging from her blouse. When someone points this out, she looks down, turns pale, and exclaims, 'Oh no! I've left my baby on the bus!' I have no idea who the woman was but, even today, I have to put up with people bringing it up, kind of slyly, as if to say: 'Don't act too stuck-up because I've seen one of your tits.' I have an answer for that, too: 'You're a bit slow, big boy. Rent Mel Brooks' *History of the World Part One* and you'll see both of them.'

You know, until yesterday when I was going through some old press cuttings, I'd completely forgotten about another public boob flash of which I'm guilty. It occurred on the Australian Broadcasting Corporation (ABC) when I appeared in a period TV drama based on a Norman Lindsay novel called *Redheap*. The sighting was extensively covered in the newspapers:

BOSOM BARED BY AUNTIE ABC – JUST FOR ART'S SAKE

It was a bare bosom all right and completely exposed on the screen for the best part of half a minute, but I couldn't believe it. This . . . was Auntie ABC's work, a dame of the airwaves who would normally frown at exposing a bit of cleavage. Yet there I was, gazing in awe at the splendid bare breast of actress Pamela Stephenson in Part 1 of *Redheap*, the second dramatization in the Norman Lindsay Festival. I had been invited to a preview of the show which goes to air at 8pm on Friday, September 29 with no warning that semi-nudity would pop up in the programme.

GASPED

And when it did happen, an unsuspecting ABC official near me, seeing the programme for the first time, gasped and almost fell out of his chair. I suppressed my own purr of appreciation and glanced across at Brian Bell, the director of the programme, but he obviously didn't want to discuss the matter right then. The scene where Miss Stephenson reveals her breast is a fantasy one, in which she is seen in a flowing Grecian gown on a swing – facing the camera. And, though stunned into almost disbelief at what I saw, I must confess it was very tastefully done . . .

Seriously? Well, it was 1972 and, back then, Australia was a pretty conservative place.

Although I privately saw myself as a toothy, short-waisted, pear-shaped munchkin with an unfortunate facial profile, I realized that, with the right make-up, hair and lighting, my looks got me a lot of attention on *NTNON*. But I worked darn hard as well, and very often disguised myself with unflattering wigs and teeth. Case in point – I donned a particularly unattractive wig and huge pair of glasses, not to mention fake teeth made from a polystyrene cup – to portray Janet Street-Porter. It was a cruel look. In fact, I think she's really a very appealing, interesting woman, and I feel sorry that, since it's when Billy and I met, she has had to endure the clip of that sketch being played again and again. The idea of the sketch was that 'Janet' was interviewing Billy, saying, 'What I don't understand is – how can people understand your accent?' But Billy turns the table on her by acting like he doesn't understand her ('Sorry?'). While we were taping, my fake teeth kept falling out, which made Billy crack up. I was rather shocked at his response. I thought he was being very unprofessional. See, I'd had excellent acting training at the National Institute of Dramatic Art in Sydney and had done a huge amount of theatre so I was imbued with performance discipline. But Billy just kept giggling and didn't care, so we had to do the scene over and over again. Nevertheless, I was very taken with him, in a womanly way. I didn't see him again for about a year after that and, by then, both our marriages were ending so we had the opportunity to be together . . . I couldn't possibly have known that, thirty odd years later, we'd be having Christmas dinner together with our children and grandchildren.

My husband is just wonderful, isn't he? Well, not always. He gave me a paper weight for Christmas. What every girl dreams of. Not just any old paper weight – one with a beautiful blue bird painted on it. 'What bird is that?' I asked, a bit mystified. 'A great tit,' he grinned pointedly, 'just ONE great tit.' Despite his questionable sense of humour, I'm still a fan. And, there I was, sitting at the other end of the table with an immobile, marble face that scared the grandkids, and trying not to put any strain on my stitches. I was still high because only sixty hours earlier, I'd been in the pre-op room with Dr Bev savagely pulling at the poppers on my gown. 'Ooh, I do love having my clothes ripped off,' I smirked. The drugs were definitely working. But Dr Bev had heard it all. He calmly picked up a large blue marker and started drawing on my body.

All I remember about the rest of that day was being helped into a car that took me to a recovery facility – let's call it 'Tranquility' – the private post-op facility I was lucky enough to be able to recover in. I know I'm spoiled, but I didn't think it was a good idea to rely on an irreverent Glaswegian comedian to help me to the bathroom, and remember my pain pills. He'd take one look at my new, swollen knockers and either faint or piss himself laughing. Either way, he'd get an hour or so of comedy material from it, but it would be totally at my expense. Tranquility's the kind of place that features a 'grey carpet parade' of celebrities shuffling along the corridor, under doctors' orders to exercise their legs to avoid DVT. You could tell from their walking style what kind of procedure each one had undergone: tummy-tuckers were doubled over with a walker, face-lifters kept their chins in the air, boob jobbers kept their arms firmly by their sides – each person accompanied by a pretty nurse ready to assist with an extra helping of Percocet. I recognized at least one person I knew a bit, but tried to hide my own face because I had emerged from surgery with one wide-awake eye and one sleepy one. It often happens because, due to the long-acting anaesthesia, the nerves in the face can become deadened in an asymmetrical fashion. But it's temporary – at least, that's the theory. Ooh er, I'd just have to wait and see.

Sharon was the only person I allowed to visit me in Tranquility. She plopped on my bed, brazenly insisted that the warm Veuve Clicquot she'd brought would go perfectly with my already volatile Vicodin/Valium cocktail and announced: 'Did I tell you, I nearly shagged my cousin?' Excellent conversation-starter. 'I wish you had,' I replied. 'As a sexologist I would have loved to know if the shattering of such a major taboo would actually enhance or hinder the experience . . .' 'But is it really taboo for us at our age?' she questioned. 'We can no longer procreate, so . . . where's the harm?' 'Quite right,' I smiled wickedly. 'From now on I'll advise any post-menopausal woman complaining about the unavailability of sexual partners to look no further than their own families . . .'

All right, now I'm fairly sure you're going, 'Really? Is she actually being so cavalier about incest? Not sure I want to read any further if that's where she's headed . . .' But, see, it's just gallows humour. Medical doctors are often privately macabre about death and illness, and Sharon and I – although we're really decent people (she's a wife, mother and psychologist, too) – that's the way we talk to each other and, although shocking to most people, I think it's so much more fun and authentic than, 'How's the pain, honey? You're so brave. Can I get you a cupcake?'

After they let me out, I had a post-surgery consultation with Dr Bev. 'I took off an awful lot of skin,' he said excitedly, showing me some thoroughly gory photos. 'Sick bag please,' I said pointedly. He peeled off some of the sterile skin-closure strips and I saw my new navel. 'What's that?' I asked, pointing at a mark just above my pubes. 'It's a scab,' said the nurse quickly. 'Yes, but from what?' I asked suspiciously. 'Oh, that's your old belly button,' confessed Dr Bev. Eughhh. 'If I have this done again,' I posed, 'will it eventually become my clitoris?'

Humour, of course, can be used as a defence mechanism, a means of avoiding the real feelings underneath. But, you know that. You're probably way ahead of me here. When it comes to self-analysis I can be painfully slow. I know, you'd think at my age I'd have a bit more self-confidence, not to mention sense, but I'm afraid I can be remarkably stupid (I may have mentioned this before but you'll see evidence of this time and time again). Case in point, it took me just one month to start regretting my surgical choices. Three days after Christmas, I flew to Brazil on a writing assignment for *Woman & Home.* I landed in the Bahian coastal town of Porto Seguro on New Year's Eve and headed for what I soon discovered was one of the noisiest beaches in the world – Beat Beach. Given my fragile physical state, the flight had been far too challenging for me. I'd had the last of my sutures removed on my way to LAX airport; how I wish I could learn not to push myself like that. Lugging my bulky scuba gear (in complete defiance of doctors' orders – I wasn't meant to lift even a water bottle), I arrived exhausted and in considerable pain. I can't emphasize enough how dumb I was to travel so soon after surgery, and how gaga I was on all those painkillers, anxiolytics and antibiotics (I ask you again: 'What is WRONG with me?').

To my horror, the frantically busy people at the Arcobaleno Hotel claimed to have no record of my booking so I spent an hour in hair-limping humidity trying to negotiate a price that was something less than extortionate for a room on their busiest week of the year. If only I could speak Portuguese. I moved into a grubby box over-looking a crowded swimming pool, where salsa music blasted from a shockingly bad speaker system, and wondered what on earth I was doing there. Why, oh why, had I left my family to their peaceful New Year celebration for this over-priced, overcrowded, overheated corner of the globe?

But a lukewarm shower, espresso, and fresh coconut juice later, I headed for the beach – where an epiphany awaited me. Women of all ages, shapes and sizes – a few even approaching perfection – were proudly sunning themselves in the tiniest bikinis I'd ever seen ('*fio dental*' the Brazilians call them, slang for thongs as skinny as dental floss). Their plump round bottoms rose proudly from the sand like thousands of freshly exfoliated hillocks. Some action-enthusiasts were dancing axé – a kind of open-air Zumba class – led by a drag queen called Butterfly wearing cut-off denim shorts and the highest platform shoes in which anyone's ever pirouetted. Young and old, these women were having a ton of fun. Their cellulite shook rhyth-mically, their tummies flopped comfortably over their pudenda, their crooked, vertical Caesarean scars were unashamedly on display. And they were so incredibly comfortable with their bodies, they totally put me to shame. If only I'd come to Brazil two months earlier! What an untimely lesson they taught me – damn, with the money I spent on surgery I could have bought a flat here. And a wardrobe of *fio dentals*.

The sun was pounding my head – fair and torturous punishment for my abject stupidity, I thought. I was now so dehydrated, fatigued and mentally self-flagellating, I was barely functioning. Mocked by a bevy of deliriously happy, middle-aged Brazilian divas, I slid to the ground and lay helpless on the searing sand. Hot granules stuck to my newly scarred neck and chin but I could no longer help myself. How on earth had I got here? I mean HERE as in 'to such an insanely ridiculous state of mind and body'? I'm an educated, insightful woman of mature years – a psychologist, for God's sake, a wife and mother. I have sailed the world, fended off pirates, guerrillas, sharks and *Strictly* judges, why on earth had I put myself through such physical and mental torment, and why did I continue to aggrieve myself in such a shockingly pathetic manner?

At least I was smart enough to know I was in trouble; at least I recognized that the answer to that vital question lay somewhere in the mire of my elusive, murky past. And it clearly lay far beyond any discoveries that had been made during the thirty-odd years of therapy I'd undergone with a dozen well-respected mental health professionals. Therapy is like peeling an onion – layer by layer by layer, until you get down to the raw centre. For some reason I'd never really got to the core. Yes, there was no other choice left: time to book an appointment with myself.

Chapter Two

THE SHRINK SHRUNK

But where on earth would I start? Usually, it would be, 'Hello, I'm Dr Connolly. Help me to understand why you've come to see me . . .' But that wasn't going to work when I was the patient as well. This could be scary. Could I be as compassionate and insightful with myself as I am with other people? Could I avoid being judgmental of myself? (If so, it would be a first.) For sure, I would know immediately if I lied, dissembled, or tried to distract the therapist with small talk, humour or flirtation. What, so I'd have to be completely honest with myself? Wow, what a concept. And near impossible. Much of what goes on in one's psyche occurs well below the level of upper consciousness, and teasing out material from the unconscious mind can be very difficult, requiring the help of therapists, shamans or dream-tenders. I've received guidance from all of the above, but the work has always been slow, painstaking and incredibly challenging. Could I manage this next phase alone?

And how exactly should I go about trying to 'shrink' myself? Should I perform self-hypnosis? Analyze my own dreams? I already do that. What about . . . delivering my 'stream of consciousness' into a Dictaphone and then analyzing it later? Or perhaps I could employ a technique used to help overly left-brained people to allow their creative, right brain to function better – it might undermine my own reserve in exactly the right way. Being right-handed, I took a pen in my left hand and positioned it over a blank piece of paper. After a few minutes it began to move, seemingly without my conscious control.

Don't know who, where, why . . . help me . . . am I she proud strong clever or am I little, unknowing?

Instant regression. That was promising. I pulled up my metaphorical therapist's chair, took my notepad, and tried to stare empathically at myself.

Why don't you start by telling me something about your childhood? Perhaps some positive memory you might have . . .?

Ah, yes. My childhood. (Deep breath.) Ahhh, where to start . . .? (Silence)

Take your time. In your mind's eye, what are you seeing?

Somewhere, I have this black-and-white, Brownie box camera photograph of myself in early 1961, wearing a woollen cardigan beneath the Egyptian sun, sharing a camel with my father. I remember feeling guilty about the wicked delight I felt when the rogue leading my mother's camel threatened, 'Pay me more, lady, or I'll make the camel dance!' Did I mention I didn't much like my mother?

Hmmm . . . Pamela, you just made a very important disclosure but couched it in a throw-away style – would you care to tell me more about that?

Later . . . I watched gleefully as she bounced around like a rag doll on a mechanical bull, wailing contemptuously. The thought of it still makes me smile – is that so wrong? (OMG I've just remembered that I kind of tricked her on to the Jurassic Park ride at Universal Studios when she was in her seventies and that had a similar effect – what an evil monster I am.)

Do you really think of yourself as evil?

In a way. I'll get to that. But, see, 1961 was the most exciting year of my childhood; not particularly because I saw someone getting the better of my mother, but it was the year both my parents took sabbaticals from their Australian university posts. We headed for London on-board the SS *Iberia*, a large P&O liner – I used to think that stood for 'Pacific and Orient' but I believe it was actually 'Peninsular and Oriental'. To be honest, 'Puking and Overbalancing' would have been more appropriate considering some of the dreadful weather we faced, but anyway I thought the *Iberia* was absolutely beautiful – gleaming white with a yellow funnel, and fresh from a new refit. She'd had several mishaps in the past, notably a collision with a tanker and running aground in the Suez Canal, but she still did the Sydney to London run in five weeks or so, stopping at Melbourne, Adelaide, Singapore, Sri Lanka (it was Ceylon in those days), Port Said (we took the option to travel overland to Cairo), Naples and Marseille. Apart from an annual Christmas holiday trip to New Zealand where I was born, we rarely went anywhere except for Sunday afternoon drives. Those regular outings had always frustrated my two younger sisters and me (even though it was unbearably hot and stuffy we were rarely allowed out of the car) and vexed my father because we bickered and fought. The trips invariably climaxed in wild attempts by my father to steer our second-hand Holden and, at the same time, reach his beefy forearm into the back seat to slap the culprits.

It's funny now, but it wasn't then. I was rather scared of him because he seemed to use corporal punishment not only to discipline us, but also to vent his general frustration. I remember running and sliding under the bed to avoid his slapping hand, and how his big hairy arm would swing like a pendulum, trying to hit its mark. (Actually, I'm very attracted to men with powerful arms now – wow, I've just realized there's probably a connection. Sorry – I digress . . .).

No need to apologize . . . you can digress as much as you want . . . And, by the way, it's common to sexualize physical aggression.

Hah! So that's my problem – a Popeye Complex! Didn't Freud prescribe spinach for that?

He certainly mentioned the tendency to use humour to deflect attention from painful memories . . .

Ah . . . OK. Straight face. Like my father, I was born in Auckland, New Zealand. My mother spent her first twelve years in Fiji but was sent away to school at Epsom Girls Grammar in New Zealand and fell for dad when they were up some mountain together chasing after rare frogs. Yes, you're right if you're thinking 'What a pair of serious nerds.' My father was a zoologist, my mother a biologist and, after they produced three girls, we moved to Sydney, Australia, where they took up lecturing positions at the University of Sydney and the University of New South Wales respectively. I was four then, so I had no say in the matter. I only mention that because I sometimes feel put on the spot about what exactly my nationality is, and towards which country my loyalties lie. I hold an Australian passport (I was naturalized in Australia when I was small) and that's where I grew up. So I'm a New Zealand-born Australian, and I feel that both countries qualify as 'home' – for different reasons.

It seems important to you that you are understood, that you don't offend anyone. Do you think you find it difficult – even painful – to tolerate the feeling that you might somehow disappoint someone?

Well that's strange, because I made an entire career out of being comically offensive . . . But you're right – not meeting someone's expectations is a big deal for me. Actually, I think I now understand where that comes from . . .

And where might that be . . .?

Not now. Anyway, eight months before we arrived in Australia, my middle sister Claire and I had been very poorly with polio. I remember the daily injections that made me scream, but I was probably very lucky that a vaccine and treatment had just become available, because I eventually made a full recovery. I'm not telling you about my illness just to get your sympathy; it's particularly relevant because once we got to Australia I was sent to have ballet lessons at the Edna Mann School of Dance at the Hunters Hill Town Hall on Saturday mornings to strengthen my limbs – which spawned my passion for dance. Best, best, best thing about my early life!

What was it like for you, being so ill?

I don't really remember much about it . . .

Hmmm. It can't have been easy . . . You've buried those feelings?

I guess so. In fact, I remember very little about my New Zealand toddler days, although three things in particular were always brought up by family members:

1. In the house where we lived in Takapuna there was a large bay window with upholstered seating facing the street, and apparently I used to enjoy parading my naked body on the other side of the curtains, visible to passersby. Just the fact that this story was told as an example of my 'exhibitionist tendencies, even at four years old – of course she went into show business!' will give you a sense of what kind of people raised me. As if a four-year-old would even be aware of what it meant socially to be seen naked! And as if anyone who saw me would either care or imagine such natural childhood behaviour to be deliberately provocative! I'm sorry to get on my high horse, but honestly . . .

2. My pre-school teacher became Sir Edmund Hillary's wife (you know Hillary, the guy who climbed Mount Everest?) At three years old my teacher's love life was completely irrelevant to me and I just knew her as 'Miss Rose'.

3. I was sick on the front seat of the Fokker Friendship plane that took us to Australia, exactly where the Duke of Edinburgh was supposed to be sitting when they picked him up in Sydney the following day. So, obviously, I had early Republican tendencies, although when I actually met the Queen's husband around forty years later I thought he was very kind to avoid bringing it up. My parents thought the incident was unfortunate, but also amusing; I had the same feelings myself when, during a London to LA flight, my first baby threw up on Joan Collins. Granted, Daisy was a little young to be so censorious, but Joan took it very nicely.

Our family moved to a small, arid, inland suburb of Sydney called Boronia Park where we'd bought an ugly, concrete-sprayed house – have you ever seen that kind of exterior work? It's hideous – like construction acne – and if you accidentally brush against it, it grazes your skin. Hide-and-seek was a truly painful affair. The whole area was just developing and I remember it as terribly hot and dusty. There was very little growing there in the early days – just a few stringy-barked gum trees and indigenous shrubs. The aural landscape was lively and loud, though; the strident humming of cicadas morning and night, the constant barking of neighbourhood dogs, and a kookaburra laughing from its usual perch on top of our clothes line.

The shape of my world at that time was a 'T'. Our house was halfway down Thompson Street, which led up a hill to Gladesville Road. To the left of that junction was the Milk Bar, where the delicious, icy, strawberry milkshakes guaranteed a brain freeze, then on the right side was a cluster of other shops – the fruit and vegetable store run by a nice Italian family, the grocery-store-cum-post-office, and finally the fish shop. The latter was my favourite. They sold hot, salty, battered fish and prawns with chips, and saveloy sausages and flat, round, battered potatoes we called 'scallops'. Oh, I loved them, and have never managed to eschew my unhealthy taste for fried food. Across the road from all of these was the knitting shop, where you could also buy greetings cards. To the left of the T junction was my primary school and opposite there was an untidy vacant lot. I really loved the wildness of that piece of land. I trekked through it every day as a shortcut to school, and there were always surprises. The sticky, paspalum grass often brushed my legs and left me with a rash, but I didn't care. There would be mysterious rustlings in the undergrowth, and sometimes I'd find a blue-tongued lizard sunning itself across my path. In February, overnight rain transformed the main track into a tiny water-filled gully, topped by soft, ochre mud that stuck to my school shoes. In spring, I might narrowly avoid stepping on a sly snake – they weren't exactly benign creatures – which would set my heart racing. Even an innocent brush against a shrub might cause my skin to be invaded by a dangerous tick. Yes, I had good reason to be afraid, yet I was sad when it became a Total petrol garage.

Next to the vacant lot was a sweet shop. That sweet shop was the sugary yin to the salty yang of the fish shop. I still love liquorice – there they had thin, coiled ropes of the stuff, and sherbet we ate from paper bags, white chocolate frogs and the squishy, white 'milk bottles' which I still think are heavenly. Even the school tuck shop had donuts. Yes, that's where my sweet tooth came from. And, partly as a result, I've battled with my weight my whole life.

Help me to understand exactly what you mean by that . . .

Well, I really like the kind of food that's not very good for you . . . Once I start eating, well, chocolate, marshmallows, jelly babies or ice cream, for example, it's very hard to stop. Food definitely equals comfort for me, especially anything sweet with a soft, squishy texture—

As if you're cushioning yourself inside?

Yes! Oh, I'm aware I use food for the wrong reasons. I've gone up and down in weight quite drastically ever since I was in my twenties . . .

What kinds of treatment have you tried for that?

Everything. Diets, gym, personal trainers, pills, nutritionists, quacks. Now I understand the psychology of eating disorders, and success-fully treat them in others, but for me personally it's just so well entrenched. In those days we drank oodles of sugary soft drinks that seemed to help cool us down – and never considered the sugar content. Hardly anyone had air conditioning in those days and in summer it was difficult for my sisters and me to fall asleep. To try to cool my legs, I would slide them up against the plaster wall beside my top bunk. I envied my school friends who lived near the beach; kids in our neighbourhood simply played with the garden hose whenever they lifted the water restrictions. Most people had sprinklers, which were fun to jump through, but they were considered a particularly wicked waste of water. Occasionally we'd go on a Sunday school picnic to Balmoral Beach where they had a decent shark net (in those days many beaches had those), or attended a barbecue birthday party at Manly, but my parents were terribly busy, even when they were at home.

You felt they were . . . unavailable . . .?

Yes, pretty much. Aside from the Sunday afternoon drives, my sisters and I stayed around the house reading, practising on the piano, or studying. There was no movie theatre, shopping mall, bowling alley, or anything like that nearby. Actually, I think there may have been a cinema not too far away because kids at school used to laugh about dropping Jaffas – round orange sweeties with a chocolate centre – on people's heads from the top balcony, but I don't remember seeing a movie until I was around eleven. I think Hitchcock's *Psycho* was the first film I saw – at a church fellowship, of all things. What were they thinking? It was traumatic – not so much due to the suspense, but because the boy I was sitting with screamed like a trapped hyena during the shower scene. Back then I would never have imagined that one day I would live in the Hollywood Hills with a hazy view of the Norman Bates Motel set at Universal Studios in the valley below.

But I don't think our family had the funds for things like cinema outings; money was to be used for education, not entertainment or luxury items. Our mother made our clothes on her Singer sewing machine. We listened to children's radio programmes, but there was no TV then. Oh, and there were a couple of dirt tennis courts in the area. We did play with the neighbourhood children – I was given a red tricycle for my sixth birthday and a small gang of us used to take it in turns to free-wheel it, helter-skelter, down the hill. I suppose that was the beginning of my addiction to adrenaline . . .

You discovered that it felt good to move fast, be scared, perhaps a little out of control?

I suppose I did. It excited me more than anything else in my life at that time. Yes, definitely it elevated my mood from everyday boredom. But apart from that, I don't really remember having very much fun. Oh, I do remember that I tried to organize the neighbourhood children into a drama club to perform plays but, very wisely, they'd have none of it. But my parents were not particularly happy people so I suppose it never occurred to them to have fun with us. I'm not exactly sure why they weren't happy. My father Neville came from a lively, down-to-earth family from the North Island of New Zealand. His father, Octavius, was the postmaster of Opotiki, a town in the eastern Bay of Plenty. Dad was the youngest of nine. Of the four boys in the family, two brothers – Ted and Norman – were killed in World War II (they were in the Allied Air Force), so I imagine there was considerable pressure on my father to make his mark in the world. I recently learned that Dad really wanted to go to war but Ted wrote him a letter from the South Pacific (where he was eventually killed) telling him in no uncertain terms to stay at home and hold the fort there.

Most of the New Zealand Stephensons I've met are pretty laid-back and good-humoured. We are descendants of Samuel Stephenson, the son of an English sea captain – also called Samuel

– who was murdered by pirates in Indonesia in 1820 when his ship *The Rosalie* ran aground. After hearing of his father's death, Samuel junior sailed from England to try to recover his father's assets in Indonesia, but when he failed to secure his inheritance, he moved on to New Zealand and established a trading post in Russell in the Bay of Islands. He married Hira Moewaka, a Maori woman from the Kapotai tribe whose father was probably Scottish (she also had a European name – Charlotte MacCauliffe), and the pair tried to settle down amid the volatile climate of fighting and land-grabbing that occurred between white colonists and Maori people in those days. Well, that's the Cliff Notes – I'm romping through this bit of family history because I already wrote a whole book about what happened to my great, great grandfather called *Murder or Mutiny?*.

My father, who told me he used to go to school bare-footed, eventually became a scientist and teamed up with my mother to form a cancer research duo. As an adult he was shy and a little insecure in social situations; however, as a parent he was a tough disciplinarian. But he had an earthy sense of humour and a rather irreverent view of the world that I regard as his greatest gift to me. I think he may have been a bit of a prankster in his youth, but I imagine my mother would have reacted pretty sourly to that kind of 'silliness'. Early pictures of him reveal his wiry, film-star looks, although his bemused expression while holding his first child – me – suggests that he may not have been quite ready for prime-time parenthood. But then, who is?

My mother Elsie spent her early childhood in Fiji. Her father was a businessman in Suva and her mother was a Methodist missionary. I was told my grandmother used to go door to door to try to persuade the Indian merchant families who had settled there to allow their girls to be educated. I've visited the property in Suva where my grandparents lived, a colonial-style house with a white, wooden gate and lush tropical garden. Early photos of my mother suggest she was a true child of the colonial empire – dressed to the nines in frilly, long-sleeved dresses and woollen socks in the tropical heat, posing coyly with her parasol. Like the children of wealthy white families in India at the time, my mother had an ayah or local woman who looked after her as a nanny, and there were probably other servants, too. But her father died suddenly when she was twelve and, immediately, her life changed. She was sent away to New Zealand alone, to board with family friends and be schooled. I imagine she was well looked after, but the sudden losses must have been traumatic, and I doubt she was happy from then on.

As an adult, my mother always seemed miserable. Now I realize she must have suffered from depression, and she was also highly anxious. She knew she had poor mothering skills (she apologized to me about that a couple of years before she died). To be honest, I always felt she didn't really like me. And the pervasive envy, bitterness and dismissiveness I felt from her – especially during my teenage years – constituted a deeply painful trauma I have only recently come to understand. It spurred a deep sense of unworthiness, guilt and fury that continues to plague me from time to time . . .

Tell me more about that . . .

My parents told me once that I was 'an experiment'. Bastards. I was always afraid to ask just how far that went. Did they deliberately deprive me of love and comfort to see how I'd turn out? Sometimes it felt that way. They had huge expectations of me, partly because some clipboard-wielding IQ tester had turned up at my kindergarten and pronounced that I was way too smart for Plasticine, paper chains and Snap (I could read when I was three). I was whisked off to a more advanced classroom where all the kids were sprouting pubic hair and talking about dating and periods, which meant that, at seven, I was a social outcast. And even though I was still near the top of my class, my father made it clear that second place was unacceptable. Yeah, I was an experiment, all right; a miserable baby-monster whose classmates didn't understand that my savage competitive streak was solely in the interests of receiving what every child deserves no matter what their exam results might be – appreciation. How I wish I'd felt loved for who I truly was, not just for what I might achieve.

I know, I know – complaining about being bright seems like I'm perversely blowing my own trumpet but, as I learned when I was studying psychology, there are many different types of cleverness, and very few of them are teased out in standard IQ tests. I think it's terrible that we expect everyone to perform the same way in school. Many absolutely brilliant people learn differently from the 'norm', but even though we now know more about learning differences than we did in the fifties, we still tend to value people who are, say, good at maths over those who are visually creative. And when it comes to dealing with life, I don't even think IQ tests relate to success. I, for one, can be remarkably stupid—OMG, there I go again, apologizing for being smart. This has bugged me my whole life. It's got more than a little to do with being female, but why exactly do I feel the need to beg your forgiveness when a) I'm sure you're just as smart as me and b) you don't catch Stephen Hawking saying, 'OK, I can explain everything about the universe, but please don't hate me cos in many ways I'm really an idiot', do you?

I had kind and helpful teachers at the Boronia Park Primary School but, because I was perceived as 'brainy', I was thoroughly disliked by my classmates. I remember burying my head in my lap to try to block out the entire class chanting 'Teacher's pet. Teacher's pet! Teacher's Pet! TEACHER'S PET!' But, by then, my tears of humiliation and frustration were tempered with some kind of inner knowledge that, one day, there would be transcendent rewards. I still marvel at that – as a young kid I really did understand envy;

after all, it was perpetrated on me by family members, friends and even my own mother. But I learned to tolerate it, and that strength has set me in good stead. Thank God that resilience never left me, despite the punishment I took – and not just for my braininess. I was just never . . . liked . . .

. . . Well, of course you would have been unpopular. When parents fail to allow a child to be herself, she will assume a false self, more invested in pleasing adults than getting on with peers, and other children will recognize that lack of authenticity.

Hmmm. Looking back, I feel so sorry for my little child self, who felt she had to try so hard to be loved. She was terribly lost. At least I had my ballet lessons, which I absolutely adored – although, like everything else, I took them way too seriously. And there were a few disasters; some have said I peed in my bear suit during a performance of 'Teddy Bears' Picnic' but, erm, I think that might have been my sister. In fact, my performing career properly began at the age of five when I danced a solo as a butterfly. I had net wings and feelers on my head made out of pipe cleaners and, naturally, I was extremely anxious about being perfectly butterflyish. (See, the fact that it was my mother who made that outfit contradicts the part of me that believes she didn't care about me, doesn't it?)

But was that what you truly needed, or was it . . . something else . . .?

You're right. I would gladly have swapped the butterfly outfit for one gentle caress. Anyway, the following year, when I was the 'Spirit of Winter' in a furry-edged tutu with sparkly snowflakes on my headdress, you could just tell I was a *Strictly* contestant in the making. Dancing was my escape. It offered me a way to slide outside my head and enjoy all the good feelings my body could provide. It was also beyond my parents' area of expertise and, therefore, not under their control. It was mine. I could not have articulated it at the time, but now I understand how important that was. I felt transported by the beauty, the passion, the music, and the exactitude of ballet, and dreamed of being Margot Fonteyn, Alicia Markova, or New Zealand prima ballerina Rowena Jackson. How I wish I'd kept it up.

But dancing also provided me with a lesson that would haunt me forever and instil in me a lifelong fear. My ballet teacher Edna Mann was a beautiful, poised woman who had a little TV show in the very early days of black-and-white Australian TV. She gave lessons to viewers, using her pupils to demonstrate barre techniques, and once or twice she chose me. The last time I appeared, she asked me to perform a short Irish dance, a gaillard, which was part of the syllabus. In my green tutu and apron, I started off confidently, but halfway through I lost my way and forgot the steps. Terrified, I glanced at Miss Mann, who got me through by smiling encouragingly, but I felt totally humiliated. I remember how embarrassed I was when I got home and heard my mother laughing about it with a neighbour outside in the street. I had learned the price of being in the spotlight.

Aside from ballet, my childhood delight lay mainly within the pages of the books I read. I liked the Noel Streatfeild ballet books, the Famous Five stories, and anything about adventure. I cringe now when I think back to some of the books I was given that are now considered racist, like *Little Black Sambo*, about a child in Africa. Although, strangely enough, I seem to remember that Sambo was presented in a very admirable way, always being able to outsmart the things that challenged him, like ferocious tigers. The Noddy books – and even some of the Tintin stories – are also considered questionable nowadays. But, at the time, I read everything I could lay my hands on, and I am so grateful that my parents provided us

girls with a comprehensive library. My mother found it very hard to
coax me to the dinner table because I was so absorbed with *Peter
Pan*, *Grimm's Fairy Tales*, and especially with a beautifully illus-
trated book I had of ancient Greek and Roman legends. I absolutely
loved those tales. I was very drawn to the convoluted soap operas of
their lives, and was tickled by the drama of the relationships between
gods and mortals, and all the bickering that went on between the
gods and their peers. Our household was a highly religious, Church
of England zone, so only in my daydreams did I dare identify with
the daring huntress Diana, the self-involved, vindictive Aphrodite,
or the clever, warlike Athena. Their stories were so much more
thrilling than anything in the Bible.

I especially loved the story about Eros and Psyche (no wonder I
eventually became a psychologist). I reread that tale recently and
was struck by the significance of the deep message it imparted; this
was so much better than the well-known 'someday my prince will
come' western fairy tale. Aside from its deeper significance – the
marriage of love and sexuality, the connection between mind, body
and spirit – this was one of the rare stories in which the protagonist
was a brave female who strived hard in myriad ways and who
successfully undertook trials and travel. In the absence of female
adventure heroines, I mainly had to imagine myself as a boy, strid-
ing off to achieve derring-do. But this girl Psyche kicked ass.

When I was around ten years old I began to write plays. I know
– I was insufferably precocious, but no one really saw them except
my grandmother, and she was nearly blind. They were all in verse
– kind of quasi-Shakespearean – but with plots and characters that
owed more to Greek literature. I would scribble away for hours and
then type them on my parents' manual typewriter, after which I
would look around for people to perform them. But I wasn't popular and had few friends, and dabbling in amateur theatre arts came
way down on everyone's list of fun things to do on a Saturday 'arvo'

– probably just below being bitten on the bum by a red-backed spider (which commonly happened in the Sydney suburbs).

My best friend (actually my only close chum at primary school) was Kathy Rosner, who lived about a mile away near Gladesville. Kathy was sweet, smart and pixie-like, with lovely curly hair and a mouth that was always turned up in a wry smile. She was as crazy about acrobatics as I was about ballet, and could flip her body in entire revolutions, sideways, backwards and forwards, which impressed me enormously. Best of all, Kathy didn't seem to mind that I was overly serious, younger than everyone else, and had parents so strict they made Stalin look liberal. At least I was allowed to stay overnight at her place from time to time. I loved being around her family – Hungarian-Jewish immigrants who told terrifyingly interesting stories about escaping from Hungary during the war. That, I decided, was true adventure. Kathy's older sister provided a novel musical education – the latest Frank Sinatra records (only classical music was played in our house), and I also received vital information I did not get elsewhere about developing bodies. It was Kathy who told me important facts of life, such as, 'If you get a cold during your first period, you'll get the sniffles every month for the rest of your life.'

My studies at Boronia Park Primary School continued to create enormous anxiety for me, and the scribbly bark tree that shaded one corner of the playground was often secretly watered by my tears. Suzanne Stubbs was my bête noire. Two or three years older than me, she came top more often than I did, and this fact was an endless source of shame. My parents did not seem to have such high expectations of my two younger sisters but, for me, second place seemed like a monumental failure. Saying my prayers, while kneeling at the edge of my sister Claire's bed at night (I slept in the top bunk), was taking longer and longer (why didn't anyone notice that my knees were always bruised?). I tried to remember to ask God to bless everyone I knew, but if I thought I might have forgotten anyone I had to start again. I now understand my general anxiety was starting to be expressed in an obsessive-compulsive manner. I felt compelled to avoid stepping on any pavement cracks, and developed a highly noticeable facial tic, in which I violently twitched my nose. People I barely knew started teasing me: 'Hey kid, what's with the rabbit faces?'

What was that like for you?

I felt terrible shame, so much so that I was in denial about it. I couldn't accept that my face was doing that, or that other people noticed. But it was unstoppable; when the urge came I just HAD to twitch. I sort of found a way to disguise it a bit, like pretending I had a cold or something, but people knew, I'm sure.

Did your parents ever mention it?

No. At least, I thought they didn't notice – but now I suppose they must have done ... I've just remembered my father had a slight stutter and no one in his family had ever done anything about that – and most people didn't really bother about treatment for such things back then. My sisters never mentioned it either. Strange. Until I was a teenager, I shared a room with Claire and Lesley, yet I felt quite isolated from them. This was partly due to the common burden of the oldest child; I was a trail-blazer who also felt a sense of responsibility for them. Perhaps I deliberately created separation from my sisters because we were so often lumped together. Being so close in age, we were collectively known as 'the girls' – and were always dressed exactly alike. George Harrison once told my husband and I how frustrating it was for him and the band to always be known as 'the boys'. I really got that.

Claire was born eighteen months after me. She was an adorable, round-faced cutie who looked exactly like my mother did at that age. She developed into a more placid, far less anxious person than I was. Throughout her childhood she was teased for not being as . . . delicately formed . . . as Lesley and I – which was terribly unfair. She wisely – and brilliantly – found escape routes, forming strong relationships with neighbours. I don't know how she did it, but I envied Claire's various local safe havens – in particular, the home of a childless couple, Mr and Mrs Peters, who lived a few doors away. Within those walls, there seemed to be comfort, warmth, iced biscuits in the shape of animals, and television. We didn't have a TV until I was a teenager. I would sometimes wander down to the Peters' house and knock on the door, hoping to be let in. Mrs Peters would answer the door in an apron, with curlers in her hair, and stand guarding the entrance. A marvellous aroma of freshly baked biscuits would fill my nostrils. Peering past Mrs Peters' slim frame I could just see Claire, stretched out lazily on the sofa in front of the TV set, munching a pastry and watching *I Love Lucy* with a satisfied grin on her face. She would glance over her shoulder and acknowledge me for an instant, secure in the knowledge that Mrs Peters would protect her sanctuary and send me packing.

Did you have some feelings about that?

Yes . . . enormous jealousy . . . and thoughts of 'Why not me?' And I bet my youngest sister Lesley felt that, too. She was highly strung like me. We called her Essie. She seemed a bit miserable and cried quite a lot, but we weren't the kind of family that talked about feelings. The three years between us seemed like a huge gap, and I remember having a strong sense of protectiveness towards her. But she and Claire were far closer to each other than I was with either of them. I'm not exactly sure why that was, although it occurs to me now that they may have interpreted the high expectations my parents placed on me – rather than on them – as favouritism. I probably got the lion's share of attention (for both positive and negative reasons) throughout our childhood, and I can understand that that might have been infuriating for my sisters.

But I know now that siblings feel more rivalry towards each other when they sense there's not enough parental love to go around – and that's certainly how I felt. It's weird but I've been thinking a lot about the Thompson Street yard, partly because it seemed to me that my parents' nurturing abilities – such as they were – went straight into that garden. The whole area of Boronia Park was a very arid, inland place – a desert, really – but my parents worked incredibly hard to create a pretty garden, and they were rightly extremely proud of it. They set it out a bit like mini botanical gardens, even leaving the names of the various tropical shrubs attached to the stems so people could identify them (well, after all, they were in the biological field). I remember there were hibiscus bushes (yellow and pink), and poisonous pink and white oleanders about which we were given stern warnings. There were poinsettia (ditto the warnings), a camellia climbing up the sprayed concrete wall, and a crimson bottlebrush, which is an indigenous Australian shrub. I was most drawn to the wonderfully bountiful frangipani tree, with its creamy-yellow blossoms harbouring an intoxicating scent; it's still my favourite flower. At some point a small rockery appeared in the front garden, while in the back yard there was a yellow wattle tree, a kumquat tree and a lemon tree – both dwarfed by an enormous, practical-but-unsightly, steel rotary clothes line.

Seasonally, my parents would plant poppies, gladioli, amaryllis, marigolds and various imported spring flowers, such as pansies, beneath the patio. These took a lot of work and lasted a very short while. I don't know why they bothered; native Australian plants were beautiful and far more hardy, although back then warratahs, kangaroo paws and banksias weren't considered as generally desirable as they are now (I suppose there was an element of European-style neighbourly competition involved). That garden had to be watered early and late; if the sun hit the plants before the water was absorbed into their roots they'd be fried. As I lay in bed at night, after our mother had read to us and turned out the lights, I would hear a pitter patter – not of rain, but of the garden hose. After my parents died, a photo album came to me with pictures from the Thompson Street days. There are forty pictures of the house and garden, five of my sisters, and none of me (although that was probably because the album was created after I'd left home). Yes, my parents loved and tended that garden with a passion.

You sound sad, bitter . . .

Yes, I am. But even though the 'hurt child' part of me is asking, 'Why didn't you spend that time tending to me instead?', my adult part understands that, in a way, they were probably just trying to recreate the lush landscape in which each had been raised; my mother in the Fijian tropics and my father, whose New Zealand family home had boasted a wonderful garden and an orchard sloping towards Takapuna Beach. I don't imagine it had been easy for either of them to relocate to Australia.

When our family returned to New Zealand for Christmas holidays we stayed in that Stephenson family house. It was a wooden, forties-style residence in Brown Street, Takapuna, and you could see the ocean from the back veranda. 'There'll be a ship along presently,' Grandma would say, taking her late husband's brass telescope and aiming it out towards Rangitoto, the peaked volcanic island opposite Takapuna Beach. My father's older sister Alice, whom we called Auntie Sally, lived there alone after my paternal grandma (whom I barely remember) passed away. I always got to stay in my father's old room, which had a lovely framed fretwork rendering of the Lord's Prayer on the wall, as well as a beautifully illuminated document congratulating my grandfather Octavius on his much-appreciated years of service as the Postmaster in Opotiki. I loved that room. Auntie Sally would always come in and hug me good-night ...

You seem happy just now ...

Mmm ... Those Takapuna summers, playing on the beach with my cousins, fishing with my uncles and aunts, having afternoon tea with the whole extended family... there was no pressure to do anything or be anything other than simply children having fun. Uncle Bill and Auntie Marjorie lived next door, with my cousins Elizabeth, Brett, Alistair, Margot and Deborah. We picnicked in the orchard under shady trees heavy with ripe peaches, pears, plums, apples and guava. I still salivate when I think of the incredible taste of those naturally grown peaches and plums. I took my children to Italy some years ago in early summer and the taste of those white peaches transported me straight back to Takapuna.

In the New Zealand outdoors there was nothing that could really hurt us – quite a consideration for children raised in Australia within biting distance of several species of indigenous killers. I eventually came to love the harshness of the Australian landscape, but as a youngster in Sydney we were always on the lookout for the savage creatures that lurked in our suburban play areas. Redback spiders were the worst; those things could jump, or so we thought. A female one's bite could definitely kill, and antivenom was not widely available then. Oh boy, we really had to know our spiders. There were the enormous brown, furry huntsmen spiders that often crept from behind the curtains and scurried across our bedroom walls. We knew they'd bite, but wouldn't kill us – same for the brown trapdoor spiders with their secret, spring-lidded burrows. But other eight-legged scuttlers were seriously threatening. We especially had to watch out for funnel-web spiders; to show who was boss, those aggressive, shiny brown beasts – purveyors of a lethal neurotoxin-filled bite – would actually stand on their back legs and bare their fangs.

In New Zealand there were no poisonous snakes, unlike the highly venomous black snakes, brown snakes and tiger snakes that sunned themselves on paths we might take to a Sydney suburb bus stop (armed with all the warnings about the dangers of the natural Australian environment, as a child I remember wondering how on earth anyone ever got to reach adulthood). Nor were there any shark nets on New Zealand beaches because, apparently, any passing bitey things were too busy migrating elsewhere to bother with us. Australians were rather shark-phobic in those days. We erroneously believed that all sharks were aggressive and liked the taste of human flesh (it was only after I became an adult scuba diver that I learned that in reality most sharks are harmless unless they're provoked or mistake you for a seal). But other Australian marine creatures could be lethal, especially salt-water crocodiles and those nasty box jellyfish you get in Queensland. In Takapuna, we suffered only mild jellyfish stings. Oh, the bees could get you, especially while stealing honey from a hive, and prickly burrs we called 'bindy-eyes' would imbed themselves in our bare feet. Apart from that, it was a predator-free zone. Even the sun was kinder.

So New Zealand provided a strong sense of safety for you, not only in the physical environment, but emotionally, too, since you were surrounded by accepting relatives ...

Mmm ... and there were so many cousins, aunts, uncles. I loved that feeling of being part of a big family – even though it was always so brief. I think they were a bit wary of us – they called us 'the Australians'– but, nevertheless, I felt a sense of belonging that was . . . almost . . . tribal. Cousin Anne (my Auntie Polly's daughter) would join us from time to time, and so would various neighbourhood chums. We'd take turns lying in the garden hammock, and playing vinyl records on Auntie Sally's portable gramophone player. We all acquired the art of winding that contraption up via the handle on the side and, when the music began to sound a bit scratchy, we knew exactly how to replace the old needle. My cheeky older cousin Alistair teased me mercilessly, but I loved it because he was the closest thing to a brother I ever knew. Older boys, I decided, were really a lot of fun.

Sometimes we all travelled north to Kerikeri to stay with Auntie Edna and Uncle Robbie. Edna was a blousy, good-humoured, chain-smoking woman with leathery skin, dark curly hair and a voice like an automatic rifle. I remember her sitting outside in her apron, gathering up my sisters and me to help her shell the peas. Her husband Robbie was a salty, taciturn man who was rarely without his sweet-smelling pipe. Very patiently, he taught me to make wonderful shell boxes, using cigar boxes, sand, varnish and small, delicate shells we found at low tide. Every now and again he would take us fishing on his wooden launch. Out in the bay, my cousins and I would dive from the boat and pick up crayfish or lobsters – well, my big cousins would pick them up; I was too afraid to touch those spiny critters with such peculiar eyes. As the sun was setting, the grown-ups would build a fire on the beach to cook them. Lobster is still my favourite food, and not because it's swish; it reminds me of the most idyllic times of my childhood.

At low tide we would gather in shallow water and 'do the twist' in the sand. When our feet met something shell-like, we'd bend down and pick up one of a variety of live 'pippies' (a bit like cockles), toss them in a bag, then steam them in a pot over the beach fire. Roaming around the Bay of Islands, even for those few days we had, was bliss;

although such times were in sharp contrast to our normal life. They always reminded me of what we were missing out on, growing up in the Australian inland without frequent access to my benevolent aunts and uncles. Oh, don't get me wrong, Sydney is a gorgeous, vibrant city that I appreciated more and more as I grew older – but early on I really envied my New Zealand cousins. They seemed to be happier and far more relaxed than we were.

In those days I never knew that I was of both European and Maori descent. I am proud that my great, great grandmother was a Maori woman but my family never mentioned it to me when I was young. Although, looking back, I had some rather brown aunts, which should have offered me a clue. Auntie Sally was my favourite. She never married and seemed to devote her life to caring for others. She lived with her mother until she died. I remember her as short and roundish, with wise, empathic brown eyes and badly fitting dentures that she nervously sucked in and out of position. As a young adult she had been a school teacher. She wore sensible skirts and blouses, and lace-up shoes and, throughout the day, would add layer upon layer of white face powder on her nose, forehead and cheeks (now I wonder whether she was consciously disguising her naturally dark complexion). But, most importantly, she was clucky, sweet and endlessly kind. In contrast to what I sensed from my parents, I knew she loved me unconditionally. Sitting at her tea table, wolfing down her thinly sliced bread and butter, her perfect scones and her springy date bread, I briefly felt the world was a safe place. Under her ample, benevolent wings, I could just be me.

Some children grow up feeling that it is unsafe to reveal their true selves. They come to understand that their job is to be what others want them to be – or there will be terrible consequences. This is not just about being good, obedient children – most parents would wish that of their offspring – you, it seems, were expected to reflect perfectly your parents . . .

Yes! And it always seemed that if I deviated from that – expressed my individuality – I would lose their love and attention (which were sparingly meted out in any case). Ballet was an exception, though. It was tolerated, although I was expected to maintain excellence. Funny, I just remembered that I once glimpsed a picture of my mother performing – maybe even dancing – in some university show, wearing a pair of harem pants. She was very embarrassed about it. She hated her body and would rarely allow anyone to photograph her. But it did make me wonder if perhaps she had a secret longing to be in the performing arts . . .

Hmmm . . . Children do sometimes act out a parent's unconscious, unfulfilled desires . . .

Ah, yes . . . She did once admit to me that she had chosen the field of biology not because it was her passion, but simply because the course was available to her for some reason or another. Perhaps I held the key to her unfulfilled desire to dance or perform; perhaps that's why she supported my 'dabbling in the arts' – up to a point.

You mentioned your mother hated her body . . . What are your thoughts about that? Do you think you might have internalized those same feelings about your own body?

Hmmm. I never thought about that before. It's not so much that I dislike my body – actually I feel very grateful that it has stood up to everything I've put it through, from childbirth to *Strictly* – no, it's more that I dislike ageing. And, actually, I have specific feelings about specific bits of me. Years ago I had some liposuction on my thighs and I remember very consciously thinking, 'I'm eliminating my mother . . .' She had 'thunder thighs' because she never exercised but she really wasn't bad looking. In fact, in her later years she looked incredibly like

Annie Lennox does now. But, ugh, it makes me shudder to see Annie, even though I like and admire her and think she's beautiful. I sat beside her on a TV show recently and felt very uncomfortable for those personal reasons. I mean, obviously I wasn't about to say, 'Hey Annie, I'm avoiding you because you look exactly like my mother!'

But Mum just wasn't . . . mumish. She seemed cold and judgmental, and her smile always seemed forced. Even nowadays, when someone wraps me in his or her arms and holds me with the genuine tenderness I absolutely melt, while at the same time I feel imbued with longing and pain for what I missed out on.

There are many ways to be a deprived child . . .

Yeah, and that's got to be the worst. I would rather have gone hungry. When I first began to study psychology I learned about Harry Harlow's famous series of experiments. You know the ones?

Mmm . . . conducted between 1957 and 1963 at the University of Wisconsin-Madison. He removed baby rhesus monkeys from their mothers and had them 'raised' by two kinds of wire 'mother' machines that dispensed milk, one made of bare mesh wire and the other covered with soft terrycloth. He found that the baby monkeys clung to the terrycloth mother whether or not it provided them with food . . .

Right! He essentially showed that a lack of contact comfort is psychologically stressful . . .

Prior to Harlow's work, people actually thought that emotions were unimportant, and that simply providing food for a child was the most important way to create a strong mother–child bond. But Harlow showed that it was actually the intimate body contact (with either mother or father) that strengthened the bond . . .

Damn. This understanding emerged a long time after I really needed it! If only Harlow had done his revolutionary 'study of love' earlier, I – and millions of other people – might have grown up much happier.

Well, when you were born, the prevailing beliefs were that it was better to limit or avoid bodily contact so as to avoid spoiling children . . .

My parents almost certainly held those views! It was the curse of the WASP, wasn't it, the white Anglo-Saxon Protestant. To be honest, it was incredibly helpful to understand finally that they did not necessarily withhold love from me because I was unloveable . . .

That is commonly how children interpret physical coldness . . .

. . . but rather, because they intellectually thought that was the best way to raise me. Of course, there was also the fact that my father thought it was OK to hit us, so I suppose I was physically terrified of him . . . That's another thing – in those days, people didn't know that smacking children is an ineffective way of disciplining them, not to mention teaching them to be violent and being wrong on so many levels. Anyway, I had a terribly strong, visceral reaction to learning about Harlow's studies – it explained so much about myself.

You're not alone. A clinical psychology degree course always contains material that triggers personal reactions; it's always much more than an academic exercise, and creates emotional learning and growth. The toilets of any good psychology department have a steady flow of crying, shaking students, privately experiencing catharses, epiphanies, and facing their demons in various ways. It's just an unofficial part of the curriculum, and essentially a good thing . . .

At least Auntie Sally hugged me. Besides her, one other adult in my life provided true, non-judgmental sanctuary: my mother's mother, my grandmother Annie Thomas. I adored Nanna, as we called her. At some point, after her life as a missionary in Fiji, she came to live with us in Thompson Street. I remember the thick stockings and high-heeled, black, lace-up brogues in which she stomped up to the shops, even in summer, and her long, grey hair which was always rolled up under a hairnet. My sisters and I would watch with great interest when she removed, bathed and replaced her glass eye.

That sounds rather bizarre . . . As a child, what did you make of that?

Well, we got used to it, like it was normal. But I felt dreadfully sorry for her. She told me a surgeon had made a mistake and irreparably damaged her eye during a cataract operation. She actually seemed rather childlike, as if she'd always been looked after and never quite grown up . . . In fact, my mother treated her a bit like a child . . .

That must have been an uncomfortable household dynamic for you to observe . . .

I didn't really think about it consciously. Not until recently. I did feel very protective of Nanna though, and I knew she felt the same about me. Our house was small, so we were all rather on top of each other. My parents eventually extended the place so they would have a larger room, Lesley and Claire would share the second bedroom, and Nanna and I would both have our own, small rooms. In Nanna's sat a carved sandalwood chest she had brought from the islands. Occasionally she would open it and out would fly the most alluring scents of the Pacific – coconut, palm, jasmine and sweet woods. Inside lay a treasure trove of intricately woven Fijian fans, a terrifying war club, a lamp made from a large, orange-pink triton shell and black-and-tan coconut mats. This chest held for me all the mystery of the ocean, the call of exotic places, and the thrill of travel and adventure. It held the promise of a future abroad.

So – perhaps even now – travel is a way of connecting you with your grandmother, someone who appreciated who you truly were . . .

I suppose it is. My travelling dreams first came true when we boarded a ship for London, just after I turned eleven in December, 1960. My darling Auntie Sally came with us, which was a great joy for me and my sisters – although it was a shame Nanna was considered too challenged by her visual impairment to accompany us. She entered a home for elderly people who needed special care and, although I didn't understand this at the time, she would never live with us again. In fact, she spent the rest of her life in relative isolation from the family.

You have a lot of feelings about that . . .?

Terrible. It still makes me sad and guilty to think about it. Most regrettably, I was so busy going through all the challenges in my own young life I did not pay her enough attention. In my adult travels I've now come across societies – especially in the South Pacific – where older people are revered, admired and never shut away or isolated from an extended family. In my opinion, that's the way it ought to be.

Sydney to London was a very long ocean voyage, but I felt at home on the sea. I loved its smell, its calm, even its fury. The Southern Cross changed position as we rolled north and, when we passed the fiery, volcanic island of Krakatoa, I was allowed to stay up late to marvel at the show as glowing lava was hurled into the night sky. I loved being on deck when we slid slowly into new, exotic ports, each with thrillingly unfamiliar sights and sounds. Men

speaking strange languages would come on board, and I was fascinated by the colour of their skin; in those days, Australian Prime
Minister Robert Menzies had introduced the 'White Australian
Policy' to keep out black immigrants and, even more shamefully,
the Aboriginal people were treated appallingly and kept well out of
sight, so I had rarely seen anyone who wasn't white.

Iberia

6th December 1960

Dear Nanna,

*We arrived at Melbourne at 4pm yesterday
and we will leave at 9pm Wednesday. Today
we ... may be seeing Captain Cook's Cottage and
the Fitzroy Gardens. We had an awful first day
with a storm going through the heads but we had
a beautiful second day. I must tell you of two
very funny incidents. The children all go to
meals by themselves which we all find is great
fun. Well, the first day we were too sick to
come down to any meals so the second day was
the day of our first meal when all the calami-
ties occurred. Firstly we were not used to the
sugar shaking out of a shaker so here are
Claire, Lesley and myself dealing out lumps of
sugar on to our cereal and laughing at everyone else because we thought that they were shaking on salt or pepper! Secondly there were two
small jugs of milk - one for our side of the
table and one for the other three children
sitting on the other side. Claire emptied our
jug on her cereal so Lesley started reaching for
the jug for the others but I stopped her in*

time. This morning we had cocoa but they made it too strong so we all put four or five lumps of sugar in it. We have made friends with the three children across the table and we play with them a lot. We now know a gentleman with a little white moustache who speaks broad Scottish so well that we can hardly understand the things he says. Our steward is English and is extremely nice. He smuggles us biscuits during the night but we don't say anything to Mum or Dad about that. I hope you're enjoying yourself at Sunset Lodge.

Your loving grandchild,
Pamela

P.S. Please excuse my writing.

At sea, even my parents seemed to relax and, when we crossed the equator and 'King Neptune' appeared on board to preside over the ceremonial games, my sisters and I witnessed our father sitting on a greasy pole battering a fellow passenger with a balloon before being forced off into the swimming pool's deep end. It was so uncharacteristic of him, we squealed with unmitigated delight. We landed at Tilbury Docks on a grey, freezing winter's day, and headed to Surrey, where my parents had rented an upstairs flat in a house overlooking a duck pond on Ham Common. The nice lady next door who invited us to tea turned out to be the mother of the spy Anthony Blunt, but we were unaware of that at the time. Had I known that, it certainly would have piqued my sense of the dramatic.

My parents took up their sabbatical posts at the Chester Beatty Research Institute in London, and my sisters were placed in a local school. But it had been decided that, since I was so ahead of my age group academically, I should take a year off; then I'd be closer to my classmates' age when I entered a Sydney high school. Perhaps my parents finally understood how socially difficult it had been for me? It's more likely their chosen grammar school would not take me until I turned twelve. Anyway, my parents very kindly placed me in a school where they thought I could take it a bit easy, learn some French, and indulge my passion for ballet. Little did they know just one year of that programme at the Arts Educational Trust at 144 Piccadilly (it's not there any more) would entirely rev up my desire to perform and render me disinterested in academic achievement for the next three decades! It was a school that provided regular lessons in the morning and theatre arts in the afternoon, and it unleashed in me a fully fledged, performing monster.

Again I was a misfit, a curiosity from Australia. The school was run in a highly formal manner. We had to curtsey to teachers whenever we passed them – 'Good morning, Miss Gracie!' – and there were strict uniform rules – for ballet we wore white tunics with a royal blue belt, white socks and pink ballet shoes. For 'character' dance classes we had black embroidered skirts over a black leotard and black character shoes with a little heel. The regular school uniform was a blue-and-white check gingham dress with a blazer, white gloves and straw hat. It was quite a culture shock for me, coming from a relaxed Australian primary school. In fact, I felt similar to the other girls purely in my adoration of our dashing French teacher, who had a thrillingly seductive accent and resembled the actor Alain Delon.

But I could hold my own when it came to ballet. Edna Mann had taught me well. I had a nice turn-out, good posture and excellent extension in my legs and arms. Ballet hurt, especially pointe work, but it was a 'good' hurt. Blisters, calluses, bunions, bleeding toes, pulled muscles – it's weird how that's all acceptable in the ballet world, even for children. The puritan ethic 'suffering's good for the soul' is very close to the raison d'être of ballet; yet I would never quibble about the value of the discipline it teaches young people.

It may also have seemed to fit with your obsessive compulsive nature . . .

That's true . . .

And all that physical exercise must have helped to reduce your anxiety . . .

Yeah. And the challenge of it excited me. The other forms of dance on the Arts Educational curriculum, including 'character', 'modern' and a bit of child-level ballroom, were new to me. The latter was very simple, with girls dancing with girls, and it bored me. For our end-of-year exam we had to bring in a party dress and I remember how hurt I was when I entered the girls' dressing room and caught everyone sniggering at my home-made ensemble – a rose pink, empire-line number trimmed with white lace, worn with a cummerbund and bolero jacket. My mother had made it from a McCall's pattern and, despite my ambivalence about my mother, I really do appreciate that she tried so hard to turn us out nicely. I just wish we three sisters hadn't all been dressed exactly alike; that was hell. No wonder I was delighted to be so gorgeously dressed by incredibly clever people for *Strictly*. It was the ultimate soothing of that early humiliation. Anyway, what I really came to love in my London year was tap dancing, and I was very proud to achieve a silver medal level. More importantly, I was also introduced to acting, which was a revelation. The notion of expressing one's self with the whole body – including the voice – was not just novel, it seemed . . . easy and natural for me. My world had changed.

17th March 1961

Dear Nanna,

We have not had snow yet ... Some very
exciting things happened this week at school.
We were having a normal ballet lesson when
in walked Ram Fopal who is a very famous
Indian dancer. Miss Wheelwright, my ballet
mistress, asked Kay and myself to dance for
him the dance we had been preparing for our
exam which was an enchainment. I wished that
I'd had my autograph book with me. You know
how the school serves hot lunches for us, well,
yesterday the junior school revolted against
the school lunches. It all started by a girl
called Adrienne going up to Matron and
saying, 'Do you think this stuff is food
because I don't think it is, I think it is
muck,' and pushed it in front of Matron's
nose. When she was sent to Miss Valerie she
told her to go and get all the children who
didn't like the school food. Three quarters of
them turned up (I didn't). At the end of the
day their stories of it had stretched so far
that one story said that the cook's arm had
been broken! Nobody got into much trouble
though. I will write again soon.

　　　　Your loving grandchild,
　　　　　　Pammey

P.S. Please excuse my writing.

Halfway through that year I wrote a musical play, *Cabbages and Kings*, which the pupils performed with full encouragement and support from the teachers. It owed more than a little something to *My Fair Lady* but I felt wonderfully appreciated. At the very end of my time at the Arts Educational Trust – once I turned twelve and was legally allowed to perform professionally – I took part in a short run of *The Nutcracker Suite* with the Festival Ballet Company at the Royal Festival Hall. All right, I didn't really dance; I just played a toy soldier (black shiny cardboard hat, navy jacket with epaulettes, white stretch stirrup trousers and shoes with spats), which involved a bit of marching and pretending to let off a fake cannon. But, for me, it was thrilling to be on a real stage and watch the proper ballerinas perform.

5th December 1961

Dear Nanna,

Thank you very much for the gift you sent me. Thank you also for the letter you sent me which contained a little hint that I should write a letter to you. I am sorry that I haven't written for such a long time but so many things have been happening that I have not had much time. Firstly I have been chosen to appear at the London Royal Festival Hall in a ballet called 'Casse Noisette' – 'The Nutcracker' – and although it is a wonderful experience it has already involved several inconveniences such as rehearsing all day every day up 'til Christmas when we have actually broken up. Then because my twelfth birthday came rather late there has been some trouble getting my licence through. Actually the ballet is on for three weeks but as we are leaving on the second of January I may only be in it for one week. I shall probably be paid about ten pounds. I have already received a long list of make-up which will cost pounds. I have written a musical play which has had three or four successful performances and last Friday a photographer came to our school to take some photos of myself with several members of the cast. I am sitting on a bench in one of Mummy's laboratories watching a lady taking the innards out of a hen. It looks so ghastly that I have turned my chair round!

Your loving grandchild,
Pamela

P.S. I hope you can understand my writing because I can't!

Like all little ballet students, I harboured a secret longing to be Clara, the young girl whose party and subsequent night-time dream forms the backbone of the *Nutcracker* story. The lucky girl who landed that role got to wear a pink, flowing nightdress, dance on pointe, and hold hands with John Gilpin, the gorgeous male dancer in a short jacket and white tights who played the prince. I noticed he had a very muscular bottom and paraded a mysterious big bulge in the front of his pants. Now, I did know that boys had penises because a primary school boy had shown me his floppy little willie on our front porch in Thompson Street, but this thing John Gilpin had was enormous, oval and immobile. 'What exactly is that?' I wondered. I had no idea.

We travelled home from England on a different ship, the SS

Canberra, a brand new liner that was the queen of the P&O fleet at that time. What is it about ships and me? I would live on a small boat if I could. My passion for the sea must have started with those liners. Although I'm not crazy about cruise ships now, back then the *Canberra* seemed incredibly romantic and endlessly exciting. A complete contrast to my Sydney life. This time, instead of travelling overland in Egypt we stayed on board and sailed through the Suez Canal. I played ping-pong on deck the entire way, keeping half an eye out for a Bedouin skirmish or a hint of an *Arabian Nights*-type of scene. Sinbad the sailor, perhaps? But no, because there was little to see but sandy banks with the occasional palm tree or camel. I had become used to the roll of the ocean, the stench of over-taxed air-conditioning units, the creak, creak of the thick, oily lines that held the ship to the dock. It seemed strangely like home. But as much as I enjoyed that return sea voyage, it was accompanied by a sense of fore-boding. I felt my hope and energy draining away as I faced the rest of my childhood in Thompson Street. I had absolutely loved that entire year in London and sobbed my heart out when I had to leave. Not only had Auntie Sally been with us the whole time, with her endless comfort and kindness, but I sensed that, for the rest of my school days, I would never find people who truly understood me. I was right.

Progress Notes – Dr P. Connolly

A good therapeutic alliance has been formed. Patient displayed unusually early regression and expression of trust. Acute vulnerability. Infantile trauma? Perhaps pre-verbal? Father appeared to be physically threatening. Revisit. One of the first significant traumatic events appears to have been serious illness, but patient seems consciously unaware of full psychological impact. Eating disorder? Binge/purge cycle? Body Dysmorphic Disorder? Assess. Maternal body-image issues appear to have been transferred to daughter. Explore. Mother disapproved of prankster personality in father – so becoming comedian may represent a rebellious stance against mother and desire to join with father? Patient is quite insightful in spurts, but entirely lacks self-awareness in other areas. Interesting blind spots. Obsessive-compulsive nature, especially expressed as anxiety-based ticks and compulsion to repeat prayers. Sister escaped parental control, why not patient?

Patient is heavily invested in pleasing everyone. Compulsive caretaker? May not be able to accept that being all things to all people is impossible.

The patient is extremely angry at parents, but feels shameful about this and has perfected a controlled exterior to hide it. Has been unable to reconcile parental expectations with sense of safety or self-efficacy. Some narcissistic rage remains. The therapy will get rocky. Anxious depression (moderate to severe) seems present. Over-focus on self-improvement may be a means of assuaging deep anxiety, while repeated elective surgical interventions may be tantamount to self-harming gestures. Inquire about self-harm, cutting? Deep sense of unworthiness, self-loathing. Acute mortality-awareness.

A good start.

Chapter Three

SINK, SWIM, SLUNG OUT

We have not been in session for a while . . . Where have you been?

Back in Australia . . .

What's it like for you to be back there?

I love it. Australia is a fantastic, diverse country and Sydney – well, as a city it's hard to beat, but for me there's always something deeply upsetting about it, too. I think it's the harbour that does it. Pitches me into a deeper brooding. It's murky in there – in my mind, I mean, not the harbour, although the part of Sydney's waterway by Circular Quay is definitely not a place to take a dip. Much as I like scuba diving around sharks, I'd avoid the hungry, big-jawed sea critters in there. I mean, I know they don't like the taste of us; they usually just take one bite and spit us out but, well, that one bite might be a rather important body part.

On the first night of my latest trip to Sydney I couldn't sleep. Jetlagged and bloated, I jogged out of my harbour-side hotel at 2am and headed south along the shoreline towards the Opera House. I calculated that from there to the Opera House and back was 3.5km (it said so on my joggers' map) so I had to do three round trips to make up 10km. See, against my better judgment, I've agreed to take part in a swimming relay across the Irish Sea, which is going to take every ounce of strength, guts and determination I have. What is WRONG with me?

We will eventually understand why you push yourself so hard, but go on . . .

OK, well, 10km was the distance I had to run to increase my fitness for the challenge. As I sprinted along the stone wall right on the harbour's edge, I was appalled to see a number of plastic bags floating close by. I stopped and looked round for a stick with which to haul them out, then suddenly I realized they were large, pale jellyfish. That sent my anxiety soaring. See, what's most daunting for me about this upcoming ocean swim is not the fact that it's three times further than the English Channel; not the fact that the water is close to freezing, or that thirty different types of sharks pass by the region; it is not even the fear that the water might still be radioactive a good thirty years after the Sellafield nuclear accident. No, it's the Lion's Mane – one of the largest species of jellyfish in the world – that is what really scares me. Did you know this giant's body alone has been known to grow to a whopping twenty centimetres, each with 800 reddish, three-metre-long tentacles? They have a terrible, blistering sting that can cause muscular cramp, even respiratory and heart problems. Since I'll be swimming partly during the night time, it will be impossible to see these trailing monsters. My sleep is frequently disturbed by visions of my opening my mouth to take a large breath and ingesting a section of three-metre-long tentacle.

You're having nightmares about the jellyfish?

Yeah, would they sting my throat, causing it to swell and constrict my windpipe and, well, game over?

Hmmm. Let's see . . . jellyfish with long, penile-shaped tentacles . . .

Oh, come on, doctor! Sometimes a jellyfish is just a jellyfish . . . But I do find myself ruminating about it . . . Perhaps between now and September I could learn how to perform – while swimming – a do-it-yourself tracheotomy. I need to work on that. I'm not kidding. See, that's who I am – I push myself. I guess I internalized my parents' work ethic that I used to despise, and now I'm one of them. I'm learning to play more and my serendipitous return to dancing has helped enormously but, basically, I'm still a nerd.

You really hate the idea of being perceived as studious and dull . . .

Mmm.

Rather like your parents . . .

Gotcha! But I want to finish telling you about my run. No one was about, and though it's quite dark around Circular Quay in parts, I knew I had to finish this circuit before the sun rose because by 9am it would be too hot to move. It crossed my mind that the shadowy corners here and there made this a little risky, and for once I was grateful for the presence of security cameras. I knew my husband would be horrified if he knew I was doing this alone, but he was asleep after a triumphant evening on stage at the famous, white-sailed building for which I was now heading. My path was lined with mauve palm tree shadows, rows of iron benches and a few forlorn coffee shops. Suddenly, I was really struck by how much Circular Quay has changed. When I was a schoolgirl, crossing the harbour every day by ferry to attend the Sydney Church of England Girls' Grammar School, I never saw a sign saying 'Have you sorbet'd today?' Sorbet'd today?! I didn't know what a sorbet was until I was at least thirty. No, Sydney in those days was very much a vanilla ice cream kind of town. I turned a corner and found myself face-to-face with the same jetty I approached every day of my secondary school life, chug-chugging to and from Woolwich, on the green-and-yellow Sydney Harbour ferries. The vessels were sitting there, empty and dark, but they seemed just the same – wooden work-horses smelling of oil, salt and sweat. As the wash swept against the jetty, I heard the clank of the gangplank and I noticed my anxiety rising. It was horribly familiar.

You think that environment triggered your anxiety? Can you remember exactly where your mind was going?

Yes. My mantras of worry were really taking hold: 'Perhaps my knees will give out. Maybe I'll have to stop after the first round trip. Maybe it'll take too long.' But the rational part of me was questioning the child within: 'What exactly is the problem? You've got until dawn, and even beyond. What else are you going to do at this time of night? It's cool now – a great opportunity.' I breathed a bit deeper. I had to tell myself: 'This is not exactly over-taxing me. Fresh from *Strictly* I am fitter than I was when I was twenty. What am I really worrying about? Why am I always so anxious to get on to the next "thing"? Why can't I just enjoy the moment? Am I just a giant rat on a cosmically operated treadmill?' On the other hand, this demon I have inside me – the one who drives, drives, drives – he has challenged me to do the myriad of extraordinary things I've done in my life, and continue to do. But, the thing is, I don't think my anxiety was just about the run; there was something else I couldn't put my finger on . . .

Hmmm. Let's see – your ferry trips began after your trip to Europe, didn't they . . .?

Yes. When I started secondary school. At that time I was really antsy. When we returned to Sydney from London at the end of 1961, I just couldn't settle down. At twelve years old, I'd seen my future and was unwilling to let it go. But for now I had to make the transition to grammar school. My parents marched me to the popular, central department store, David Jones, and bought my new school uniform: navy smock, white blouse, tie, straw hat and gloves. And (this is hard to believe) they had my feet x-rayed to ensure my school shoes fit, a well-dodgy practice that was considered useful and safe in those days. But everything had to be right. At the Sydney Church of England Girls' Grammar School (SCEGGS), the wearing of the uniform was serious business. All pupils carried cards that a teacher or prefect could sign if they saw you breaking a rule, such as taking off your hat in public (three signatures led to detention). I sat outside on the ferry twice a day, every school day for many years, firmly holding my hat on in the blustering winds. Oh, I was a rule-keeper all right – until I finally snapped (fasten your seat-belt now, because my teenage story is going to get a bit rocky).

I'm so afraid of telling this next bit. See, initially, I went through the motions of following the rigorous academic studies in that school for high-flyers, but, internally, I was raging at my parents. Maths, Latin, Science. Didn't they understand it just wasn't possible to do what they had done? Expose someone to an environment where they feel truly appreciated, then whisk it all away again. It was like a one-time exposure to crack cocaine. No one thought I was special at my new school, in fact, I felt I was largely despised for not being like everyone else. I became aware of yet another reason why my classmates might reject me: they tended to be from wealthy families and lived in lovely sandstone houses in fashionable North

Shore suburbs; I was not, did not. No one at school had heard of Boronia Park, but it was near Gladesville and Ryde, which were decidedly unswish.

Worst of all, there was nowhere to continue my acting classes, and finding a suitable ballet class was difficult. I joined a dance school in the centre of Sydney, but that meant walking there after school and not getting home until very late. I already travelled three hours' round trip to school (bus to Hunter's Hill, then a cross-harbour ferry, then another bus to Darlinghurst) and, with all the homework I was given, I was often exhausted. But one of the deepest regrets of my whole life is giving up ballet. It was a huge loss in my life, and I think it must have made me quite depressed.

Well, all that hard physical exercise had helped keep your anxiety at bay. But without it . . .

Oh yes . . . I was struggling in many ways. My nightly prayer regime continued to be overwhelmingly long and comprehensive, making my knees stiff and raw. The self-flagellating practices of medieval monks would have made perfect sense to me. I began to have trouble concentrating and started slipping from being an excellent student to a mediocre one who sometimes neglected her homework. I began to tell lies to my fellow classmates in a pitiful attempt to fit in: 'I go surfing every weekend. I have an aqua and white surfboard. I have a gorgeous blonde boyfriend.' But they didn't buy a word of it; I was pasty-white with pimples, had short, lank, mousy hair and braces on my teeth. Popular girls were pretty, tanned and athletic, with clear skin and real boyfriends. I did have two or three school friends: Pinkie, Pauline and a lovely Dutch girl called Phillipa. They were remarkably tolerant of my weird, miserable self. As for my sisters, I felt isolated from them. Deep down I may even have resented them for having escaped the expectations that were placed on me. But it also seemed to me that I shouldered a burden I should not inflict on them: at some level I understood that by being the oldest, the 'guinea pig', I was protecting them from misery.

When my father became the organist and choir master at a local Anglican church, my mother and I were seconded as choir members. That meant endless singing practice around the piano with my father. He tried to train me to sound like the boy sopranos whose pure, clear voices he much preferred. Since I had a natural, female vibrato, this was an impossible and frustrating task. At school we had chapel every morning and, for reasons I cannot fathom, I also joined the school choir. That was an awful lot of church, and sometimes it seemed to me that I lived not in the bright Australian sunlight, but in shadowy, darkwood choir stalls surrounded by cool, grey stone. I was sent to piano lessons from the age of thirteen. I was quite musical and eventually trained at Sydney's Conservatorium of Music, but I hated it because it meant more pressure, higher expectations, and even more practising. And when our local Sunday school fell short of a pianist I was asked to step in to accompany the hymns, which led to torturous Sunday mornings. Wracked with anxiety, I would flee red-faced after making dreadfully obvious mistakes every time.

I pleaded for a guitar and was thrilled when I finally received one for my fourteenth birthday. I spent hour upon hour sitting on my bed producing soulful renderings of Joan Baez and Peter, Paul and Mary songs. My voice was high and warbling – painful for the listener, I imagine – but it was the true beginning of my teenage bid for individualism and it felt comforting and real. I discovered Bob Dylan, who was a revelation and could almost be credited with saving me from complete despair. His poetry spoke to me, and it seemed like something personal I had that did not belong to my parents. Well, they'd never relate to: 'Yes, and how many years can some people exist / Before they're allowed to be free?' But I certainly did.

I tried to fit in at school by keeping up with popular trends, but I did not have access to pop music at home (I learned folk songs by reading sheet music with chord charts). When the Beatles visited Sydney in June 1964 (I was fourteen) I was aware that my class-mates were crazy about them, and joined the pack of truants who went along to chant 'John! Paul! George! Ringo!' outside their hotel in King's Cross, but when everyone started singing 'Love, love me do', I was probably the only one in the crowd who didn't know the words. I could never have predicted that a decade or two later I would get to know Paul and George – or that Ringo and his wife Barbara would attend my wedding.

One day a notice was posted on the school bulletin board, encouraging girls to try out for a musical play, *Down in the Valley* by Kurt Weill, a co-production with a nearby boys' school, Cranbrook. I turned up and sang for Gilbert Jones, the teacher who was direct-ing it, and was immediately cast as the *ingénue*. Suddenly, there was hope in my life again. I absolutely loved performing at Cranbrook. Not only was it a chance to return to the stage, but I was able to socialize with boys – something that had been largely missing from my life. I definitely liked boys; in fact, I was a thorough, budding sexpot (still am). *Down in the Valley* was a great success, and it revived my spirits. I followed that by joining the cast of *Our Town* and then appearing in a poetry evening, and came to understand that I really belonged in the performing arts.

But when my thespian fun at Cranbrook ended, I became misera-ble again. I hated school and, except for English, found the lessons boring and tedious. Oh, don't get me wrong, SCEGGS was an excel-lent school that provided a fine education for almost every girl who attended it. But, given my state of mind – my confusion, frustration, and often despair – I needed serious help in order to take advantage of it. At home, my parents seemed to be struggling. I noticed tension between them, and sometimes there were loud fights. I gathered most of this was about work – they had teamed up professionally at the same university so I guess that brought its own challenges. After dinner they sat together at the kitchen table with photographs they'd taken of microscopic samples, anxiously counting cancerous cells. Fun times. I suppose it was a case of 'publish or perish'.

I searched for ways to escape the house, and managed to get a job pumping petrol on Saturday mornings at the local Total station. I was seriously crap at this – in fact, I was a liability – because I knew nothing about engines. But I had begun to secretly pad my bra and wear a little make-up, so I suppose Ken the proprietor thought I might be a kind of 'jailbait' asset. Actually, he was a kind man who tried hard to teach me about cars. I seem to remember making a couple of dreadful mistakes, including pouring oil into the wrong part of the engine, which he never punished me for. I think he felt sorry for me. He had a Morgan dealership, and I did love it when one of those gleaming beauties purred into the garage – although he very wisely made sure I never went near it.

My physical development and attempts at beautification seemed to enrage my mother. It seemed as if she disapproved of my becoming a woman. From twelve years old I was desperate for her to provide me with a bra – if only to cover the shame of my budding nipples. But it was as if such things were best ignored, and certainly never discussed. Maturing seemed to be a sinful process. I remember being in a car with a school friend and being amazed when her mother said, 'Put on some lipstick, honey; it will make you feel better.' I could never have imagined that someone would actually support such a womanly 'vice'.

At school, I was plotting some salvation. At SCEGGS, girls were grouped into houses and the house captains were the ones who produced the end-of-year house plays, which I badly wanted to do. I knew I was not prefect material – and most house captains were also prefects – but since house captains were chosen by house votes, all I had to do was make myself popular and prove myself as a leader. 'All I had to do'! This was a monumental task and I'm not exactly sure how I managed it. But, oh, how hard I worked on it! Drawing on my acting skills (for my fellow students couldn't possibly have started to like the real me, could they?), I assumed the character of a jolly, netball-loving pal-to-all and finally achieved my goal. Although, maybe it was simply a matter of there being no one else who wanted the job. Who wanted to produce a stupid house play when there were dances to attend, outfits to design and boys to make out with? Well, I did, and I chose Bernard Shaw's *Passion, Poison, and Petrifaction*, which I knew would be popular. I released my inner megalomaniac – produced and directed the whole thing, and cast myself as the leading man, Adolphus. It was a riotous romp that I accurately predicted would be a huge success. My wig fell off half-way through, which earned me even more laughs. I think it was my first experience of pure comedy, and I absolutely adored it.

But when that was over, it was back to boredom, antipathy and frustration. My physical development was racing ahead, but no one fully explained the process. Though wary of my interest in boys, my parents had allowed me to go on one or two afternoon dates (with a strongly enforced curfew) and I met a couple of young men at the Church Fellowship with whom I went to the movies and even the beach. But I was in full adolescent angst and craved more freedom. I noticed that was more forthcoming if a boy charmed my mother and was respectful to my father, so I searched for suitable candidates. My first real boyfriend ticked my parents' boxes and was also sweet to me. We attended school football matches and dances, and he introduced me to motorbikes. His Dutch family was incredibly liberal compared to mine, and I was amazed at how accepting his parents were of his

– and my – burgeoning sexuality. But he finally dumped me because I would not have intercourse with him. I was actually quite willing to accommodate him in any way; I just didn't know how. No one had ever told me how sex worked, and it hurt my feelings when he called me 'selfish'.

One evening my parents – surprisingly – allowed me to go to a party with a Cranbrook boy, who picked me up in his parents' Cadillac. We had convinced them that the party would be fully supervised, but it wasn't. There was a lot of beer. This was a new situation for me and it seemed rather exciting, although I did not drink because I hated the taste of alcohol. But we left the party well after my curfew and headed for my house. I remember thinking the stars were spectacularly bright that night, but I would soon see them whirling fast to the music of crashing metal.

As we crossed a bridge, I was very abruptly pitched into terror, panic, and a heart-pumping surge of adrenaline, as my young driver suddenly hit the brakes in an attempt to avoid an oncoming vehicle. He failed, and we hit a small car head on. Six people were crammed into that car. Two of them were killed outright, including the driver. Another couple of victims died on the road while waiting for the ambulance, and the others were seriously injured. I remember their moans of agony, their pleas for help and the last pitiful whimpers of those slipping into unconsciousness.

Then there was a terrible, seemingly endless silence before the sirens approached. I remember the horrors of the ambulance, the glare and shock of the busy hospital, the questioning by the police, and my parents turning up at my emergency room bedside. My date, who (unlike me) had been wearing a seat belt, walked away unharmed. After having been pitched violently against the dash-board, I was left gasping, winded and trying to breathe, with fractured ribs, cheekbone and coccyx. This was the worst thing that had ever happened to me and, naturally, I looked to my parents for help and comfort. 'If you'd only left the party on time,' said my mother, 'you wouldn't be suffering like this, and all those people would still be alive.'

This was more than I could bear – the guilt of believing I had been responsible for four people's deaths. It was clearly all my fault. Now I hated myself with a vengeance. I was bad. I was loathsome. I deserved nothing good. Whatever my parents did to me now would be insignificant in comparison to my own self-punishment. Unconsciously, I looked around for a suitably painful way to harm myself.

My hormones were circulating like mad and, at sixteen, I discovered the thrill of sneaking out at night. It was easy. I'd wait until everyone else in the house was asleep and then prize open my window and jump on to the flowerbed below. At first I met up with fellow teenage folksingers and sat in a local park strumming for hours, but eventually I found my way to older, more exciting – and dangerous – men. I would hitch-hike into wicked King's Cross – the centre of Sydney's well-established and considerably powerful 'vice ring' – and wander around attracting people who did not have my best interests at heart. Now I understand that the adrenaline rush I was getting from being so bravely disobedient was helping to mitigate my depression; if only someone had noticed how troubled I was. I seem to remember my parents expressing some suspicions about my behaviour, but they never really confronted me. I imagine they would have found it hard to believe that I was doing what I was doing. Certainly, I was a thoroughly contrary teenager, often fighting openly with my mother. She would scream at me if I stayed on the phone too long and, in typical teenage fashion, I felt entirely unappreciated and misunderstood.

Nowadays it is better understood that it's wise to give teenagers a bit of slack – a moratorium on their behaviour, to some extent, since their sulky contrariness usually serves an important purpose in their development. But my parents had grown up in a far more conservative society, and I suppose they didn't know how to handle me.

I blossomed into a slim, peroxide-blonde babe with the deep tan all SCEGGS girls aspired to. 'You look quite Negroid,' said my mother when she saw me sunning myself in the back garden. 'It's most unattractive.' I suppose her early days as a white colonial child in a country populated by dark-skinned people had instilled deep prejudice.

I liked to wear my naturally wavy hair straight, but we did not have hair straighteners in those days, so I managed to contort my body sufficiently to lay my hair on an ironing board, cover it with a cloth, and steam it with the iron. Now I marvel at the hand–eye co-ordination that required – although I did burn my arm from time to time. But my breasts were not co-operating; they remained small and bud-like. I stuffed my bikini top with rolled-up school socks, but going in the surf with such poorly improvised augmentation led to an excessive amount of water-retention, shape-distortion and subsequent embarrassment. Sadly, the invention of the Wonderbra was a good few years away.

I was still a virgin at this point. I was fairly ignorant about sex, but I had an inkling that it might be the route to my desired destruction, so when I met a 35-year-old heroin junkie who lured me into his flat, I put up little resistance. It was a horrible, painful experience, out of which I got nothing but glandular fever and gonorrhoea. I suppose it was rape. What was the age of consent back then? I don't even know. I don't want to know. It was just terrible, but I thought I deserved it, and worse. I told no one, but when I became dreadfully ill our family doctor informed my parents of the truth about my ailments. I gave no excuse. My father came to me as I lay sick in bed. 'You were supposed to keep yourself clean until marriage,' he said, with such cold fury I could barely take it in. 'You are no longer my daughter.'

Without further discussion, my parents kicked me out of the house.

(Long silence.)
What was that like for you?

I remember the feeling very well, because I still experience it every time someone rejects me, even in some relatively small way ... You'd think after all these years, all this work I've done, that I'd handle it better ...

Oh, it takes as long as it takes. Tell me, in your mind is there a relationship between ageing and rejection?

(Extremely pregnant silence.)
Oh my God ... that's it! Why didn't I think of that? Since our society is rather negative about people in middle age and beyond, the better, the younger I look, the more likely I am to avoid the pain of being rejected on the basis of my age. And, since rejection is terrifyingly painful for me, of COURSE I'm going to do everything I can to appear youthful!

Good God, doctor, you're brilliant.

Chapter Four

THE DEVIL, DRAG QUEENS AND DANGER

I'm wondering exactly how you survived your charity swim . . . I don't mean physically but rather how did you manage your anxiety?

I did my best to keep it at bay, mainly by sleeping as much as possible whenever I wasn't swimming. I suppose everyone thought I was a bit antisocial, but the whole experience was pretty terrifying and I had to soothe myself as best I could. There I was, in a boat on the Irish Sea – it was 7am and I had been asleep for only three hours. I was shaken awake to take my turn swimming for an hour in the cold and murky waters. Not that I could really complain. After all, I was wearing a wetsuit, whereas the real, professional swimmers were just in their Speedos. But several of the team had already been stung by Lion's Mane jellyfish and had huge red welts to show for it. I was nervous and frightened but, most of all, I hoped I wouldn't make a fool of myself by being unable to complete my hour's swim; that would have been the worst. I told myself that, compared to some things I've endured in my life, this would be a breeze.

Hmmm. Interesting reframe. You've started to turn trauma into triumph – good sign.

At least the sun was out. Jenny, the team member who had been swimming ahead of me was wigged about Lion's Mane sightings and exited the water early. With a fair bit of trepidation, I took over and began to swim, as slowly as I could to begin with, so I could warm up and assess the situation. Luckily, the visibility had improved so I could see objects in the water at a range of three to four metres. But there were several Lion's Mane jellyfish in my vicinity. 'Breathe, Pamela,' I instructed myself. 'You can do this.' Picking my way between the critters, I kept a watchful eye out for trailing tentacles and swam as conservatively as possible. I was shocked to note that some of the beasts actually seemed to be swimming upside down, so their nearly invisible stingers were pointing up towards me.

I thought of my favourite book: Homer's *Odyssey*. The protagonist of that story has always inspired me. In my mind, I would cast myself as Ulysses, braving the treachery of the sea. I would pick my way between these floating islands of danger, and find a way to survive. I could do this. I had already been stung by a Portuguese man-of-war, off shore in the Caribbean some years ago. It wrapped itself around me and, although I immediately went into shock and experienced excruciating pain, I had managed to get ashore and treat myself. (I half-seriously begged Billy to pee on the angry swelling because I'd heard that urine assuaged the pain but, understandably, he refused so I had to make a dash for some vinegar!)

Before my Irish Sea swimming hour was up, I encountered dozens of those hazardous, flame-red creatures. But I picked my way around them – sometimes having to keep my arms at my sides, turn my head sideways, and simply float away from danger. Those beasts tested me just like the Sirens, Circe and Cyclops challenged Ulysses. But thanks to all those who have rejected, abandoned and ill-treated me, I've learned to act calm in the face of threats.

Hmmm. In a sense, that swim was a metaphor for your whole life. But as a teenager, were you calm after your parents kicked you out? And how did you manage to look after yourself?

Well, I wasn't exactly left to fend for myself on the street – my parents would not have wanted that. Instead, they put me in a kind of hostel, several miles away, run by Catholic nuns. God may have been there, but He wasn't with me, and He couldn't help. He had abandoned me, along with my father. Now I was a child of the devil. I had even killed people. I was supposed to continue attending school by myself, but that was well-nigh impossible; instead, I just got into more trouble. Nobody cared, anyway. Nobody insisted that I spend the night in the hostel – in fact, the rule was that if you did not get home by midnight you had to wait until morning! My parents never intervened. They visited me occasionally, but they'd really given up. And they were about to take off on another sabbatical year abroad, so they were gone for over a year after that. They did make arrangements for me to see a psychiatrist, but he behaved in a seductive manner towards me, which only compounded my problems.

In some ways, the fact that my parents had completely turned their back on me actually seemed to be a relief. Completely lost, I spent more and more time wandering around the shadowy streets of King's Cross. I felt at home there because it was well-known to be full of bad people. Yes, I belonged in the shadiest part of town. I was befriended by some of the inhabitants: criminals. The con men, drug pushers, heavies – those people actually seemed kinder and more understanding than my own family. I had a particular boyfriend who, although a con man, treated me like a kind father. All right, he had other girlfriends (who were all sex workers) but I was able to overlook that. Hmmm. I've just realized he must have been a pimp. Anyway, in my mind, I deserved nothing good; in fact, I deserved to be ignored, hurt and ill-treated. Looking back, it was extraordinary that I never became a drug or alcohol addict, never engaged in prostitution or turned to crime myself, and that I managed to survive. I was alienated from my sisters and former school friends and, when I learned that one of my very best school friends had been killed on a motor scooter, it barely registered.

Depression is often experienced as numbness, an inability to feel anything...

Mmm, I suppose that must have been it. I was sort of going through the motions, but not very effectively. When it was time for my final exams at school, even though I had been largely absent from school, I managed to pass. I couldn't tell you exactly how, although I do remember staying up all night in a King's Cross coffee shop to read *King Lear* for my English exam, then putting on my uniform and going straight to school in the morning. Somehow, despite the mess I was in, I knew I had to keep my options open.

I managed to get into the Bachelor of Arts programme at the University of New South Wales, but I had no scholarship so I took jobs working in King's Cross night clubs. I worked as a bartender at Whisky a Go Go, a job I soon discovered required therapist skills just as much as cocktail mixing. It was the time of the Vietnam War and the young soldiers came over to Sydney for some R & R. Americans, Australians ... they were all so incredibly young to be experiencing that brutal world of jungle warfare. They cried bitterly into their Mai Tais and it was hard to know how to comfort them, although I did try. Given the casualty rate in Vietnam, I knew most of them would be dead before the year was up.

Later I became a cocktail waitress at Les Girls, which was a club where drag artists performed, a bit like La Cage aux Folles. It was my first experience of people who were transgendered and I was intrigued by them. Given my background, the whole environment seemed outrageously wicked – in a fun way – and I loved it. I thought the 'girls' were hilarious, bitchy and fantastically glamorous – especially Carlotta, the star of the show. A couple of them took me aside one night and gave me a full make over. They were warm and maternal, and I've had a penchant for false eyelashes ever since.

When I took a job at the new Caesar's Palace nightclub, I became more aware of the society of organized crime that surrounded me back then. In those days, Sydney was a bit like Chicago in the thirties, with mafia-like bosses running things in a way the police could not control. Heavy-set men with foreign accents would enter the club and sit doing business throughout the night, and there was a sinister vibe to the whole scene. I couldn't work out what was really going on but, whatever it was, it was brutal. In my off-the-shoulder, sequinned mini-toga, I once hid behind a partition and witnessed a fellow waitress being thrown through the glass ticket-window. I was quite relieved when I was fired for doing my homework on the sly.

You're telling this story without emotion, as if it had become 'normal' for you to experience such things . . .

Yes. Again, I suppose I had become numbed to it all, beyond feeling anything, no matter how awful or crazy my life became. And I was terribly tired . . .

Another common symptom of depression . . .

Yes, although to some extent perhaps I was courting exhaustion because I did have to support myself. I worked in those clubs until 3am every night except Sunday, so it was very hard to follow my university programme. Truthfully, I was fairly disinterested in continuing the degree, since I had discovered that the drama course was disappointingly theoretical, with little chance to act. Also, I had become involved with a thoroughly nasty German man I met at Caesar's Palace who was a good deal older than me. But I think I understand why I chose such a cruel, inappropriate man . . .

Cruel. Hmmm. Well, when women are conflicted about their fathers – especially if they have been abandoned or rejected by them – they may unconsciously try to repeat the experience by choosing someone who similarly ill-treats them in an attempt to gain mastery over the experience. It's a complicated, thankless task . . .

Mmm, I must have been attempting that at the time. I'm lucky that, over the years, I've had an opportunity to heal from the abuse Helmut perpetrated on me; it was far from pretty . . .

I'm wondering about the emotional aftermath. You still have many feelings about that time? Post-traumatic responses that linger? Tell me a bit about the nature of his cruelty . . .

Well, I mean, the man was a thorough sadist. He tortured and beat me with great regularity, slamming me against the wardrobe, and abusing me verbally, mentally and physically. I took all this punishment meekly; after all, wasn't this exactly what I deserved? Even my own father had abandoned me – that just proved I was worthless. Helmut commanded every ounce of my attention and energy. I dropped out of university and spent my days and nights trying to please him. I gave him the money I earned at the nightclubs and believed I loved him.

Given your deep sense of unworthiness, that is understandable . . .

In fact, I nearly ended my own life over that man. One night, when I came home at the usual late hour, I found him in bed with a dark-haired beauty. I ran off into the night and cried for hours, sitting poised for action by the cliffs at Vaucluse – a famous 'lovers' leap' that was conveniently located in my very neighbourhood.

Help me to understand what stopped you, saved you . . .?

It would have been so easy to end my agony in one fatal leap; in fact, too easy. I suppose I felt I did not deserve respite. I suppose it seemed to me at the time that ending it all would have been a reward. I needed to stay alive in order to receive more pain and punishment; I had not yet paid full price for my essential badness. The next day Helmut insisted the woman in my bed had just been in my imagination, and he returned to the business of beating and threatening me. It's hard to believe I stayed with him for about a year. Every now and then I would come to my senses and try to leave, but he had warned me he would always find me – and hurt me even more.

That must have been a very, very frightening time for you. And you were so young, with no one to talk to. How on earth, do you think, did you manage to survive it?

I'm not quite sure. More importantly, how had I transitioned from goody-goody teacher's pet and star pupil to a disgraced, depressed and desperate young woman, tolerating a horribly abusive relationship – in just six years?

You must be aware that the trauma of abandonment by your parents left you with a self-hating, self-destructive sensibility, and probably severe depression . . . And no one seems to have helped you at all?

Not really. In my capacity as psychotherapist, I've often treated highly troubled adolescents, and I have been very glad to be able to help many women who have survived physical and mental abuse. I believe my own experience of it all has helped me understand what they were going through. The cycle of violence, the essential lack of self-esteem that leads one to tolerate it, the misguided beliefs that one can change one's abuser . . . these were all things I myself had to come to terms with and heal from. Many people think I became a therapist because I needed to understand my unusual husband, but that's not true at all. I became a therapist because I had witnessed the power of psychological healing in my own self, my own life. And I am enormously grateful to the therapists who eventually helped me to heal as well as to the writers of certain important books. Yeah, my journey into mental health began long before I embarked on studies to enter the field. It was my inspiration for eventually becoming a healer myself . . .

Well, that's common. Many of us are . . . wounded healers. But, again, I'm wondering if any one person helped you at that time?

As a matter of fact, it wasn't a human being who saved me initially, although I am thankful to my friend Robert, a young man I'd met on one of my rare appearances on the university campus, who learned what I was going through and tried to help me get away. No, something else saved me: drama school. I don't really know how or why I managed to apply. I was so incredibly lost, and felt so powerless, I am amazed I actually filled out the application form for the National Institute of Dramatic Art (NIDA), a widely respected programme that produced most of Australia's best actors. Of the thousands of people who applied every year, they took only forty applicants, so my chances were very slim. I was offered an audition slot and prepared my monologue in secret because I knew Helmut would not allow me to do anything that was unlikely to benefit him. But when the appointed day arrived, he instructed me to do his washing and I was too afraid to disobey. The following day I called the office and pleaded with the registrar to let me reschedule. Luckily she relented. I managed to sneak off and performed my heart out for the stern panel of theatre experts who would decide my destiny. Somehow, I must have known it would be my escape.

The day the letter arrived announcing that I had won a coveted place at NIDA was the day a tiny light became visible in my future. Deep in my heart I began to believe that I might be worth something after all. With Robert's help, I stealthily packed a bag and sneaked off to a safe haven he had arranged for me. I never looked back. I would never again allow a man to ill-treat me. I would survive and thrive.

Chapter Five

SURVIVAL

Where have your thoughts taken you this past week?

Well, revisiting my experience of physical and mental abuse really
made me think more about my time in the Congo. I went there in
2012, to the Democratic Republic of Congo, because the people
at Merlin, a wonderful charity with a long-term approach to
health care in war-ravaged countries or disaster areas, asked me
to go and help draw attention to the situation there – especially
the amazing work being done by local health workers whom
Merlin supports. In the Congo I heard terrible stories from
women who had been brutalized by men . . . Beyond shocking . . .
In such a situation, my professional skills were barely adequate,
but at least I felt that, because of my own history of violence at
the hand of a man, I was personally in a position to understand
the terrible feeling of shame that lingers in one's psyche. Of
course, what I experienced was nowhere near as horrible as what
Congolese women faced. If I told people some of the things I
heard they'd just want to throw up . . .

First of all, it's a mistake to compare one's personal experience with that of another. But you're sighing deeply. Was the DRC really that bad?

Yeah, absolutely terrible. It's a really troubled country, a war-ravaged zone with a legacy of brutal colonial mistreatment. I really didn't know what I was getting into, although my brave pal, Australian film maker George Gittoes, who had once been locked up there for photographing something politically sensitive, came round to our New York apartment and, in Billy's presence, warned me that if I went there I'd be dragged into a dark room and interrogated. 'You'll be lucky to see the light of day, ever again,' he said. Needless to say, my husband absolutely forbade me to go. But, by now, you should know me well enough to predict whether his laying down of the law had any effect on me whatsoever!

I jumped on a plane for Africa (my first trip to any part of that continent that lies south of Morocco) and landed in Nairobi. So far so good, I thought; well hello, there was a shopping mall at the airport. And cappuccinos. I met up with Sally, the Merlin official who would be my companion and guide. She spoke Swahili which seemed like an excellent asset; I wished I'd acquired it, too. Our next flight winged us to Kigali, Rwanda. Although this region still held the terrible legacy of genocide in living memory (not to mention a terrifying movie with brutal images that were still fresh in my mind), I was pleasantly surprised by the excellent roads and the generally impressive infra-structure of the countryside. Driving the entire length of Rwanda – necessary in order to get to Goma and enter the DRC which is a land-locked country without a safe airport – I was forced to wonder, 'Perhaps genocide is actually profitable!' It was a disgusting thought but, given the enormous amount of cash that flowed into the country after the Tutsi and the Hutu had finished battling it out in such a desperately savage way, I think I could be forgiven for it. At least the

The missionary and the merchant – Grandma ('Nanna') and Grandpa Thomas in Fiji.

Silly hats aboard ship – Mum and Dad, and Auntie Sally opposite, New Year's Eve 1960.

'What exactly do I do with this?' Dad and me.

'Let me out of here!' Me in New Zealand.

The family in Singapore. Mum is hiding behind me, Auntie Sally between Claire and Lesley.

Marine biology lesson from Dad at Coromandel, New Zealand.

'What? Another one?' Lesley's arrival, 1952.

It's a hard life, being a butterfly.

'Peas in a pod' – my sisters and me (*far right*) in the Boronia Park garden, Australia.

Told you I hate Christmas!

'Is this right?' Copying the big girls
– winter ballet concert, 1957.

'Wanna play
chicken?' In New
Zealand.

Four triangles. My favourite is Rangitoto, the volcanic island in the background. Takapuna, circa 1964.

Prodigal return – Boronia Park garden during my drama school years.

At seventeen.

The year after being kicked out, at my school leaving dance. I hand-sewed my dress, and took my 30-year-old boyfriend.

NTNON publicity shot.

Why is *Rowan* holding the trophy?

Sassy stand-up, 1981.

Born to be wild…
Except I wasn't really
riding that and the
outfit wasn't mine!
At sixteen.

Trompe l'oeil flash!

Siren with double-jointed elbow.

In Bali, 1980, trying to forget the hairy Scotsman.

money actually did seem to have been spent on improvements, rather than ending up in some dictator's Swiss bank account.

I didn't feel at all safe in the Congo, though. In fact, I felt uncomfortably visible. You don't want to be blonde there. And you don't want to be a woman either. As soon as I arrived, a security officer advised me: 'You might want to cover your . . . female assets.' He wasn't kidding. Sexual violence against women is ubiquitous, and the utterly terrible style of the rapes is hard even to contemplate. I travelled around the countryside to Merlin-funded health clinics and spoke with women who had barely survived the atrocities. They sat stoically with clouded eyes, whispering details of being inhumanely surprised in their villages, homes, on the way to market and in the fields that they were trying to cultivate.

In that colonially desecrated, war-ravaged land there are multiple dangers – malaria, yellow fever, malnutrition, or crossing the burst Rutshuru River with a heart-stopping ravine just inches from the wheels of your bus. The food was unsafe, so I tried to live on the cereal bars I'd brought. Everyone seemed to be carrying a gun – except us because Merlin's policy is to be unarmed. I longed for my Glock (I'm pretty handy with guns, since I had to learn to defend myself from pirates during a sailing trip I'll tell you about later). I was constantly on the alert, which is necessary in a place where the regular police here carry rocket launchers, where you're just as likely to be robbed, raped or kidnapped by members of the Congolese army as by paramilitary groups or bandits. I travelled only between 10am and 4pm, in convoy, in vehicles with sat-phones, VHF radios and hiding places. I was taught to keep my windows up and doors locked. If stopped, I was briefed to show my ID through the window, put my hands up and try to smile. NGO workers had been pulled out of cars the week before I arrived, robbed and raped.

My security briefing was shockingly to-the-point. 'If you get ambushed on the road,' warned the jaded Frenchman who briefed me, 'your driver will run away. Wear trousers and trainers you can run in. If they start firing, get out of the car on whichever side is furthest from the gunfire and hide behind the nearest wheel. When you hear them pause to reload, run for your life to the next point of cover.' To be honest, I was so unfit at that time I could never have run fast enough to save my own life, and this fact pitched me straight back to the gym the minute I returned home.

In South Kivu alone, a woman is sexually assaulted every two hours – often by men in uniform. 'How does one become a soldier here?' I had asked the security adviser. '*C'est compliqué,*' he replied with a wry smile. 'They give you a uniform, a Kalashnikov [AK-47] – and off you go!' The extraordinary women I met completely humbled me. I knew from personal experience what it was like to be helpless, to be at the mercy of a cruel man, but my own negative experiences paled into insignificance when I heard these survivors' stories. Compared to them, I had been incredibly lucky. I'd had the opportunity to learn to read and write. I'd been to school, been clothed, and there was always food on the table. I'd had the resources to create a career for myself, through attending an excellent drama school, and that experience gave me the confidence and strength to walk in the world with my head held high. How I wished the women I met in the Congo could have the same opportunities.

You said that drama school saved you . . .

Yes – although NIDA was certainly challenging. But I enjoyed everything about it – the movement lessons, the acting coaching, the voice classes, the improvisation sessions, and especially the productions. It was a completely new culture, too. However, after what I'd just been through it took some time to relax, trust my teachers and fellow students, and realize no one was going to beat or mistreat me.

I was often cast most strangely – as the tinker in *A Midsummer Night's Dream*, for example – and I believe it was a good school policy to cast against type for a while – but I finally earned decent roles, as Helen in *Look Back in Anger* and Maggie in *Cat on a Hot Tin Roof*. My tutors were extremely demanding, but they were also very clever and supportive. And I sensed true benevolence from them. I blossomed.

Half the student group was always asked to leave after the first year. When it was crunch time, I went nervously to sit before the panel of serious faces who would decide my fate. I was expecting rejection, but instead I was met with smiles and encouragement. 'We thought you'd only last a few weeks,' they said, 'but you're still here and you've improved so much . . .' Little did they know those were the most helpful words I could possibly have heard. They showed me that, unlike my parents, no one there had high expecta-tions of me. That meant I was able to develop, feel free, accomplish. I felt I had permission to make mistakes, and that I would be appre-ciated. Yes, it was exactly the right environment for me. How lucky I was to find it, and still be there! I thoroughly enjoyed my final year. After our last production – Lorca's *Blood Wedding*, in which I played an elderly woman as a kind of weird bird, all trussed up in latex with wings under my cloak – I graduated in 1970. I adapted a passage from Jeremy Sandford's book *Synthetic Fun* as my audition monologue – a funny and poignant piece as a character who appeared in a strip club as a topless highwayman – and presented myself to the world as a professional actor.

Straight away I acquired an excellent agent and was in demand for TV, film and stage work. I accepted an offer to join the Perth Playhouse repertory company run by British director Edgar Metcalfe. It was a wonderful start: I played six leading roles in a row, including Dixie in David Mercer's *Flint*, Linda in Tom Stoppard's *Enter a Free Man* and Celia in Christopher Hampton's *The*

Philanthropist. I was well received in all those comedies, and discovered how much I loved to be funny. I particularly liked playing Dixie – a troubled teenager to whom I could certainly relate. She was funny, brave and optimistic – qualities I was grasping for in myself.

I noticed that, unlike drama, comedy brought immediate audience rewards. But the final play I did in Perth was a serious piece – Australian playwright Lance Peter's *Assault with a Deadly Weapon.* It transferred to the centre of Sydney, which meant that I was immediately starring in the Australian equivalent of London's West End. This was the chance I'd been hoping for. I worked hard at my career and promoted myself with a vengeance. Newspapers carried my picture quite frequently – after all, I was pretty easy on the eye at that time – and I was always posing in a terribly dated, fifties starlet manner. At one point I even paraded for the cameras wearing a white mink bikini. Seriously, Pamela?

Recently, I was confronted by an image of myself in a very early TV interview – it's on YouTube – and I was really struck by my voice. I had such a strange, fake accent – a bit like old British B movies. Why on earth was I talking like that? I have no idea. Perhaps it was the result of the NIDA voice production classes; in those days, the more English you sounded the better. I never really had a strong Australian accent but, honestly, I sound like Prunella Scales with a poker up her arse.

No wonder that, behind my back, people called me 'Plastic Pam'. Well, I suppose at the time I was trying on different personalities to see what fitted – no wonder I came across as inauthentic. Understandably, I really didn't know who I was. I had stuffed down all the pain of my father's abandonment, all my fury at my mother, my ill-treatment by Helmut, and was vengefully doing everything I could to make my mark in the world and prove that I was worth something. At the same time, this seemed to help assuage my anxiety. I was characteristically very, very serious about every aspect of

my career. I worked particularly hard at presenting myself attrac-
tively – those were the days when the 'dolly bird' style was in vogue
in Sydney (originally made popular by British icons Mary Quant,
Twiggy and Pattie Boyd), so I became adept at donning the tiniest
miniskirts, the highest platform boots and the most enormous false
eyelashes, top and bottom. I relished the power that decorating my
face and body like that seemed to bring me, both personally and
professionally.

At some level, perhaps it seemed to be a safeguard against
abandonment . . .

You're right. It did seem that way. And I never stopped. I appeared
in quite a few TV detective shows (they were very popular in
Australia at the time); in fact, I became rather in demand for guest
spots in such shows. Oh, now I'm getting chills because I just
remembered that one day a script arrived that horrified me because
it appeared that I'd be expected to drive a car. At the time I couldn't
drive at all – but I was determined to keep the part. I telephoned a
friend of a friend who was a racing driver. He turned up with a
lovely, expensive sports car and kindly gave me my first driving
lesson. But I imagine he thought better of it when I nearly parked
his four-wheeled pride and joy in the pond of a local park – I'm
blushing now just to think of it – and, well, lesson over.

So, I still couldn't drive when I arrived on the set a couple of days
later. Why on earth didn't I just 'fess up? I was just praying that no
one would ask me for my driver's licence (to be honest, they didn't
really care in those days!). But, even worse, it turned out that I was
actually expected to perform something akin to a stunt: while a
man was trying to drag me out of an open sports car by my right
arm, I had to start the engine with my left hand and perform a hill
start, then roar away from my attacker – spinning him away and

narrowly missing the parked car in front! Nowadays they'd never ask an actor to do a scene like this and it seems an incredible 'ask', even in those days, but I was so determined to stay in the programme, I focused hard and actually managed to do it rather well – on the second take! Now, that wasn't necessarily a good thing, because then my problems were compounded; I'd made a name for myself as a bit of a stunt-driving actor and was offered even more driving roles. I quickly took my driving test – and, of course, I failed!

A similar thing happened with horse riding; I couldn't ride, but aspired to certain parts that required equestrian skills. After being thrown off a horse a couple of times, under thoroughly precarious conditions, I realized that commanding living beasts was a bit more difficult to fake than simply driving a vehicle – and potentially even more dangerous. Frankly, I was really lucky to avoid serious injury, but it was entirely consistent with my risk-taking, ambitious character and determined mindset at the time that I felt I had to either succeed at everything I tried – or die trying.

So no change there, then? You still like to take risks?

Absolutely!

It's not unusual for someone who has faced physical abuse to subsequently deliberately place herself in danger. It can become a compulsion to prove one's efficacy in surviving, time and time again . . .

Well, that certainly rings some bells for me. But I did settle down a bit for a while when I landed a permanent role as a detective's secretary in a popular new series called *Ryan*. I played the power-behind-the-throne type of girl, who occasionally solved the mystery before the boss did. It was pretty silly, and I became bored. I appeared in a couple of experimental, low-budget films, such as *Private Collection*, and even dabbled in musicals, doing a run as June in *Gypsy* (again, I over-challenged myself by saying I could do the splits when my legs really weren't quite that loose, and ended up with ripped tendons). But I was more interested in serious theatre at the time, and was thrilled to be invited eventually to join Australia's foremost theatre company, The Old Tote. I played Lucrezia in Machiavelli's comedy *La Mandragola*, Cordelia in Edward Bond's *Lear*, Solveig in *Peer Gynt* and, when the Sydney Opera House opened, I starred in two plays in the launch season at the Drama Theatre – Queen Isabel in Shakespeare's *Richard II*, and as Polly Peachum in Jim Sharman's production of Brecht's *The Threepenny Opera*, set in Australia in the thirties. This was a really big deal. At twenty-six years old, as a serious young actress, I suppose I had arrived.

Bizarrely, at this point my parents seemed rather proud of my success and wanted to be part of my life again. That actually started to happen during my second year at drama school. They realized that I was moving up in the world and was less of a threat to their peace and sanity, so they invited me to move back to the house. The idea was that I could have a solid, inexpensive base, but I felt very ambivalent about it. It was weird and uncomfortable, to pretend nothing had ever happened, and everyone being fairly nice to me. I still desperately needed their approval, so I was happy they wanted me again, but I was understandably suspicious of the sudden turna-round. Nevertheless, it meant that I no longer had to work at night, which was becoming impossible with all the evening performances I had. Funny thing, fame – it changes every relationship in a person's life. I bet my sisters felt angry with me when I turned up back in Thompson Street – and understandably so. It was a modern re-enactment of the prodigal son's return. But there was so much left unspoken in the household. Even before I graduated I realized it was too hard to be around my parents at my age, and so I moved into a rented house in the arty suburb of Paddington.

I remember eagerly seeking out the company of young men – in keeping with the zeitgeist of sexual promiscuity at the time. But, although I really enjoyed sex, I suspect that physical pleasure was not really my uppermost desire. Being held tenderly, caressed, seemingly adored – even briefly – those things were probably more important to a young woman like me who was so strongly imbued with longing. Lying in a man's arms seemed to provide the only true peace I could summon at that time.

Hmmm. That's known as pseudosexuality . . .

It also felt like pseudolove because, well, I never seemed to be able to keep those guys around. I imagine my excessive neediness at that time scared them off. Outside my little attic bedroom in Paddington, there was plenty of stimulation. There were some interesting things going on I was also inspired to explore. I became aware of a society of Sydney and Melbourne artists – not just the actors I met, but wonderful painters like the late Brett Whiteley, a charismatic vision on roller skates whom I encountered briefly at that time. Many years later – not long before his untimely death from a heroin overdose in 1992 – he became friendly with Billy. But in the late sixties and early seventies there was a terraced house somewhere in Macleay Street, Potts Point, that became known as The Yellow House (presumably named after the subject of the famous Van Gogh painting), and it attracted all kinds of fascinating people. In my patchwork maxi skirt, floppy hat, leather jerkin and beads ('dolly bird' style eventually gave way to 'hippie' clothes), I could turn up there any time and witness something stimulating and unusual – it was a kind of full-time 'happening'. I remember walking in one day and seeing two terribly sleepy pianists playing Erik Satie's 'Trois Gymnopédies' exactly the way they are meant to be played – gravely and dolorously, in a marathon of repetition. Yes, there was something cool and exciting going on I wanted to be a part of. I'm still a bit like that – never want to miss out on anything . . .

Fear of rejection again?

Mmm. Maybe. But it was more than that. I craved something I'd rarely had – fun. But also, there was a side of me – the creative artist – who craved the company and support of like-minded souls. Since drama school, I had become aware that there were some thoroughly edgy people around who could make me feel more . . . normal. I especially admired artist Martin Sharp, who was producing extraordinarily clever underground cartoons (he actually started the Yellow House artists' collective). People were wearing clothing made of crushed velvet, denim and Union Jacks. They were smoking pot and listening to Dylan's 'Lay Lady Lay' (I remember we were all worried that his motorcycle accident might have affected his ability to produce another *Blonde on Blonde*). I actually performed as a folk singer myself in a couple of basement dives but, although I had a friendly guitarist supporting me, it was a bit too much like my horrid Sunday school experience, trying not to make mistakes on my guitar. I thought the early seventies folk scene was cool (although we didn't use that word then) and, even though I felt inadequate, I was drawn to it.

Perhaps you wanted to belong to something, as teenagers tend to do. It's a way of finding out exactly who they are. You had partially missed out on that developmental stage, due to the trauma you experienced at the time.

Yes, but there was a lot going on in the zeitgeist. I think most people sensed the excitement, as the 'age of Aquarius' dawned. See, Australia was a little behind the UK and USA; we had the sixties in the seventies.

However, I was mainly very focused on my acting career. As I grew in stature as an actor, my family continued to take quite an interest. I guess by now they may have begun to feel a bit guilty about kicking me out. But I still felt ambivalent about it all. My parents came to see my performances at the Sydney Opera House, and seemed pleased about my success. But no one gets perfect reviews and I did notice that every time something a bit disparaging was said about me, they took it personally and called me to complain that I'd embarrassed them. I was relieved when they told me they had inherited a house in the UK, from mum's cousins Millie and Marie, and had decided to sell up and live there in Surrey.

For the following few years I was a bit of a gypsy, living in whichever part of Australia I was working, and travelling quite a lot. I took a trip to Bali – a common holiday destination for young Australians – and was entranced by it. I adored the culture, the religious involvement with flowers, incense and decoration, the ceremonies, the legends, the colourful clothing. In true Conrad fashion, I sought out its nooks and crannies with a passion. While staying with the local music master's family, I learned to play a Balinese instrument that makes a sound like a frog (well, why not? No practising required).

The Balinese have an extraordinarily well-developed dance style, as well as masked plays and gamelan orchestras. Rarely seeing other white people, I based myself in Peliatan – far from the tourist areas – and attended daily dance classes. I sat with three-year-olds, trying to bend my adult fingers into the intricate shapes of a legong dancer, but to no avail; the dance form must be mastered before the age of twelve or it cannot possibly be achieved. I even managed to witness some special ceremonies, such as a tooth-filing, a cremation and a wedding. This was all so fascinating to me, I became a closet anthropologist; I still am.

My longing for travel was omnipresent, and since I'd been

earning money, I had some means for buying tickets. I had been living with a well-known Australian actor – let's call him Gareth – who had been successful on Broadway in *Oliver!* Gareth was quite a bit older than me, and I appreciated that. There was a paternal edge to him that made me feel safe and protected, and he was a very good man. He educated me in many ways . . .

Sounds a bit like the father you always wanted . . .

Yes. It was all that. I was very much in love with him but, deep down, I knew I would not be with him forever. I set off on a trip around the world, promising Gareth I'd be back in a few months. But I wasn't. As a matter of fact, I never again returned to live permanently on Australian shores.

You were ready to fly the nest . . .

Mmm, it felt a bit like that. Although it was scary, travelling the world alone. I still seem drawn to hostile environments, somehow wanting to test myself against the odds. Like the Congo, with the extreme personal danger to which I was exposed there. And then there was that terrible feeling of being out of my depth in a professional sense . . .

How so?

Well, as the days went by in the DRC and I met more and more survivors, I realized I was observing psychological dynamics that were far more serious than those most western psychologists have ever seen – yet none of these women had received mental health treatment. That was professionally and personally extremely challenging. As I listened to the survivors' stories a terrible sense of hopelessness seeped into my own psyche. See, I'd never been unable to help anyone before, and that terrible feeling has haunted me ever since . . .

Understandable. You of all people really NEED to be able to help . . .

Yes, I hear you. It's compulsive. And I am also aware that help is something I really want for myself but don't know how to get. But at the same time in the dire DRC situation, help was sorely needed. And there was no crisis-intervention team here, no system for the healing of massive and widespread trauma. Given the enormity of the problem – the huge numbers of women affected, the severity of their psychological conditions – I seemed irrelevant, a lone psychologist without the time, resources or clinical framework to help. It took me a long time to recover from that life-changing trip. One of the feelings I had in the aftermath was shame at having once contemplated suicide. 'How is it,' I asked a Congolese doctor, 'that these women are still alive?' I was told: 'African women don't kill themselves. They have too many responsibilities.' I thought back to the time I nearly jumped over a cliff because of a cheating lover and felt very, very ashamed.

He wasn't just a cheating lover, Pamela. In your traumatized mind he represented a stern father, meting out punishment you believed you deserved. Choosing another woman was tantamount to repeating your real father's rejection – powerfully damaging, re-traumatizing stuff. Try to be kinder to yourself.

Yes, doctor. I will try . . .

Chapter Six

ADVENTURE

So . . . your passion for travel is clear and understandable. It has its origin in your first voyage to the UK, when you were first exposed to a wider world of new experiences, adventures and other cultures – which you adored. But this tendency of yours actively to seek to travel in hostile environments – I'm wondering about the risks you have been taking. Shall we explore what you might be trying to achieve through facing such dangers?

Mmm. I am definitely drawn to extreme adventure . . .

Close your eyes and take a moment to allow yourself to revisit somewhere you've been, somewhere you felt afraid to be, yet were gripped by the power of the experience . . .

OK . . .

What are you seeing?

Mmm . . . Well, it's still dark . . . A little bit of light creeping in . . .

What are you hearing?

Mosquitoes . . . Dozens of them. As usual, they're up well before me. I can hear them buzzing all around my mosquito net . . .

What are you feeling?

Scared. Maybe one got inside and bit me during the night . . . I don't want to get dengue fever again. I have to put my arm outside the net to reach under my sleeping mat for my special water bottle – not just any water holder, but one a member of my camera crew fashioned for me yesterday into a portable loo. 'Here's your "she-wee",' he'd said with a grin. As a New Zealander, he pronounced it 'shay way', but I wasn't going to snigger. Thank God. I would no longer have to take my pants down and give the bugs full munching rights on my backside.

Where are you?

Um . . . in a tree house, somewhere up the Sepik River in Papua New Guinea. Malaria, Japanese encephalitis and dengue are rife here. I'm worried. My anti-malarial tablets and the vaccination I had last month will probably protect me against the first two, but there's no prophylactic for dengue fever; I was very ill with it three years earlier in Samoa and definitely don'twant to run the risk of contracting a haemorrhagic version. That can kill you.

I peed, dressed, ate a protein bar, took my pills, cleaned my teeth, did my hair, put on make-up and sprayed DEET all over me – all within the confines of my netted bed. I'm getting better at this.

What are you seeing?

The first rays of sun are cracking their way through the coconut wood slats of the tree house . . .

What can you smell?

Um . . . coffee . . . and eggs. Our guide is making breakfast. But I don't want to eat. 'Just bottled water for me, thanks!' 'OK,' he said. 'Then come and meet my son. He's waiting for you . . .'

And where are you now?

Down by the river. I'm standing right where our dugout canoe's waiting. We've been travelling on the water for three days now.

What are you seeing now?

Hmm . . . A young man. He's . . . he is undressing for me . . .

Nice work if you can get it . . .

What? No, seriously this is all in the name of anthropological inquiry.

Oh. Right. Well? Go on . . .

He casually unbuttons his jeans and removes his T-shirt. Now he's turning round so I can see the markings on his back and buttocks. Hah! No bug-worries for him.

How are you feeling?

Uncomfortable . . . I'm just trying to ignore the awkward,

cross-cultural subtext of this encounter. Now I'm venturing closer. 'May I touch please?' He nods shyly so I reach out and ran my fingers along the raised tracks of keloids that are running vertically down the left side of his back, all the way to the middle of his buttock. It's a beautifully designed, deliberate scar. The effect's just as I've been told – remarkably like the dorsal side of a crocodile . . . At the base of the design, I can make out an asymmetrical star shape. 'What's this?' I ask. 'This is the sign of a female crocodile,' he says. 'The men can choose male or female during the initiation ceremony.' The markings went over his shoulder and around one nipple. 'That's the crocodile's eye.'

Where are you now?

I'm at the Sing-Sing now. The festival. There are crocodile-scarred backs everywhere and . . . wow, and, in fact, everywhere I look there are live crocodiles. I can't believe . . . people are wearing them around their necks as jewellery. People are actu-ally dancing with them. Oh . . .! Now I've been given a baby croc to hold . . . I'm cradling it. It's much softer than I'd have thought . . . Although I have to say, it's not exactly engendering my maternal instincts. Oh my God . . . I can see several men in the crowd walking around with huge, vicious, salt-water crocs on a flimsy lead . . . Aggghhh!

What happened? You came out of the hypnotic trance very suddenly just then . . .

Well, one just escaped into the crowd! Got away from its owner . . . Wow, that was a heart-stopping moment. My husband says having a salt-water croc after you is like being chased by a hungry train.

You really do have a special interest in ethnographic anthropology, don't you?

Yes! So fascinating! The people from certain tribes along the Sepik River believe the crocodiles are their ancestors. In special 'spirit houses' young men undergo an initiation rite that involves re-enacting their own births and making them physically connected to their reptilian past. Held protectively by an uncle, they are cut and scarred until their backs resemble those of their scaled ancestors. Oh boy, it must be enormously painful. And so must be an attack from one of the dwindling population of present-day crocodiles that inhabit the Sepik. I saw them from time to time, basking in the mud at noon, or hunting at night with glittery eyes caught in the glare of my torch. They say those critters have a nasty habit of getting under your canoe and upending it so neatly the passengers flip right into their jaws.

After several days' canoe trip up the Sepik River, I reached my destination – Ambunti, with its Crocodile Sing-Sing Festival. It started with a warm, tropical downpour that delayed the festivities because no one wanted to get their fine, feathered headdress wet. Well, people had worked for a whole year to produce their costumes. For some, this had involved a long process of luring special bright green beetles inside their houses then making them into shiny beads to cover each tribesman's busby-style helmet. I watched men painting each other's faces with clay (some were cheating by using modern finger-paints). Others were stringing shells, leaves and feathers around their bodies and jamming their penises into pointed gourds that would shake as they danced. Now that's not something you see every day. And this was normally no place for a woman; however, my presence was strangely tolerated (it's good to be an older, white woman!).

At one point, a terrible cry emanated from the show ground; a pig had been tied to a stake in readiness for its presentation to the main sponsors – the World Wildlife Fund. My sense of irony fully engaged, I found a young woman who was representing the charity and asked, 'What will you do with this unfortunate creature?' I expected the answer to be, 'Let it go' or 'Put it out of its misery', but instead she grinned hungrily, 'Have a big feast!'

I wandered among the tribes people, searching for the 'mud men', a fascinating group of people who cover themselves with ash and grey mud. When I found them, they were waiting patiently for their turn to dance. In contrast to their grey bodies, hair and faces, their mouths were bright red from chewing the ubiquitous beetle nut that invokes an amphetamine-style 'high' and destroys one's teeth. One group of mud men were carrying a closed canvas stretcher in which a child was cowering. Hmmm. There is a strong history of cannibalism in these parts and only a week ago the local newspaper carried a story about a man who ate a baby. 'Why would a man eat a baby?' I had asked a local chief. The answer was chilling: 'The baby was fat and the man was hungry.' Ask a silly question . . .

You travelled alone for some time after you left Australia, didn't you? Was that intrepid-style travel, too?

If I could have, I would have travelled by balloon. It was 1975 when I set off to explore the world alone, and I'd seen the movie based on the Jules Verne novel *Around the World in 80 Days*; that really whet-ted my appetite for a bit of similar, cross-continental madness. Instead of a balloon, I flew by commercial airline from Sydney to Manila in the Philippines. Actually, although I had thought the place would be interesting, I was immediately disappointed to discover it was a shambolic, traffic-laden and fairly westernized place. I didn't stay long. But my next stop, Japan, was a different story. I was fascinated by Tokyo, and was especially tickled by the startling juxtaposition between ancient and modern Japanese culture – punk teenagers in kimonos made from black plastic bin liners were smoking weed within spitting distance of robed monks performing a morning chanting ceremony at a central Shinto shrine. I saw businessmen, in grey western suits and briefcases, installing prayer cards (presumably hoping to land that big client account) in the designated cubby holes outside an ancient Buddhist temple.

How exactly does being in the presence of people whose culture is vastly different from your own speak to you?

I'm really not sure. Perhaps because I was deprived of that growing up in such a homogenous, WASP society, or perhaps because I have this other, foreign culture inside me – my Maori roots – that I have never explored and is so mysterious to me . . . But experiencing and getting to know people from other cultures is something that I have loved since that first sea voyage when I was eleven. And despite my ambivalence about my parents, I do have to thank them for instilling in me a curiosity and enjoyment for the wider world, and an appreciation of the diversity of its inhabitants.

But as a young actress, I was also very keen to see the way different peoples of the world performed. I was determined to see theatre wherever I travelled. For example, when I was in Tokyo I found my way to a kabuki performance. The production was slow and indecipherable, but I sat transfixed. The show takes many hours, with a long break in the middle for a meal, although I had not known that when I bought my ticket. The ticket-box vendor kept showing me plates of weird plastic food and wouldn't stop until I picked one. When the lights came up for the interval I followed everyone else to an enormous canteen full of tables bearing Japanese numbers, and I stood there confused – until I saw a man waving and pointing to the only table in the place with a lonely little flag bearing an English number '1', beneath which sat a bento box containing the edible version of my plastic food choice. That just tickled me.

I was entranced by the extreme theatricality of that kabuki performance, the histrionic characterizations, the highly elaborate costumes and make-up, and the magical way the actors changed on stage before our very eyes. The scenery was also elaborate, and actors made surprise entrances from trapdoors hidden at various points on the revolving stage. I was intrigued to see how long the performers could hold their traditional poses – with open mouths, flared nostrils and eyes crossed. Craig Revel Horwood would be in his element! It was a bit like a cross between early Shakespeare performances and English pantomime. Oh, and *EastEnders.* The audience seemed perfectly familiar with the story. Even though it was apparently in an ancient form of Japanese, some of them got quite noisy and shouted back at the actors from time to time. Highbrow Japanese hecklers – what a concept! Not knowing that most western people dip into a kabuki show for half an hour then make a run for the nearest sake bar, I returned for the afternoon portion of the show, and actually stuck it out until the bitter end. Apparently you can now get earphones with an English translation which, I must say, would have been nice.

But sitting there in the kabuki theatre, watching that highly melodramatic, all-male performance, I was trying to imagine what it must have been like 400 years ago when it was an all-female extravaganza. Apparently those women were sex workers and their sensual performances were so popular they caused riots – which led to their being banned by the Shogun's officials. So men took over the performing, and I imagine kabuki theatre became a perfect home for male-to-female transgendered people; however, they too were in demand as prostitutes and the audience mayhem they inspired led to another clamping-down. I wish I'd seen it in its heyday. In a way, it seems a shame that kabuki theatre is now so formal and respectable. But some of the actors who play female roles (*onnagata*), are extremely famous in Japan – even revered as 'National Living Treasures'. Honoured transvestites? Well, I suppose the British value their pantomime dames. I thought of Les Girls and wished Australian society appreciated them more, rather than considering them simply to be tacky figures of fun. Strange that, years later, I would conduct a psychological study of transgenderism as it is expressed by people in various cultures throughout the world.

I was inspired to seek theatre in every place I visited during my trip. In fact, that was my main focus. I was a terribly serious young performer. Everything had to be a 'valuable experience'. Other young Australians who hit the hippy trail would be partying and getting laid – but 'having a good time' was way off my radar. I've just realized that's why I love a party now; I completely missed all that fun when I was young.

You are beginning to allow yourself to play . . . ?

Yes, it's only taken forty years. And I never feel quite right about it – there's still someone inside me wagging her finger . . .

And who exactly is that person?

Ah. Yes. Mum gets everywhere, doesn't she? Even Bangkok back then – the ultimate party town – did not summon a desire in me to cut loose and enjoy myself. Well, then again, I suppose it was always a male-focused place. But the smog-filled, overcrowded city certainly offered an eclectic range of performing events, from the highbrow, traditional Thai temple dancing, with its intricate finger gestures and eye movements, to the shocking, sleazy sex shows I witnessed in compounds on the city's outskirts. I tried to view the latter without judgment, but I felt very conflicted about it. These were family businesses and the people performing live sex acts were related to each other. And these places had evolved largely due to the demand of westerners who would pay top dollar to attend. It seemed abusive to even watch. On the other hand, I reasoned, Thai society has a more relaxed attitude towards sexuality than many other cultures. I learned, for example, that Thai men could openly take their mistresses to official events – and, by law, they had to provide for them. But was this a good thing? Did it help the position of women generally in that society or not? What about the growing prevalence of sexually transmitted diseases? Even back then, I was intrigued by sexual mores. And in Bangkok, there was certainly a lot to think about.

It doesn't really surprise me that you were fascinated by it, that you wanted to study sexuality and eventually made it one of your professional fields. After all, the most significant moment of trauma in your life – being kicked out of home – occurred as a direct result of sexual behaviour, didn't it? As a result of not just the behaviour itself, but the attitudes and beliefs and mores concerning what happened that were held by your parents – as products of their own upbringing and society ... I suspect that even then you were bright enough to be able to see that it wasn't just you; you were a product of your environment, and the prevailing zeitgeist strongly influenced those events ...?

I guess ... to some extent. And I suppose that's actually why I always wanted to search for answers concerning all kinds of human behaviour, not just sexuality. And that's one of the things that spurred me to travel. And to experience different kinds of relationships with different kinds of people. For example, after Bankok I flew to India where, in Delhi, I was sidetracked from my theatre studies by a brief and heady romance with a young American peace worker called Jerry.

Well, that was just bound to happen, wasn't it?

Yep! With curly, long, blond hair and a beard, an electric blue, crushed velvet suit, strings of coloured beads around his neck and a guitar slung over his shoulder, he was a vision of seventies splendour, and I was unable to resist. I remember he had an amazingly confident, maverick approach, and I saw far more of his well-toned body than I did of the fascinating Indian capital. I felt guilty about Gareth, but reasoned that if something like this could happen so quickly and easily, I had been kidding myself to think I was still in love with him. Besides, he had already been married twice, and had two children. He wanted to settle down with me, but I just wasn't ready. Perhaps this whole trip was really about finding a way to leave him.

Anyway, I managed to wrench myself away from Jerry's arms to catch my planned flight to Moscow, but I was so sexed-up and discombobulated, I boarded the late-night Aeroflot flight wearing a sleeveless summer dress – forgetting that the temperature in Russia would be minus thirty-two degrees. Twenty minutes before we landed, the flight attendant tapped me on the shoulder. 'You have a coat?' she asked. 'Afraid not,' I replied. In fact, I did have one, a black rabbit fur I was extremely proud of, but it was locked in my checked-in suitcase. I don't remember how I managed to survive the intense cold of that winter arrival. The aircraft steps and tarmac were pure ice and I was wearing flip flops. The handle of my suitcase had frozen off, so I had to carry it under my arm as best I could. It was brutal.

In those days it was very unusual for a single woman to travel alone anywhere behind the Iron Curtain, and I can't imagine that anywhere could have been more uncomfortable than in Moscow. I was OK inside the hotel, though. I was staying at the art nouveau Hotel Metropol, which seemed like a set from *Dr Zhivago*. Sitting alone at supper in the dining room, men in military uniforms would send oranges to my table initially (highly prized in the Russian winter time), then turn up at my side, click their heels, bow, and then whirl me awkwardly around the dance floor. At first I was oblivious to the fact that I was being observed – rather, spied on – by the KGB. I was terribly naïve about the political climate at the time and I made some stupid mistakes, such as thinking it was OK to speak to ordinary citizens (at least I thought they were ordinary – who knows?). I found it very hard to get around the city with no signposts or maps and the lack of help from Intourist (I imagine that was a KGB-run 'tourist bureau'). It was impossible to know what to do when people offered me black market exchange rates for my dollars. Eventually, even I could not help noticing that there were some glaring hypocrisies; when I attended the opera and saw important members of the KGB sitting in the best seats beside their wives who wore the latest Paris fashions, I understood that I had seen the reality behind George Orwell's *Animal Farm*. Under the Russian Communist regime, all were equal, but some were more equal than others.

I tried to see good theatre and naïvely thought Chekhov would be playing somewhere. But instead of sending me to *Cherry Orchard*, as I had requested, Intourist sold me tickets to a dreadfully cheesy Russian variety show. However, the KGB was not responsible for my worst moment of confusion. At one point I was searching for a taxi outside the hotel. Night had fallen and it was absolutely freezing. I was desperate for transport. Eventually, I spied a dark car with a sign above it, waiting on the corner. I ran thankfully towards it and hopped in, handing the driver a paper on which was written my desired address. But his reaction was a long way from what I expected. Instead of nodding accommodatingly, he stared at me furiously, with flared nostrils. 'Nyet taxi!' he snorted. It was a military police car.

I took the Orient Express from Moscow to Budapest. I have since visited the twin cities of Buda and Pest and found them attractive and charming, but for some reason that was not how I found things the first time. For a start, I was getting a little low on funds and had to board in a decrepit building where a bomb had fallen during World War II. I swiftly moved on to Warsaw, where things were very different. I was enormously impressed by Poland and its citizens. In particular, I found the painters, cartoonists, film directors and actors were highly original and tremendously exciting. I met people I really liked and admired, and didn't want to leave. I was lucky enough to meet Alex Brooking, an Australian diplomat stationed in Warsaw, who, I suppose, was detailed to keep an eye on me (I was amazed to discover Alex had grown up in Boronia Park). Knowledgeable and passionate about Polish film and art, Alex was extremely kind and informative. I gradually discovered the underground political theatre and found it absolutely thrilling.

In those days, a strong anti-Russian sensibility abounded in Polish society, and this was reflected in the satire. There was an underground political cabaret company called the Pod Egida ('Winking Eye') to which I managed to find my way. In order to avoid discovery, Pod Egida performances took place at the last minute, in a forest on a Sunday afternoon or in someone's house. I saw one of those clandestine performances in the basement of a small café. The backdrop was a satirical rendering of Da Vinci's 'Last Supper', except that the faces of Jesus and His disciples were replaced with members of the Politburo, the Polish United Workers' (Communist) Party that many in the audience had decided was too bureaucratic and essentially Russian in style. Someone I met there translated for me, and I my heart began to beat faster and faster at the thrill of seeing such a dark and biting comedy that truly meant something important to this audience. At one point a man leapt to his feet and shouted '*Solidarność*!' Others followed suit, until the place was chaotic. The feeling in the audience was absolutely electric. I think it was at that moment I truly understood the thrilling, life-changing power a performance could wield under certain circumstances. I did not know it then, but it was the beginning of the anti-bureaucratic social movement 'Solidarity'. Five years later, Lech Wałęsa would form the first non-Communist-party-controlled trade union in a Warsaw Pact country, and eventually become President of Poland. But the power of that performance profoundly affected me. I had never before seen theatre that could stir people like that. It was the true beginning of my passion for satire.

When I arrived at my next destination, Berlin, I immediately realized a long-term dream by crossing the Wall to East Berlin and attending a performance at Bertolt Brecht's theatre, the Berliner Ensemble. This world-famous theatre was where *The Threepenny Opera* (which I'd performed in at the Sydney Opera House) had been conceived and first staged, along with other Brecht plays, such as *The Caucasian Chalk Circle*, in which I had also performed. After the show I waited to speak to the actors and asked if anyone could speak English. I was very lucky to meet the director, who invited me to observe rehearsals for the next production, *Mother Courage and Her Children*. I was lucky to receive this invitation. Here I was, in a theatre setting I had admired for years, watching some of the best works by satirical masters Brecht and Weill. These were the most outstanding, politically motivated performances you could find anywhere in the world. I was in heaven.

But there was one problem: I could not get a visa to stay in East Germany, so I had to cross the Wall twice a day, every day. I remember my daily arrival at Friedrichstrasse checkpoint, with its stern, armed guards with their Alsatian dogs, and the endless waiting.

Nevertheless, it was worth it. The director and cast were kind to me. I learned a great deal from watching their painstaking work, and they helped me to understand their methodology. I admired them tremendously and wanted to emulate them – especially their dedication, focus and attention to detail – in my future career.

Now that I had found a branch of theatre that truly moved me, I sought it out wherever I went. When I arrived in Istanbul, a military coup was underway and the political events were reflected in the extraordinary street theatre I saw at that time. Again, it was vital and thrilling, and I wanted more. Ancient Greek theatre moved me, too, especially when it reflected issues that were also pertinent to modern Greek society – which happened to be remarkably often. However, in Milan, opera at the famous La Scala and the stylized theatre form *Commedia dell'Arte*, which was born in Italy in the sixteenth century, were now far less interesting to me than the edgy political cabarets to which I inevitably found my way. I also saw wonderful classical theatre and musical performances in Vienna and Zurich, but they paled beside the electric contemporary satire I'd previously seen. Even in Paris, I yawned at Feydeau's farces, the lively nineteenth-century theatrical confections that were first mounted there. They were well done and interesting, but they were museum pieces.

During my travels I had received a fantastic, broad theatre education. Most significantly, I had found where I belonged. I had acquired a true passion for contemporary political theatre, and had now seen the finest in the world. As I stepped on board a flight for London, I was, quite simply, ready for my next reincarnation.

That's all very well, but it occurs to me that you were travelling alone, a very pretty and apparently vulnerable young western woman – were you ever in danger?

Yes, some young soldiers began to assault me when I was on an empty Hungarian train . . . I screamed and fought them off as best I could. It could have been a lot worse, but fortunately we were disturbed by an officer who ordered them off. That was a nasty experience . . . It was the arrogant way they obviously thought they could do whatever they liked with me. I remember thinking, 'Pamela, you're alone in a country where no one cares what happens to you; and no one back home even knows you're here. You could just disappear without trace.'

Travel can be so much safer now we have email . . . I mean, even up the Sepik River in Papua New Guinea they had cell phone towers. They are actually causing problems in the locality. One village chief complained that, very suddenly, the people in his village were getting porn images on their phones and being exposed to things they'd never seen or heard of before – culturally shocking. I'll never forget the words he used – so interesting. He said, 'Sex is becoming very popular now.' I said, 'What? Was it unpopular before?' After all, I had just been inside a spirit house, climbing stairs that were carved like penises, and had watched tribes people shaking their genitals at each other in ritual dance. But the chief didn't answer me.

But, Pamela, can you see that your travels – especially those you undertook early in your life – served an important purpose?

Hmmm. I suppose that seeing the world – and observing how people behave cross-culturally – was always enormously soothing for me. Not just an education, but more... I suppose I felt that it helped me to grasp not just how diverse human beings are, but more importantly that the weird, unaccepted, 'alien' person I always felt myself to be – so different from everyone else in my family – wasn't really so strange in the context of the wider world, with its myriad societies full of strikingly different individuals. And, at the same time, I witnessed and felt the important similarities, the basic things that make us human… Yes, travel was – and still is – vitally important to me.

But there's more. In your family of origin, feeling like an unappreci-ated, misunderstood outsider was not only painful, it was an unbear-able mystery. Travel seems to reaffirm your rightful place in the family – the wider human family. And somehow, the more different the people and their culture, the stronger your relief and delight when they are friendly and accepting. You actually seek this – and danger – as a means of gaining mastery over your early traumas. Paradoxically, for you, intrepid travel – even when highly precarious – was, and contin-ues to be, a powerful way for you to feel safe.

Chapter Seven

FOB

It occurs to me, Pamela, that you deliberately search for a lifestyle that is the antithesis of what most people want. For example, you are comfortably off – earn your own living and are married to a well-known man with a flourishing career – yet you appear to eschew luxury in favour of, say, a tree house in Papua New Guinea.

Yeah, well, I know I am lucky to be able to have that choice. But, for example, staying on a yacht in Cannes harbour during the Festival in May 1978, and hanging out with stars like Marcello Mastroianni, Harvey Keitel, John Hurt, Robbie Robertson and Martin Scorsese (it was the year *The Last Waltz* was released), might seem like it was a glamorous and desirable experience, but it affected me like a camper who's unwittingly pitched her tent on an ant hill. After just a few days of such a heady lifestyle, I glanced around at my fellow passengers – happily sipping champagne over brunch – and put some dry clothes in a plastic bag on my back and slipped off the boat into the water. A couple of miles away was the island of Ile Saint-Honorat on which sat a monastery. I have no idea what drew me to it, but it appeared in the distance as a beacon of peace and clarity.

I was exhausted after my long swim. I lay on the rocky beach for a bit, then, once the sun had warmed and dried me, I dressed and began to walk along a path lined with vineyards to an ancient stone building with a bell tower. A couple of monks were working in the fields but they ignored me. Perhaps they'd taken a vow of silence. I climbed the tower and sat there, high in the sun, a contemporary Quasimodo contemplating my future. The day before, I had met the Polish film director Jerzy Skolimowski, who that year took the Grand Prix for *The Shout* (shared with Marco Ferreri for *Ciao Maschio*). I was hugely taken by Jerzy, having long admired his screenplay for Roman Polanski's film *Knife in Water*, which I thought was psychologically profound, and spent a long evening with him. To be honest, I believe he actually helped me out of a gutter on the Croisette, but I'm not entirely sure how I got there in the first place. Perhaps it was the merlot.

I fully expected him to try to sleep with me but he didn't. Instead, he spoke to me respectfully about my creative core. This was a first. 'Unless you have honesty and authenticity in your own life,' he said, 'you will not have it in your art.' I thought long and hard about that. In trying so hard to fit in with the high style and heady glamour of Cannes, I had lost sight of who I really was. 'This isn't me,' I told myself from my perch on the tower. 'I'm behaving like a C-movie starlet, when I'm really an experienced, serious actor. Look at all the work I've done.' There and then, I took a vow to protect my creative talent the best way I could.

As I sat lecturing myself high in the stone clock tower of Ile Saint-Honorat, what lay ahead of me in just a few months – being cast in a highly popular BBC2 topical comedy show – was pretty unimaginable. Right now, I was a relatively unknown Australian actress who could not get a break. All the work I had done in Australia seemed to mean nothing. In this new, bigger pond I had to start all over again and try to prove my worth. It was terribly daunting. Evening began to fall and the swallows began to circle. I had been so transfixed by my reverie I had failed to consider that dusk might not be the best time to start that long swim back to the boat. Fortunately, two kind friends arrived to save me, with a couple of sea scooters.

The ride back was cold but mercifully brief. On board the yacht, the partying continued, but I remained withdrawn, remote. Ile Saint-Honorat had reconnected me with myself. My meta-analysis continued in London, where I reread Eric Berne's *Games People Play* (having first read it in my early twenties) and, three weeks afterwards on 20 June 1978, I scribbled an important passage in my notepad:

Each person . . . has a preconscious life plan, or script, by which he structures longer periods of time – months, years, or his whole life – filling them with ritual activities, pastimes, and games, which further the script while giving immediate satisfaction, usually interrupted by periods of withdrawal and sometimes by periods of intimacy.

Scripts are usually based on childlike illusions which may persist throughout a whole lifetime; but in more sensitive, perceptive and intelligent people these illusions dissolve one by one, leading to various life crises described by Erikson. Among these crises are the adolescent reappraisal of parents; the protests, often bizarre, of middle age; and the emergence of philosophy after that.

Sometimes, however, overly desperate attempts to maintain the illusions in later life lead to depression or spiritualism, while the abandonment of all illusions may lead to despair.

I'm wondering . . . which part of that passage was most important to you?

I'm not even sure, although actually, I find it acutely to the point at this time in my life too – 'desperate attempts to maintain the illusions' certainly speaks to me. I had already been profoundly affected by reading Arthur Janov's book *The Primal Scream* several years previously. That was the first time I was made aware of the notion that the unconscious mind harbours all kinds of traumatic memories from childhood that subtly influence our behaviour. I tried Janov's method of abreacting trauma – having a good old scream when no one was around – but I'm not sure how helpful that was. Not recommended while driving either (in Australia I used to let loose in my car).

But at Ile Saint-Honorat I was reminded where I had been, and where I hoped to go. I was not a party girl, I was a dedicated performer. All right, you might think this is a bit on the hokey side, but, in a way, I sort of knew something was about to happen. I could just feel it in my sea-chilled bones.

But, explain to me, why exactly did you feel you needed to protect your talent? Was it under threat?

Most people I met in London just after I arrived did not understand that, due to my training, my work in Australian theatre, TV and film – and all my informal theatre studies in various countries – I was pretty experienced. I felt I was rather . . . accomplished . . . but I wasn't good at proving it. Well, after all, a young British woman of my age probably would not have had the same opportunities for professional experience as I'd had in the less crowded arena of the Australian theatre scene. However, I didn't present myself the right way; in my high heels, heavy make-up, brightly coloured clothing and long, bleached hair, I looked more like a contender for the Eurovision song contest than the kind of person you'd see wandering around the RSC. Then there was my Australian accent, which tended to make people guffaw. I was upset at how snobbish people were about 'Antipodeans'.

It had certainly been tough for me when I first arrived. I hadn't planned to stay in London but I was flat broke, having already spent all my money travelling thus far. I remember standing at a public phone at Heathrow airport, trying to find a very cheap hostel. I had roughly twenty pounds in my pocket. A man who overheard me took pity on me and arranged accommodation for me at a female friend's house. Now, of course, that could have been a rather dodgy scenario, but I had been travelling for a long time by myself and had learned to size people up pretty fast. This guy, John, was all right. In fact, he was a very kind person who really was as good as his word. His friend turned out to be a beautiful blonde model and I stayed first with her in the centre of London, and then with her sister in Fulham. And John introduced me to a young man called David who became a loving, protective and enormously supportive boyfriend for some time (we're still friends). Boy, was I lucky to fall on my feet like that!

But it was hard to get used to being around urbane, well-off and sophisticated people like David and his brother, not to mention his brother's terrifyingly chic girlfriend who worked for a Parisian fashion house. David tried to groom me as best he could, but I think it was amusing to them that I was so ignorant about fine food, cars, art or fashion, and frequently put my foot in it. The jetsettish side of life was a complete mystery to me. What the hell was a truffle? Who were Georgio and Karl? I pretended I knew. It was a bit like being back at SCEGGS, trying not to appear too crass beside all my fellow students from ritzier suburbs. I remember David trying to explain the concept of a Fabergé egg to me, but it was quite baffling. 'I don't get it,' I said. 'Why would anyone bother?' I was mortified when, on our first date, he jumped out of his Porsche to buy me two dozen red roses from a street stall. Two dozen? That would pay my rent for a week. I was a kind of female Crocodile Dundee.

David kindly took me on holiday to Ibiza with several friends and we all stayed in a wonderful villa overlooking the sea. The girls all took off their tops to sunbathe and I felt obliged to do the same. Burnt nipples from the Mediterranean sun? Backgammon by the pool played on a leather Asprey's travel case? Did I want my sea bass on or off the bone in that trendy beach restaurant on Formantera? It was all so heady, confusing, and way out of my league. One day David told me a story about an American couple who had been somewhere outside London – Manchester, I think – and stopped a local person in the street. 'Excuse me,' they said, 'is there a Harrods around here?' He thought it was hilarious, but the humour completely escaped me. I was a FOB (that's short for 'Fresh Off the Boat') but I wouldn't even have known that at the time!

And getting work in the UK was a whole other challenge. I was offered a few modelling jobs, but that was not what I was trained to do – and certainly not what I desired. A theatrical agent called Peter Dunlop, of Fraser & Dunlop, had seen me perform in *The Threepenny Opera* at the Sydney Opera House, so he took me on as a client of the agency. I appeared in a few commercials and took guest roles in some popular TV series, but for someone who had proved herself in serious roles it was a bit embarrassing to play the girl with a grenade down her bra in *The Professionals*. I seemed only able to get 'glamour' roles in popular TV series such as *Space 1999*, *The New Avengers* and *Target*.

I really shouldn't complain, because I was lucky to be earning money, but it was also excruciatingly uncomfortable to appear in truly dreadful C movies, like *The Comeback* with American singer Jack Jones. Eventually there were better things: *The Man from the South* in the Roald Dahl series (shot in Jamaica – director David Mallet was the first person in the UK to give me a decent job), a play at the Crucible Theatre in Sheffield – *Celestina* by Rojas – and eventually the role of Iris in the period drama *Funny Man* for Thames

TV. I tried to get BBC drama work, but producers usually smirked when I went in to White City and read for them with my Australian accent. And, apparently, being straight off the banana boat was not just amusing, it was also slightly threatening. I had the feeling women in the UK were supposed to be sweet and unchallenging – and I was neither.

For example, at a dinner party David took me to I was appalled to witness the host making fun of his girlfriend's breasts. I hated to see her meekly putting up with this, so I loudly inquired, 'Well, why don't you tell us a bit about James' cock? How big is it, and does it work?' There was a terrible clanging as forks dropped, then silence. Everyone looked at James for a rebuttal. 'The awkward thing about Awwstralians,' he murmured, 'is you can't quite place them, socially.'

Class was something I just could not understand. As an Australian, I had no point of reference for the notion. Oh, I had long recognized the hierarchy that can be created by levels of wealth, but that didn't seem to apply in the UK. Why did people from different areas of such a small island group act and sound so different? There was a massive smugness about certain people, a kind of security of birth that truly irked me because it seemed unearned. But people at the other end of the scale seemed equally annoying in their willingness to kowtow to people they deemed 'above their station'. I did, however, like the fact that, being from a classless society, I was given a little licence to ignore those boundaries myself.

I was particularly mystified by what seemed to be a secret set of rules I could never learn, and hurt by the sniggers I received when I got it wrong. Bit by bit, I learned things like how one was supposed to eat artichokes and asparagus, how to compose a 'thank you' letter; that 'serviette' was bad, 'napkin' good; 'lounge' bad, 'drawing room' good. There was no end to the stupid protocol. 'Who said it has to be "supper"?' I would demand. 'Who made up that rule, and why does it matter?' It was as though a secret army of etiquette police might turn up any moment and snatch your fish knife from your middle-class fingers. 'Seriously?' I thought. 'Does anyone really care?' But it turned out they did. And I'm still confused about lavatory/loo/toilet/crapper/ bathroom/restroom. Might as well revert to the Australian 'dunny'. The only thing I REALLY needed to know, I decided, was that a 'stiffie' wasn't necessarily a sign some man was inordinately pleased to see me.

With that attitude, my social education therefore made slow progress. And frankly, I still get it horribly wrong. I was actually oblivious to just how badly until fairly recently Prince Charles hit the nail on the head with 'Pamela, your social skills are improving!' It was a hilarious back-handed compliment that gave me a tiny insight into the depth of my Etiquette Deficiency Disorder. What is WRONG with me?

My attempts to land work also made slow progress. One of the most ridiculous jobs I had in those days was making a commercial for a type of pen. The selling point for this pen was that it could write upside down – a dubious quality (who would need that?) but I was so eager for work I didn't even question it. At the casting meeting, it was explained to me that if I were given the role I would be taken up in a World War II biplane. The pilot would perform a manoeuvre known as a 'barrel roll' and, when I was upside down, I would smile into the camera, demonstrate writing with the pen, and say some dialogue. I can't even imagine what made me agree to such craziness, although, to be honest, it really didn't seem that weird after the things I'd experienced in my life. And I seem to remember that I was so amused by their nonchalant effrontery that I sort of felt drawn to accept the challenge . . .

Oh, come on, Pamela. Surely this was your adrenaline-junkie side, the part that uses the rush of danger and excitement to assuage your anxiety . . . ?

I suppose you're right. But I was not afraid of aeroplanes. My sister Claire had recently acquired her pilot's licence (in fact, she had married an Australian teaching pilot), so I suppose I was thinking something along the lines of 'How bad could it be?'

I would soon find out. When the filming day arrived, I was taken to a small airfield somewhere in the countryside and introduced to a rather uninspiring pilot who seemed to have a problem with his middle ear. Now, just that fact alone would make most people run a mile, but I meekly followed him on to the tarmac, past all the rather well-maintained aircraft, until we reached something that looked as though it had been out of operation since Hitler was a threat. 'We'd prefer you didn't wear a flying helmet,' said the director. 'We want you to look as glamorous as possible. So you won't be able to communicate verbally with the pilot when you're in the air. But you can signal him in his dashboard mirror.' 'Why would I need to signal him exactly?' I gingerly inquired. 'Well, he'll give you the thumbs up when the sun is at the right angle to light you and he's ready to do the barrel roll. You signal back if you're ready to switch on the camera.' 'Switch on the camera?' I asked in amazement. 'Isn't there going to be a camera person on board?' 'Well, no,' smiled the director uncomfortably. 'There's only room for two people.' Duh. This was a biplane. The pilot was in the front seat and I'd be in the back. They had mounted a camera on the side, so I'd be responsible for switching it on. Then I'd do my dialogue, write with the pen while the plane was flying upside down and switch the camera off again when we were the right side up to save the battery. Easy peasy.

Why in the world, I wonder now, didn't an enormous red light start flashing inside my head at that moment? Amazingly, I just went along with it, trying to be as professional as I could. After I was clicked into my safety harness and given instructions about activating the parachute they'd attached to my back, we taxied to the runway and set off. At first I enjoyed the feeling of being in an open cockpit, unencumbered by a ceiling – or anything else that might prevent me from hurtling many thousands of feet to the ground below. The countryside was a patchwork of farms, fields, cottages and streams. Then, once the sunlight hit my right cheek it was time to try for a take. I returned the pilot's signal and switched on the camera. Within a few seconds, the plane began to roll. Let me tell you, there is no feeling like that on earth. I had given little thought to what it would be like to hang upside down in a safety harness in a hurtling aircraft – let alone trying to write and say dialogue into a camera at the same time. The g-force pulled my facial skin backwards until I resembled a carp against a current. The blood rushed to my head, my brain barely functioned, and my limbs lost their motor skills. How did I manage to collect myself enough to carry out my ridiculous duties? I have no idea.

We repeated the exercise several more times, then landed so the director could check the camera. 'How are you doing?' he asked. 'Just dandy,' I replied cheerily. The endorphins were beginning to click in. We took off again and continued to do those stunts – for that's what they truly were – time and time again until the sun began to disappear. What, oh what, is WRONG with me?

What did you learn about yourself?

After we landed for the last time, the pilot confessed that this was the second attempt at making the commercial. The first attempt – with a model – had ended when the plane developed a mechanical problem and he'd been forced to land in a field. The model had decided life was too short and walked off in a huff. Smart girl, but obviously not someone who loves adrenaline as much as I do . . .

Pamela, what did you learn about yourself?

OK . . . At the end of that utterly mad day, I understood new truths about life and the human experience: 1. Adrenaline is powerful, fun, and thoroughly cheers you up. 2. Facing your mortality is powerful, fun, and thoroughly cheers you up. 3. Adventure, derring-do and even a little craziness are what make life worth living. I was on a high for weeks after that. I read Aleister Crowley's *Diary of a Drug Fiend* twice (the protagonist is a pilot) and thought, like him, that I'd discovered the secret of the universe.

I was sitting at home when the commercial came on TV some months later, and the friends I was with remarked that, apart from my weird, flapping cheeks, it looked like a studio set-up. So much for reality. When I told Billy that story – many years later – he gave me words of wisdom that have set himself in good stead whenever he's enduring turbulence at 30,000 feet: 'Och, it's all OK – as long as you're above maiming height.'

So in London, it seems you not only began to throw yourself into estab-lishing your career there, but it seems you continued your focus on personal growth and learning . . . ?

No question. And I was lucky to come into contact with many people who influenced and helped me with that. For example, about a year after I first arrived in London a fellow Australian introduced me to Dr Germaine Greer. I was thrilled to meet one of my idols, and even more thrilled when, not long after, she very kindly allowed me to stay at her place. I was absolutely in awe of her. Not only had she been extremely inspirational to me from a distance, but up close and personal she was unbelievably brilliant. And she was formidable; I felt I could never match her in confidence, and was afraid of disappoint-ing her through being a far-from-ideal lodger. In fact, I began to be a little scared of her. One day she saw a press picture of me posing provocatively (black lacy dress, knickers showing) and expressed her distaste. I couldn't even formulate the question I wanted to ask her, which was how could I present myself in a way that would get me noticed in order to get jobs, without coming across as a bimbo. I was so grateful for Germaine's support, but I now understand she unwittingly reminded me of my mother, which stirred up painful feelings of being bad, unworthy and judged. And then . . . oh yes, she happened to say something disparaging about me publically that was actually pretty innocuous but I took it very badly . . .

Certainly sounds like you projected your mother issues onto her . . .

Yes. I did. And around about this time I started having fears about my body – especially about becoming seriously ill. At some level I actually knew it was irrational, but I still felt very afraid and imagined all kinds of things were wrong with me. I was constantly reading medical text-books, which just made it worse, and a couple of times I consulted doctors who told me nothing was wrong . . . but I didn't believe them . . .

Your anxiety had begun to take the form of hypochondriasis?

Yes. It was only for a short time – a few months at most - but now, when I have patients who suffer from it, I really feel I can understand them. It's terrible to be so sure you're about to linger and die yet no one will take you seriously . . . God almighty – I'm realizing just how many kinds of mental health problems I've had – although it all really boils down to anxiety, doesn't it? And trauma, which was really inflicted on me, wasn't it?

Hmm. What would it be like to think that you yourself were somehow at fault . . . ?

Just terrible, although I suppose, if I could take some responsibility, I'd have a sense that next time it could be controlled . . .

Well yes, but it's important for you to understand that anxiety and many of the ways in which it's expressed, such as OCD and some eating disorders, tends to run in families. Your essential anxiety was part of your mental constitution. You had it, your mother had it, and probably others in the family did as well. You were not to blame for it . . . and by the way, neither was your mother. And the trauma you sustained as a child and teenager – that was not your fault either. You were just a child!

My head – my cognition – gets that, but there's this deep shame about it too . . .

How does that shame manifest itself?

Well, it's like this: a voice inside tells me that if only I had been more . . . loveable . . . those bad things wouldn't have happened to me . . .

You know very well that's the way children tend to think when they're trying to make sense of rejection, abandonment and abuse. They cannot allow themselves to rail against the adults who were responsible, so they turn their fury inwards instead . . .

It's taken me some time to understand that my long, childhood period of feeling unappreciated and unloved constituted a traumatic injury. Previously I had thought of trauma as always being the result of a single, scary event, like being nearly drowned or being attacked by a stranger . . .

It's a common misperception . . .

As I grew into an adult I definitely began to have this very unusual feeling that I might actually deserve to be happy – even successful. This wasn't easy to believe, but it was definitely dawning on me. By 1979, for example, when I was twenty-eight years old, my confidence was growing . . . I was gradually getting more used to being in London, and came to understand a bit more about how things worked. I stumbled into my role in *Not The Nine O'Clock News*, a TV show developed at the BBC by a gang of elite Oxbridge blokes. It's quite true that I met the boyish, ebullient and clever producer John Lloyd at a party, but I didn't shag him (as many people thought). No one could understand why a brash Australian Sheila got such a big break in British television, and unkindly assumed it was for the wrong reasons. However, it happened through a serendipitous – and well-boundaried – social meeting. There I was, in a relaxed mood among friends, doing some impressions of newscasters I'd seen in the USA, and apparently John Lloyd was quite taken with my sense of satire and invited me to go to the BBC and audition for him and co-producer Sean Hardie. At the time, I didn't really pay John much attention, but I finally trotted into Television Centre at White City and improvised a few characters, read a few scripts. To be honest, I thought they seemed a bit disorganized and lackadaisical. They were surprisingly open about the fact that they had never done TV comedy before. I may not have been in the famous Cambridge Footlights like them (I'd never heard of that at the time), but I had done a fair bit of TV in Australia – and, most importantly, the time I had spent during my travels seeking and studying local satire in countries like Russia, Poland, Turkey and Indonesia made me well qualified to perform topical comedy.

Luckily, John and Sean took me seriously and decided to cast me. The show started and it quickly became popular. Looking back, it was quite clever of them to choose me, because a nice British girl might have been afraid to do some of the things I did – taking on icons like the newsreader Angela Rippon, for example. But see, I had no idea who anyone was so I wasn't afraid. I didn't understand British society or politics, and I didn't know or care if I was offending anyone.

Coming to public attention – with all the attendant razzmatazz and discomfort – occurred very quickly. I barely understood what was happening until years later. But just before I was cast in *Not The Nine O'Clock News* I had come to embrace the Buddhist philosophy, which helped me to stay relatively centred – at least at first. It was a wonderful antidote to the worrying brand of Christianity I'd experienced earlier in life. In Buddhism, there was no such thing as original sin; you started out good and had a decent chance to remain that way. For an Anglican-raised person that was quite a novel concept! Buddhist precepts are based on the idea that, well, there are set guidelines if you want to be happy, but it's your choice, and there is a minimum of agonizing expectations to be met – no wonder it was so attractive and helpful to me. Plus I found the meditation practices I acquired at the London Buddhist Centre in Bethnal Green, like the Mindfulness of Breathing, truly helped to assuage my escalating anxiety.

You were becoming more anxious again, just at that point?

Absolutely. Well, my life had changed so drastically. There had been all that travel, then a relocation to London, and now becoming successful . . . There was a part of me still going, 'You're unworthy, you don't deserve that . . . Who do you think you are?'

And whose voice was that, do you think . . . ?

I suppose it was my mother's or my father's voice . . . Those voices could seriously interrupt my concentration. On the very first day's

shoot I simply could not get my lines right (later, John Lloyd told
me he thought then and there he'd made a terrible mistake – I
suppose I was lucky he didn't fire me on the spot). But, with the
help of the meditation techniques I had learned, I very quickly got
into my stride. I can't imagine what the others thought I was up to,
isolating myself in a corner of the set, but I was desperately trying
to calm myself and enter a useful creative state. There was a sketch
in which I played a weird animal rights campaigner who barged
into restaurants to 'rescue' cooked chickens and perform mouth-
to-mouth resuscitation (I know, I know . . . it doesn't sound funny,
but you had to be there!) and after one long, largely improvised
scene, our director called 'Cut!' and I suddenly became aware that
the crew was applauding. 'OK, I can do this,' I thought happily. 'I
may not have gone to Oxford, but I'm ready.'

After just a couple of weeks, *NTNON* gained a momentum –
and notoriety – that got us well and truly noticed. As producers,
John Lloyd and Sean Hardie cleverly pushed boundaries just as far
as they could, while keeping the material smart and with broad
appeal – even if it was pretty puerile at times. Talent-wise, we
performers were a mixed bag, with Rowan Atkinson being largely
a solo artist, Chris Langham (who was in the first series but did
not continue on with it) being more of a self-contained writer and
stand-up, and Mel Smith and myself approaching the work more
as actors. Once Griff Rhys Jones replaced Chris we all began working more as a group but, like all performing groups, there were
tensions and rivalries.

But the *NTNON* team involved far more than four performers.
Many writers and a talented production team helped to craft classic
scenes such as 'The Gorilla Sketch', in which I played a TV anchor
interviewing a curiously articulate gorilla called Gerald (played by
Rowan) who had a quirky relationship with a zoologist (played by
Mel). I've noticed that sketch still seems to hold its appeal, whereas

the more topical offerings – such as another spoof BBC interview we did in which serious-minded people debated whether or not the Monty Python movie *Life of Brian* was blasphemous or not – were extremely funny at the time, but are now mystifying.

One day I became aware that *NTNON* producers were particularly excited – as were my fellow cast members – because they had an appointment to meet a Scottish comedian called Billy Connolly, who they wanted as a guest on the show. I'd never heard of Billy, but I dutifully went along with the gang to meet him at his manager's office. We all shook hands with this hairy stranger, then walked round to Geales fish restaurant for lunch. I was shocked. You know how sometimes you meet someone and have a completely unexpected reaction, a kind of secret knowledge? Some people would call it 'love at first sight' and I suppose it was. I was extremely taken with him. He was so different from the men I had met during *NTNON* – well-educated, genteel males without that edge of danger that Billy had. I was (unknowingly) very strongly attracted to him.

'Danger' . . . interesting word . . .

Mmm, I take your point. At lunch he ate his fish with his bare hands and I remember thinking, 'What an animal!' He was thrilling; a savage gypsy lover with a voice like gravel and honey, but I learned he was married. Oh, yes, that's right – so was I.

I had been married to the actor Nicholas Ball for about a year. He was a delightful man whom I truly loved, but we were not quite right for each other, and things were getting pretty tense at home. I had met him when he was the star of a TV detective series called *Hazel* and was enormously taken by him. We got on well for a while, but my sudden success in *NTNON* eventually meant I was unable to give him the time and focus he deserved.

In Billy, you may have unconsciously recognized a fellow survivor . . .

Yes! We matched and consoled each other but, right from the start, there were some big problems . . .

I'm not surprised. But it was partly your previous abuse at the hand of a crazy, dangerous man that made it possible for you to be with Billy, wasn't it? I don't mean that he was like Helmut, but he was headed on a highly self-destructive path, which you came to recognize, didn't you?

Well, yes. And I had vowed never to put myself at the mercy of a violent man again, so when Billy showed signs that he was capable of out-of-control behaviour (i.e. under the influence of alcohol), I set a firm boundary and was prepared to walk away. I definitely fell in love with him the minute I met him, but at the time when I met Billy, my career was extremely important to me. I think he recognized that. Incidentally, I'm wondering now if perhaps John and Sean noticed we had a connection, because they got us to do a sketch in which Billy played an Iranian Ayatollah to whom I sang a love song as a naïve guerrilla. 'There's a man / In Iran / That I can't ignore . . .' Very silly, but hilarious and highly topical (the Iranian Embassy siege meant the sketch had to be withdrawn for a week until things were resolved), and you can see there was a spark between us.

But as I said, I was conscious that *NTNON* was an extraordinary opportunity for me, and I was thoroughly focused on it. It was the perfect job for someone who was passionate about satire and had thoroughly studied it – and I was thrilled and proud to be part of it. However, it was also a pretty stressful work environment.

Right from the start, I felt like an outsider. Not only was I the only female in the cast, but I was culturally quite different. Half the time, I didn't understand what the others were laughing about. I was completely mystified about the British class system, British politicians and their political parties, and the nuances of life in the UK generally. In some ways I suppose that might have been a good thing because, until I caught up, I focused on what I could do: impersonations. I had never done them before, but using my acting skills and my musical ear (which helped me achieve vocal accuracy), I developed into a startling copy-cat.

The BBC had an amazing in-house wig and make-up team at that time. I was especially helped by Kezia de Winne to look like the people I was impersonating, notably: newscasters Angela Rippon and Anna Ford, TV presenters such as Annie Nightingale, politicians like Margaret Thatcher, and pop icons like Olivia Newton-John, Kate Bush and Agnetha from ABBA. I loved crafting those impersonations. I took them so seriously I tried to forget they were meant to be funny – until I performed them for the live audience. Once I heard strangers laugh I knew they were good, and then I thoroughly enjoyed their approval. That's the great thing about comedy – instant gratification! But I played everything very straight, never camping it up, and that helped to make the sketches even more powerful. My self-education in the political theatrical environments I'd visited during my travels had set me in good stead. And I understood that risk and danger in performance provided an edge that could be riveting to an audience.

In fact, I played a huge range of characters on the show, not just impersonations, and was grateful that John and Sean were classy enough to allow and encourage me. After all, I could have just been a token woman. But instead of playing, say, the nurse, I was the doctor, and plenty of our sketches inverted – and even made fun of – traditional female roles. I didn't have much to measure this against, but I sensed that this was a new quality of female support from male producers and I really appreciated it. John and Sean also provided me with an amazing opportunity to show my characterization skills. They seemed genuinely excited to watch me develop as a comic actor.

Naturally, there were complexities in the group's performing dynamics. Right from the start, I felt Mel and I worked particularly well together. He was a real actor and I think we understood how each other worked. Of course, Rowan Atkinson and Griff Rhys Jones were extremely funny but, in many ways, I wish Chris Langham had remained in the cast. I thought he was extraordinarily talented and was really more grown up than the rest of us. Perhaps that was his downfall, as it set him a little apart from the team.

I'd like to say I played every female role but, in typical British style, the boys also loved to get into a dress whenever possible. 'All right, very funny, ha, ha, ha,' I'd say sourly. I don't really blame them for wanting to cross-dress, because it guaranteed some serious laughs – especially for Mel – but at the time I found it really annoying. And I just didn't quite get it. I was barely aware of the British pantomime dame tradition, hated Benny Hill and thought the whole idea of dressing as a woman if you weren't actually transgendered – or received erotic pleasure from it – was really tacky. The boys and John tended to look slightly guilty whenever they were working on a drag sketch – well, they would, wouldn't they, with me pouting furiously in the corner? They were all collapsing with mirth, while I made no attempt to conceal my pique.

To be honest, I think they could be forgiven for deciding that, off-screen, I had no sense of humour. I remember being very thin at the time, and very edgy. I chain-smoked and ate very pure food – no salt, sugar or fat, if I could help it. I've mentioned that I had become a practising Buddhist and spent a lot of time meditating – which did help my focus and performance anxiety – but I wasn't exactly fun to be around. I wish I could have just lightened up and enjoyed myself, but I couldn't. It was all so overwhelming. And I did feel such a misfit. Well, what else was new? I'd been feeling that my whole life. Also, I was increasingly affected by occasional unkind comments in the press, which seemed to confirm the deep self-loathing I had never fully managed to eradicate.

In achieving such success, and reaching such a central position in the limelight, you also risked massive rejection, didn't you?

Good point. And I really had no one to talk to in the early days; I was too busy to have friends and I was going through a very painful withdrawal and separation from Nicholas. The *NTNON* boys and I were a team in the professional comedy sense, but that was as far as our contact went. Actually, I'm not even sure I could use the word 'professional'! We put the show together in a seemingly haphazard way. I remember our early rehearsals, in a big, chilly room some-where near Hammersmith. There was a Space Invaders machine we all used to take turns at, non-stop. We'd start rehearsing a bit late, then halfway through the morning Richard Curtis would turn up with a crumpled bit of paper – something he'd handwritten for Rowan. Rowan would read it and, next thing, John Lloyd would be doubling over with his high-pitched laugh. The rest of us would roll our eyes because we wished Richard would write something bril-liant for us, too. Now John would be in a great mood and Rowan would be smirking, Mel would be playing Space Invaders, and Griff would be eating an iced bun out of a paper bag, but I would be morose and plotting in a corner. I desperately wished I could write sketches that would blow them all away. I was like Ringo Starr, who used to think he'd come up with a good Beatles song, but when he turned up to play it for the band he'd walk in and Paul would be playing 'Yesterday'. None of us could write like Richard, although together we were good at developing what other writers had drafted. Eventually, more writers would shuffle in and John would start reading what they'd been working on. If he broke into a giggle at any point the three boys and I would saunter over to see who could swipe that line. Oh yes, comedians will sell their mothers for a laugh – and we were no exception.

Usually these groups, like your comedy team, end up replicating dysfunctional families, and the individuals often behave in ways that are triggered by the group dynamic . . . You were slotting into your familiar role of family outsider, weren't you?

Ah, yes. Now that I am a psychologist I understand a lot more about groups, and I wish I'd understood that process back then. Nowadays, I'm especially interested in comedy troupes and musical bands and, professionally, I have often helped members of such collectives to deal with the stresses and problems that arise under such pressured conditions . . .

Well, many people regress – and destructive competitiveness can be inspired by quite innocent acts: for example, assigning a particular role to one person may cause another to feel injured and resentful, even though the adult part of him may understand it's for the greater good and he'll get his turn.

Yes. I know there were complicated issues – even a kind of sibling rivalry – swirling around all our psyches; and with John and Sean as 'daddy' and 'mummy' there were bound to be fireworks. Of course, now I understand that it must have been my deep fear of rejection that often caused me acute pain in that situation. Fortunately, all these feelings were kept in check – under the surface. Cross words were never spoken as far as I know . . .

Maybe they should have been . . .

Yes, I suppose it would have created more authentic relationships between us. To be honest, I don't think any of my fellow cast members liked me at all. And I don't blame them. Well, what would they have liked about me? I imagine the kind of women they would have liked were upper middle class, fun, matey, essentially lovely, accommodating types, like, well, Emma Thompson, who had come from the same background as them. I was far from accommodating and in *NTNON* I tended to steal the limelight a bit by being sexually provocative (the sketches sometimes demanded that). And I made the mistake of behaving competitively towards the boys, which didn't go down too well. I really hadn't learned how to get on with men who weren't my boyfriends. Yes, the chaps disliked me. I wasn't 'one of them', we were never friends, and we have not kept in touch. Also, I discovered after a couple of series that I was being paid a lot less than them. That seriously pissed me off.

You still have feelings about that?

You betcha. But I genuinely appreciate how well and benevolently they tolerated my prickliness. Looking back now, I realize I was really struggling. For example, it was really weird to have such a novel perception of myself – created largely through others. Apparently I was some kind of a phenomenon. I discovered this because people said extraordinary things to me at the time. They said, 'I've never seen a pretty girl being funny before.' Seriously? Sometimes this would even be posed as a question in the press: 'But can an attractive woman really be funny?' That really surprised – and insulted – me. After all, I was being funny, wasn't I? Well, I was doing my best. I didn't even think I was particularly pretty; in fact, I always found fault with my appearance. I mean, I understood that what I was doing was new and slightly threatening, but I resented the question. My personal comedy heroines were Lucille Ball and Goldie Hawn – both beautiful, funny women – so I certainly didn't think there was anything unusual about me. Well, perhaps it was new for Britain at that time.

I'm wondering . . . now that you understand how traumatic it is for the mind when a person rockets to public attention, are you able to reflect about some of the feelings you were having at the time and put them in that context?

Oh yes . . . I now recognize them as par for the curse – wow, Freudian slip, I meant 'course'. But in a way fame is a curse, because it's rather a hollow victory. While appreciating the good things fame can bring, one also tends to maintain private terror – that it will go away, that you'll be 'found out' as unworthy of it, and that the real person you know yourself to be deep inside can never match up to the scintillating personage others now think you are. I knew, for example that I was personally nowhere near as funny as I was on *NTNON*, but somehow strangers seemed to expect that I would be. 'Go on, make me laugh!' was what they seemed to demand, whether that was on the street, in a cab, or in a public ladies' room. And the embarrassment! I was once trying to avoid the stares in a doctor's waiting room when a nurse came in and very publically handed me a small, clear bottle 'Miss Stephenson? The doctor would like a urine sample.' 'Me too,' I quipped. Brazening it out, I waved the bottle at my wide-eyed fellow patients. 'Any takers?'

You made the best of it on that occasion, but it can't have been easy – all over again, you became acutely aware of people's high expectations of you . . . That has historically had a negative effect on you, hampering your ability to be productive . . .

And of course, I wasn't the only one who had that problem. One day Mel Smith turned up for filming in a state of total panic and announced that, for the first time ever, he'd been asked to give an after-dinner speech – but he had nothing prepared. He had to face this group of 250 Barclays Bank managers that very evening so, in between scenes, the four of us sat crouched over a paraffin heater in a make-up van, desperately trying to think of a decent joke or two. As the day wore on, Mel became more and more terrified – because nothing much materialized from any of us. It struck me as being highly ironic that four people who were supposed to be among the top British comedy-makers were unable to think of a single thing. We were all trying to remember every joke we'd ever heard – even really stupid stuff from our school days. 'Knock knock . . . ?' It was sooo pathetic.

But being in a hit show at the BBC was fantastic, and I was terribly lucky to be a part of it. Really – that's not just a PR line. And it got me some of the attention I most wanted; Billy called me after I did a sketch in which I parodied pop singer Kate Bush ('*Oh England . . . my leotard . . .*') and told me he thought I was very talented. Wow. From a man I'd never seen perform but the people I was in competition with thought was a comic genius! That meant a great deal to me. Of course, I could be cynical now and tell myself he just really fancied me in that leotard . . .

Pamela! You're way too harsh with yourself . . .

Really? I thought it was Billy I was being harsh with . . . But anyway, my husband's leotard fetish aside, four series of *NTNON*, several records, plus a stage version of the show called *Not In Front Of The Audience* truly launched me as a comedian in the UK. It wasn't easy and I remember how nerve-wracking it was to perform live every week with so little preparation. But, then again, I'd survived worse.

So, in many ways, your early trauma and the survival skills you developed to deal with it really helped you to handle difficult situations you subsequently faced – both personal and professional. In fact, one could say they contributed to your success . . . ?

Well, yes. I do now see myself as a survivor, but it wasn't always like that. I have mainly seen myself a bit like a racing driver who is not quite ready for the race she's in, gripping the steering wheel and hanging on for all she's worth. At any moment, she could lose control of the car and it could skid into a corner. Frankly, I still struggle with that. Will I ever be free?

Chapter Eight

KING OF COMEDY
KINDA LINGERS

Consistently being on the edge as you describe, compelled to place yourself in danger, is not a comfortable way to live – do you ever see respite looming?

Ahh . . . I'm always grasping for it . . .

Yes . . . I watch myself doing it over and over again, but feel powerless to stop it. For example, I was in Fiji a couple of years ago. Now, if you're going to face destruction in the path of a tropical cyclone, it would be nice if they took the trouble to name it. Serious storms I've read about in newspapers – and even the few I've faced before – were respectfully called 'Hurricane Francis', 'Arlene' or 'Todd'. But sitting on an alarmingly low-lying Fijian atoll, constantly ducking flying coconuts is particularly upsetting when the aggressor is simply known as 'Nineteen P'. Waiting out weather of any kind has always had limited appeal. As I stare at the boiling sea, protectively clutching my fourth cup of rain-infused tea, an irresistible idea forms.

Idiodynamism – the tendency of an idea to become action – is my bête noire. Determinedly, I stride to the edge of the water, wrestle an ocean kayak from its wooden holster and launch it into the waves. I grab the paddle and make a dive for the middle of the plastic vessel – just as it is upended by a vicious wave. I hang on stubbornly (they don't sink easily) and manage to right it. With my body finally centred in the canvas seat, I strike away from shore. Adrenaline – oh yeah! That's what I'm talking about! Perhaps it's what I really live for. Suddenly I'm excited, inspired, challenged. Out of the corner of my eye I see a local man gesticulating furiously. He's trying to wave me back, while another concerned person is running along the jetty with a life jacket in hand. I laugh at their earnestness; they don't know me. They see a middle-aged, crazy woman, but I know who I am: a perfectly sensible, elated, extreme risk-taker. This part of the South Pacific Ocean is choppier than I imagined, and I seem to have hit a cross-current. I have a sober moment of abject fear, but then I tell myself I've been in worse conditions. At first I'm struggling to steer the kayak and keep it upright, but eventually I find the perfect groove in the waves. I mount each white-capped water-monster at a thirty-five degree angle, then slide down the other side with a thrilling twist. I glance over my shoulder. Now I have an audience on shore, as tourists and locals have been stirred from their shelters to watch the mad white woman commit suicide before their very eyes. Then it strikes me: what am I doing? Where exactly am I going? What is the point of this?

Well, aside from unconsciously trying to gain mastery over early trauma, you must be aware of the relationship between the summoning of adrenaline and depression. Do you think it's possible that the adrenaline or endorphin rush you get from taking risks is important because it can mitigate a depressed mood?

That may well have been the case – and not just regarding physical risks. It was probably true of my edgy comedy work after *Not The Nine O'Clock News*, when I started doing stand-up. But many comedians I've met seemed to be depressed people who 'self-medicated' one way or another, including simply through doing stand-up – one of the scariest jobs in the world! Much of the comedy I did after *NTNON* involved high risk-taking that made the BBC show look safe. In fact, John Cleese once chided me because he thought one of my acts was 'more disturbing than funny'. It was during the Secret Policeman's Ball charity concert for Amnesty International and, for some reason, I had decided it would be funny to do a sketch in which my breasts were haunted. Holding a seance with your tits was not your usual Oxbridge-type skit, and John Cleese finally came to my dressing room and banned it. Well, it may not have been John's cup of tea, but Sting was in the audience and he later told me it was one of the funniest things he'd ever seen. So there. I'll always be grateful to him for that.

Of course you understand where your bitterness about that comes from . . . ?

Well, all right, we can factor or in my rejection issues, but frankly I was bucking against the prevailing notion that only a certain type of comedy was 'the right kind'. And it was largely the stuff driven by middle-class males – with a notable exception, of course, being Billy. 'The boys' club' as I called it, looked down on most working-class comics – people like Les Dawson, who'd been making people laugh heartily well before the rest of us were born. And as far as women were concerned, there had been few examples of females on the British comedy scene doing outrageous comedy in their own right. In Monty Python, for example, poor Carol Cleveland was always 'The Crumpet'. Of course, the wonderful Joyce Grenfell

certainly had her day, the *Carry On* crew did lots of smutty jokes at
Barbara Windsor's expense, and there was Eleanor Bron who was
funny in a gentle, intellectual kind of way. But brash, smart, in-your-
face comedy from a woman on British shores? There had been no
Lucille Ball or Carol Burnett here. Just hadn't happened.

French and Saunders were starting out, though. I saw them at the
Comic Strip on the few occasions that I performed there. I was
impressed that they had the courage to do softer, female-friendly
material they'd written together. It wasn't easy to handle that crowd.
I remember waiting in the wings to go on and wanting to shit
myself. I was thinking: I have no armament to please these people.
Alexei Sayle would have just rocked the house with his strident
chanting: 'Ullo, John, got a new motor?' And Rik Mayall's pants
would probably be round his ankles just as I was about to walk on.
It was hellish. No point trying anything subtle; you had to bring out
your toughest material just to stay alive. I did abrasive sets, as shocking as possible, but they were very hit-or-miss. Once Billy phoned
and said he would come to see me at the Comic Strip the following
week, but that terrified me more than the audience so I pulled out.
I couldn't bear for him to see me fail.

You'd think I might have been more self-confident at this point.
After all, I'd been part of a comedy team that had affected people's
lives; I know this, because recently I met a woman who told me that
she was a schoolgirl when *Not The Nine O'Clock News* was on television. At some point – it may even have been the very last episode we
made – we sang a song called 'The Memory Kinda Lingers'. Now,
'Kinda Lingers' was a double entendre for 'cunnilingus', and people
smirked when they heard it. Well, not everybody. This woman I
met, who was a young teenager at the time, apparently went to
school with a serious mission. At the end of every lesson, when the
teacher asked 'Any questions?' she put up her hand. 'Please Miss,
could you tell me what "kindalingers" really means?' But no teacher

would tell her. Finally, at the end of the day, she went to the librarian, who took pity on her and told her the truth. Thirty years later, this woman still feels mortified about it – I guess she'd prefer her memory to have a kinder kinda linger.

One memory of my own that I would prefer to be kinder is that of my association with a hero of mine, the late Peter Sellers. In July 1980 his 'people' called my 'people' to suggest that we meet to discuss a role he was keen for me to play in a new Clouseau movie. It was a character called Anastasia. In this new script, Clouseau fell in love with her, and ends up leaving the police force for her. I was enormously flattered that such a genius as Peter was interested in working with me. But when I turned up to meet him at the Dorchester, I was surprised to see him sitting in the lobby, anxiously watching the door for my arrival. That seemed a bit bizarre. We exchanged pleasantries for a bit and he said some very nice things about work I'd done on *Not The Nine O'Clock News*. To be honest he seemed a little odd – but then, people had told me he was highly superstitious. 'Don't wear green whatever you do,' my agent had said. 'He thinks it's really unlucky.' Sporting a safe choice of pink and blue, I followed Peter round the corner to a Chinese restaurant where we met Clive Donner who was going to direct the film. When the two of them offered me the part then and there, I was completely bowled over. 'I'll read some of the script to you,' said Peter, who seemed worried that I might say 'No'. 'You really don't have to convince me to do this . . .' I murmured, completely mystified by his apparent desire to please me. But he launched into a scene where Clouseau and Anastasia are on a date and the hapless detective accidentally sets fire to his beard. As he read, Peter was giggling madly in a terribly endearing way, and I could just tell it would be enormous fun to work with him . I wasn't even deterred by my sense that the man was clearly crazy.

After dinner, feeling rather disbelieving of the whole situation, I sat down with Peter in his suite to hear more about the project.

'Now, you're going to hear some things,' he said, suddenly turning serious. 'I'm going to LA tomorrow to have a big operation. But, whatever you hear, don't worry. This movie will happen.' He walked me to my car and pressed a copy of the script in my hand. 'Read it immediately, please,' he said. 'Of course,' I promised. 'As soon as you get home?' he pleaded. 'Then call me and tell me what you think ... It doesn't matter what time.' Again, it seemed utterly weird that he was so anxious, but I dutifully read the script that night. I loved it, but by the time I reached the last page it was 3.30am. I thought it would be best not to bother Peter until morning.

At 10.15am I called my agent. She had already been telephoned with contractual details and I was verbally engaged to do the movie. It was so exciting – this seemed like an absolutely perfect fit for me. But at around 11am, as I was on my way to rehearsals for something else, I heard an announcement on the radio. 'Well-known movie star Peter Sellers suffered a heart attack last night. His family is gathering around him.' I didn't believe it could be serious because Peter had warned me that I might hear 'things', and had promised me the movie would go ahead. But throughout the day the news bulletins became more and more worrying and, by the afternoon, he had passed away.

What feelings did you have about that?

Agh! On the one hand I was terribly sorry about his passing. From what I had seen of him, he was a delightful and enormously talented person. But there was a part of me that was also railing against my own loss – and yet I felt quite guilty about that. I wondered if I had caused him greater anxiety by not calling him after I finished reading the script. Had I contributed to his final heart attack? I felt horrible about that possibility. But to get so close to such an enormous break in my career and have it whisked away all within a matter of hours was a particularly difficult experience, and one that took me years to get over. Oh, and there was also a rather nasty insinuation from some quarters that, well, what was I doing in his suite so late, and had I exacerbated his heart condition by – dot-dot-dot? Oh, please! Being so weird and fragile, Peter had inspired my caretaking instincts – but certainly not my lust.

Thankfully, a few other things were happening in my career – people began to invite me to appear in other movies – and there was a major development in my personal life: Billy and I got together. This happened roughly a year after we first met. I was filming in Brighton and a young man approached me on the street: 'Did you know Billy Connolly's here? He's playing at the Dome.' I have no idea who that young man was but Billy and I always joke half-seriously that he was an angel. The minute he said those words I knew what I had to do – find Billy immediately and try to reconnect with him. Strange, eh? Previously I'd had no conscious understanding of the depth of my feelings for him. At least we were both in the process of marital separation, although for both of us things were still jolly complicated. I got to the theatre before Billy arrived. When he turned up the same young man was at the door. 'Pamela Stephenson's inside,' he said. Freaky, huh?

As I sat on the wash basin in his dressing room (there was only one chair and his clothes and banjo were on it), we chatted as if we'd always known each other. Then I went into the auditorium and watched his show. I just couldn't believe it. How on earth could one person manage to keep the attention of that wild, well-tanked crowd? It was such a difficult space to play. People were walking in and out, spilling beer over each other. They were loudly heckling Billy too, although they did so at their peril because Billy was totally on the offensive. 'You don't get out much, do you?' he'd scoff. If someone stood up in his eye line he would mock them mercilessly. 'Edna is wearing . . .' Emulating a fashion announcer he would provide a hilarious running commentary of some poor woman's appearance as she tried to scuttle up the aisle to the bathroom.

I especially loved two particular stories he told that night: one about a 'wee woman in a fat coat' who was pitched off a bus into a shrubbery, and another about a budgie that got loose in a pub. The extraordinary pictures he created for the audience, the world into which he invited us, the colour and insanity of it all – were breath-taking. At that point in my professional life I had been so involved in the making of comedy, I was far from a comic's favourite audience member. At other comedians' shows I tended to sit there being quite analytical and watching them work, rather than being swept up in the performance. But with Billy, I was totally engaged, and left the theatre at the end clutching my hurting stomach, just like everybody else. It didn't even matter that I only understood every third word. He was angry as hell, but beneath it all there was a philosophical angst – not to mention a palpable, deep wound. When he talked about his father smacking him in a rhythmic fashion to match his diatribe, and being hit so hard he flew over a couch, I felt enormous empathy towards him, even though I was laughing hard along with everyone else. He touched everyone in the room in a most powerful fashion, and I knew then he truly was a genius. It hadn't been hyperbole from the *NTNON* crew after all; I had seen it with my own eyes. So I'm afraid it was very hard to resist when he popped the question: 'Come to my hotel room and save my life . . . ?' He was quoting Loudon Wainwright but, in a way, he meant exactly that.

We fell in love very quickly; in fact, as I have already implied, we had probably became (somewhat unwillingly) enamoured of each other the second we met. When I wrote my husband's biography, *Billy*, I naturally put the focus on his early story of abuse, and on his courage and survival. But now you know that I too was an abandoned child, you'll understand how fitting it was that we should have met. Joined at the wound, we were. But there was one really big problem; the man drank. In a way, it was impressive; I had never seen a man imbibe as many whiskys as he did that night and still be able to make a girl happy. At first, I thought his excessive drinking was just nerves, but I soon discovered he was not only adorable, loving and delightfully vulnerable, he was also anxious, trauma-tized and bent on self-destruction. I kept flip-flopping between thinking, 'This man is a nightmare' and 'I want to have his babies.' As a cautionary message to self, I copied a passage from the Buddhist scripture the *Dhammapada* into my notebook:

'There is no fire like lust, and no chains like those of hate. There is no net like illusion, and no rushing torrent like desire.'

Fortunately, my early illusory state gave way to a slightly better grip on the reality of Billy Connolly. I became aware that my attitude towards him waxed and waned depending on whether he was drunk or sober when we met up. He was highly unpredictable and, most alarmingly, under the influence of quite a lot of alcohol he seemed to undergo a personality change, becoming a rather mean version of himself. I jokingly referred to that dark alter ego as 'beastie' but, to be honest, it was no joke. I suppose, to some extent, I found his complexity fascinating, but it was also scary. Sometimes I even worried for my own safety. Eventually, I decided he was too hard to handle and ran away to Bali to try to forget him. But, predictably, that didn't work.

Bali 27th December 19??

Slowing down slowly
Maybe I'll go to Ubud tomorrow. Take too long today.
I like not talking.

The gecko and I have an interesting form of communication.
Mutual surprised fear . . . familiar feeling.
Is it true that I don't have one friend?
Hungry ghost. Neurotic craving for . . . once it was success . . .
now it's more success . . . but solidly linked to specific human
need . . . which has no real future. I'm losing my own strength to
that craving.
Meditate. Get strong again.
I'm still thinking only of my return. I can't really think beyond
next meeting (with Billy). This is totally destructive and negative.
Problems foreseeable? 1. His drinking. 2. My ego. 3. Both tired a
lot from working. 4. His guilt about his family. 5. Fears of Press
discovery.
What's the answer?
It would be better to break it off now. THIS KIND OF ROMANTIC
CRAVING BELONGS TO THE WORLD OF THE HUNGRY
GHOSTS. CAN ONLY LEAD TO UNHAPPINESS.

And . . . how did that resolve work out for you?

Ha! I just could not stop thinking about him. And Bali was a disappointment on this, my second visit. See, I hadn't just fled from Billy.

For the first time on my life, I'd escaped Christmas. Narrowly.
Collapsed onto a 747 on the 23rd December and woke up 30 hours
later in a full-stop in the Indian Ocean where Christmas is a mere
myth from the World of the Tourists. Arrived just before midnight
at the Bali Beach Hotel in Sanur. Crawled to my bed in a concrete
bunker high above the palm trees, and woke with the surf pounding away below. I've done it! No tinsel, no carols, no Noel hype . . .
NO CHRISTMAS TELEVISION!

I didn't write down the worst thing that could happen to me at Christmas – a family get-together – but I imagine that was upper-most in my mind. My parents were now living in Epsom, Surrey, and wanted me to turn up for festive fun and fake familiarity. Awful. My sister Lesley was now an opera singer, living relatively nearby in Zurich, so I guess they had a fantasy of playing happy families in their retirement years. Hmm. Not on your nelly . . .

Again, such bitterness. And you know, your prolonged anger towards them hides deep, continued sadness that you'd be a lot better off without . . .

Yep. I know, it would be wonderful to be able to let it go. If only insight alone were enough to release it. Hopefully, one day . . .

Actually, I tell a lie. A family get-together was not the worst thing that could happen at Christmas. I'd already experienced the ulti-mate disappointment, and I'm not talking about a crap present. One Christmas Eve . . . I must have just turned six or so . . . I was lying awake trying to figure out something. See, my bright little logical brain just couldn't figure out certain things I'd been told. For example, when that footman went around with Cinderella's slipper, looking for a girl who might fit into it, I knew it was highly unlikely that no one except Cinderella could slip it on . . . unless, of course she had a foot the size of a pencil sharpener. It simply didn't make sense. Why, oh why, I wondered, hadn't the writers of the story thought that through? Couldn't they have come up with something like: 'She had a very unusually shaped foot, with seven-teen toes'? Then it would have made sense. But anyway, this partic-ular Christmas Eve I was unable to sleep because, by now, I was fully aware of the size of the world population, and – even allowing for time changes – I just couldn't figure out how Santa was going to get around to every child's chimney in the same night. I called my mother and asked her to explain. 'Well, he doesn't,' was her blunt reply. 'What do you mean, "He doesn't"?' I asked. 'He just doesn't do that,' she said again. I still couldn't understand – or perhaps I just didn't want to. 'Look,' she finally said, somewhat impatiently, 'you know all those Christmas cards and pictures of Santa? Well, they're just made up. He doesn't really exist.'

How'd you take that . . . ?

Very, very badly. It seemed like the end of my childhood. To be honest, she might as well have ripped my heart out with her sensibly short nails. It actually took a while to sink in, but once it did, I was devastated . . . Seriously? Christmas Eve? I mean, something like 'Because he's magic!' would have sufficed. A mug of cocoa . . . a hug . . . I would have been asleep in no time. But as it was, I was going: 'Well, what else is fake? Is my real mother the Ice Queen?'

What do you think was her reasoning?

That's beyond me. I mean, they still expected me to believe in that 'loaves and fishes' thing, not to mention people being turned into pillars of salt, and even raised from the dead . . . So why, oh why, couldn't I have hung onto Santa just a bit longer?

But I suppose, in a way, my mother was giving me a compliment. Her scientist's brain valued logic above everything else, and she obviously thought she was providing me with what I needed at that particular moment . . . But, traumatic though it was, I definitely learned from it; even when my children became adults I was still saying: 'If you don't believe in Santa, he won't fill your stocking!'

So you see why – for me – Christmas was best avoided? But in Bali, my best attempts were thwarted.

Christmas morning
I leapt out of bed and wrenched open the curtains, gulping
lungfuls of balmy air, and expecting to see the Bounty ad
paradise stretched out before me . . . no such luck. Despite the
fact that this is largely a Hindu island, the biggest bloody
Christmas tree in the world was sitting right below me on the
jetty. I repacked my bags and fled, aided by dozens of obsequious
Hindus bleating Christian slogans and advising me of Mass
times. I saw just enough of this vast hotel to motivate me to
return when feeling stronger, just for the curiosity value. Exactly
what kind of hotel-planning genius inspired someone to include,
on this site of rare and luscious natural beauty, a SWISS
restaurant (Rosti and Appenzeller music in the tropical heat)
and a penthouse club, 'featuring Buddy Loren! Impressionist
Extraordinaire! Special Christmas Show with Traditional Turkey
Dinner only 30 Dollars per head Black Tie!'

In fact, I returned to that hotel sooner than expected to get myself
jabbed by the resident doctor, having finally bothered to read the
small print on a leaflet handed to me at the airport: 'IF YOU
HAPPEN TO CONTACT TYPHOID, CHOLERA, OR MALARIA
DURING YOUR VISIT TO BALI, PLEASE CONTACT THE LOCAL
AUTHORITIES. HAVE A NICE STAY.

I hadn't been inoculated against anything at all (last minute rush
– hard-hitting impersonation of Princess Anne for the Mike
Yarwood Christmas TV Show, personal life in tatters, usual stuff!)
but I decided that, on chance of hepatitis from the needle beat the
deadlier alternatives. I questioned whether maybe my karma might
have been good enough to arm me against the wrath of the gods,
but then I thought about Angela Rippon, Princess Anne and other

well-wishers back home back in Britain, and I thought, 'No . . . Go for that jab!'

Actually, that Christmas Princess Anne skit, in which I wore really large fake teeth made from orange peel and neighed like a horse, inspired a wonderfully bitchy response from a member of the public. At least I think it was a member of the public; it was so witty, it might just have been the royal victim herself:

> Dear Miss Stephenson,
> When I saw a programme where you were, as I thought, mocking Princess Anne, I thought how very cruel and unkind it was of you but I must apologize to you profusely as when I saw you in Barry Norman's show I realized they were your own teeth.
> Yours sincerely,
> Kathleen Williams

Although I had nothing personally against the Princess Royal, I definitely deserved that. And as for my dentition, erm, it's true that I have fairly . . . substantial teeth. All right, I have bloody enormous choppers. My husband calls them 'the fridge doors'. Even the late Leonard Rossiter remarked: 'Young lady, you have far more teeth than you're entitled to.' Funny, funny man.

Anyway, I had my jabs, although probably the worst diseases on the island of Bali were to be found among the Western colony at Kuta Beach. After its famous postcard sunset, the bars along the main drag wailing tinny, bootleg disco sounds, would fill up with lascivious young beachcombers – all Piz Buin and herpes – Swedes, Germans, Dutch, but mainly Australians. Everywhere Australians.

I am beginning to think I am prejudiced against my own kind. At the very least, I want to persuade them to stop using Bali as their very own Costa del Sol. Overheard on a local bus (please recite with flattened vowels): 'What, is that rice over there? Is there meant to be all that water?' There are plenty of Americans too, who tend, of an evening, to gravitate to Poppies Bar and Restaurant. For a dive that does you a magic mushroom omelette on request, the proprietor's notice seemed a little superfluous: 'PLEASE DON'T GET LOADED AT POPPIES.' I sidled onto a bar stool, my corn-rope plaits zinging round my neighbour's ears. 'Hi Bo!' he winked, absurdly linking me to Bo Derek in the movie *Arthur*. 'Oh piss off,' I hinted. We made friends later, though. An accountant from Santa Barbara, who seemed to be having a good time. 'Yeah,' he said, 'I reckon it's a great place to just veg-out!' Well, I must admit, he did remind me of a radish. Bright crimson forehead, and a white patch on top where his hat had sat. Bound to be a sick boy tomorrow. But if you sun too much, drink too much, anything too much, all you have to do in the morning is make it to the beach. There you can be massaged, soothed with coconut milk, dog-haired, coked up – whatever it takes. But as soon as you come round it's time to move or you will definitely be sold something: 'You want a bikini? I give you good price. You buy bracelet? Wood carving? What about dope? I give you cheap!' Yes, regarding the latter, I know for a fact you can buy the best Harpic in the Southern Hemisphere right there on Kuta Beach.

But I tire easily of such an excess of sex, drugs and rock 'n' roll – cheap though they all were – so I went to visit my eccentric English friend Victor, who lives in Pennestan Village with a Balinese stunner and their two children. 'Oh, hello,' he said, not particularly surprised to see me, 'I've just been listening to you on the *Private Eye* record.' Now, is that fame? Or is that Fame? I *just hadn't previously thought that the world went as far as Bali . . .*

The Balinese, on the other hand, believe that Bali IS the world – actually a giant tortoise that sits on a rock surrounded by sea – and that beyond it lies a different place, the World of the Tourists, populated by travellers of all nationalities who do nothing but fly round in aeroplanes with their suitcases, occasionally dropping in on Bali. Six years earlier I had spent three idyllic months on the island, and I hated seeing how much it had changed. I considered it a tiny precious jewel, a magic place with a unique and astonishing culture. Why, I wondered, wasn't someone doing something to preserve it? The first time I visited Bali I stumbled on a gathering at night in a remote village, where I saw a dance in which some young girls, wearing ornate sarongs and gold leaf jewellery entwined in their hair, were put into a trance by village priests. They were not trained dancers, and only people who had practised since the age of three could do the challenging Legong, but nevertheless they danced it, after a fashion, for several hours. The explanation for this phenomenon was that 'heavenly spirits' were instructing them through the medium of trance. I had been riveted by this extremely powerful event, and felt privileged to have witnessed it, but now, six years on, anyone could catch a 'Trance Dance'on Tues. or Fri. in Bona Village . . . Bus leaves Kuta 5pm, 7,500 Rupia. Alternatively, you could get a 'Quality Cremation' for eight dollars Australian. Yes, I hated seeing that amazing culture being destroyed so quickly.

I tried to go to the island of Komodo, which had always taken my fancy because it was inhabited by giant 'dragons'. Tour operators said the seas were too rough to complete the crossing, but I discovered that was just a cover-up. Apparently, on a recent expedition, one of those fascinating monsters had eaten a Japanese tourist. I met quite a few Japanese tourists while I was staying at Kuta – my diary entry reveals a tongue-in-cheek awareness of my apparent sexual power.

These intriguing individuals arrive regularly in large groups, all neatly kitted out with Louis Vuitton surfboard covers and Gucci First Aid kits. My problem is simply one of popularity – and nothing to do with *Not The Nine O' Clock News*. Every morning, as I sit alone on the verandah of my bungalow, there's a steady stream of requests from these little Asian studs, that they should be photographed, one at a time, sitting at breakfast beside me with smug, toothy smiles – the morning-after mock-up routine. They seem so pathetic I usually agree. So I'm now famous in Japan, not as a comedian but as the holiday squeeze of hundreds.

That became boring after a while, so I moved inland, to spend the rest of my stay in a remote hut in the middle of a rice field. On New Year's Eve, instead of disco-dancing on the Kuta strip, I was catching eels by firefly light. Lovely. I rested, I became serene, I discovered that it does a girl good to go to bed early.

As for my plan to forget about Billy – I really struggled with all my might, but after a month or so of agony I returned to his side. I'd had no experience of alcohol addiction, and I needed a crash course. I read Alcoholics Anonymous's *The Big Book* bible from cover to cover, from which I learned that it would be foolish to imagine I could stop him drinking if he didn't want to. I gave him an ultimatum: 'It's drink or me.' I was prepared to give him up – OK, I know what you're thinking . . . but at least I would have given it a darn good try.

Fortunately, Billy decided that he was going to plump for personal happiness and changed his life to a sober one. It didn't happen all at once; 'one day at a time' was very much the way it went, but he was essentially strong and resolved and, to this day, has not touched alcohol or drugs for nearly thirty years. Billy never entered a rehab programme. He tells people, 'I decided to quit drinking while it was still my idea.' And that's pretty much the way it was.

But while I was teaching Billy about his inner beastie, he taught me things about comedy. He never actually sat down and said, 'This is how it works' – he's the last person you could ask to analyze how comedy is constructed (in fact, he would vehemently resist that) – but he was enormously generous about other people's work, if he thought it was good, and scathing about what he disliked, so I was able to internalize his comic taste. Billy admired my other heroes at the time, Robin Williams and Steve Martin ('wild and crazy guy').

I didn't mind being irreverent myself, and I went through a phase of performing truly outrageous comedy stunts, such as the time I conspired with Bob Monkhouse's producer to destroy his set. Have a look on YouTube and you'll see me pretending to have a broken leg and walking on that show to do something very different from what we'd rehearsed. Bob Monkhouse truly had no idea. With the help of a brilliant special effects team, his producer John Fisher and I rehearsed it when the star of the show was absent from the set and that's why it works – no pretence. I just love the look of panic in Bob's eyes when he thinks he's on live television with a crazy, fully armed nutcase. He even covers his genitals in case I destroy his manhood. At least I think that's what his hands were doing there; he confessed later: 'I had to change my underwear.'

I gained notoriety for performing comedy stunts, although some people mistakenly thought they were unplanned pieces of spontaneous anarchy. Well, some of them sort of were – like when I threw raw eggs around on breakfast television (anchor Anne Diamond's face was a picture), debagged a dazed TV journalist, and climbed into underpants-for-two with David Frost and Selina Scott (no, not all together, with each person on separate occasions – we wouldn't have all fitted!). But these things were all done in the name of humour and entertainment, not bloody-mindedness. I saw all that as an immediate and edgy style of improvised comedy, and I was far from the only one in the world interested in it – Ken Campbell in London was an aficionado. In LA there was Bobcat Goldthwait, and Sam Kinison, who liked to set fire to TV set couches. And Robin Williams, of course. When a comic did something unexpected and shocking, the energy in the room became electrified. I loved that feeling. And I knew that it was no bad thing to create a sense of excitement so that audiences were excited about seeing me perform live; they knew, for sure, it would not be dull.

And of course, for you it would summon a great deal of extra adrenaline . . .

Point taken. I was certainly eager for more stimulation. I had actually become a bit bored doing TV and was looking towards the American movie world. When we had breaks from *NTNON*, cast members did other work. After the second series, I trotted off to Hollywood to meet Mel Brooks, who was casting for his new movie *History of the World Part One*. He greeted me in his trailer on the Universal back lot. I remember being amazed that, because of the noise, they had to stop shooting whenever the tourist trams came by. It was my first inkling that Hollywood is more than just a movie town; that associated businesses sometimes command equal dollars and, therefore, equal power.

I immediately loved Mel Brooks. He seemed childlike, with an enormous twinkle in his eye. I had admired his work ever since I first saw *Vertigo* and *Blazing Saddles*. He was warm and encouraging and was very nice about my work on *Not The Nine O'Clock News*. I was surprised he'd seen it. He said, 'I loved the Gorilla sketch. Who are those guys?' I told him. Then he said, 'You're funny. Are you OK about being half nude?' With rash bravado, I replied: 'I'll do anything for a laugh.' Maybe that wasn't such a good idea, but it seemed to impress Mel. 'Is that mostly you?' he asked, looking at my chest. It was a bit difficult to answer that, considering my history, but I nodded. I was hoping he wasn't going to ask for a look.

I loved working on that movie. Many of my heroes were in it; in fact, it was cast with gods and goddesses from the *Who's Who* of comedy. I worked directly with Harvey Korman, Cloris Leachman, Gregory Hines and Spike Milligan – all thorough idols of mine. But I was particularly fascinated to see how Mel Brooks worked. Directing AND acting in a movie is extremely challenging – what a responsibility! He would arrive on the set very early and greet his actors. 'Hello Pamela!' he'd say to me in front of everyone, faking a *mea culpa* shame. 'I'm sorry about last night – I behaved like an animal . . .' He said it time and time again but I still found it hilarious. Mel would block the first scene and set up the shot, then disappear to change and be made up. As soon as he returned, the cameras would roll, and he would ping-pong between acting and observing the scene straight after on playback, then direct changes. Believing that the funniest takes occur when the actors are right on the edge of cracking up, Mel occasionally encouraged the actors to create skits that were nothing to do with the film. Then, when we were boiling over with laughter, we'd return to the scripted scene and do it with heightened comic energy.

Spike Milligan played my father. He was an extraordinary man, with a truly original sense of humour. I didn't always understand it (the Goons were incomprehensible to me), but he did come up with one fantastically memorable line. We were at Blenheim Palace, filming a scene that occurred right near the end of the movie. It was an enormously complicated crowd scene in which Mel, Spike and I were saved from the guillotine by African-American actor Gregory Hines, who rode up on a white horse and cart. There were around a hundred people in the crowd and the set-up for Gregory's ride to save us required very careful choreography. Finally, everything was rehearsed and the cameras rolled. 'Action!' As Mel, Spike and I were being pushed towards the guillotine by henchmen, the crowd parted and Gregory galloped towards us on his white horse. It should have been a one-take relief for all, but Spike just couldn't resist improvising. 'No, no!' he cried. 'Stop! We ordered a BLACK horse and a WHITE driver!'

While we were shooting at Blenheim Palace, Mel, Spike and I were invited round to drinks with the people who lived there – the Duke and Duchess of Kent. We turned up in our period costumes – me in a pink crinoline and Mel in a satin footman's outfit – with powdered wigs. It must have been amusing for the staff. Our hosts asked Mel to tell the story of the movie, which was a bit racy to say the least. More particularly, the character Mel was playing that day was Jacques the Piss Boy from the time of the French Revolution. Mel didn't feel it would be appropriate to mention urine, but well, avoiding that subject was – nigh on impossible! As I witnessed him trying to water down the story for their Royal selves I started giggling nervously, and eventually became completely hysterical. I pulled him aside. 'Mel,' I tried to soothe him, 'you don't have to worry about the British upper classes; they wrote the book!'

After the final series of *Not The Nine O'Clock News*, John Lloyd created a solo TV show for me. My diary of some filming days reveals that I was struggling with the public attention I was receiving, and with another, very familiar issue: my eating disorder. Since I left drama school I'd been struggling with a form of bulimia (without the vomiting bit). I would purge by severely restricting my food until a filming day, then binge heavily afterwards. At the time, I told myself that it was a professional necessity to keep my weight very low – and that was true up to a point because television cameras tended to add around ten pounds. But it would have been far healthier to have maintained a constant weight via a steady, nutritious, low-calorie programme, coupled with moderate exercise, rather than the binge–purge cycle I followed for many years. And what's more, my body image problem was growing.

My TV Show Diary
First day's rehearsal:
Miners' routine. I'm working with Hot Gossip so looking round at immaculate bodies. Ugh. Comparing sizes. I do feel silly. And fat. Taps shoes too tight. Later, I am obsessed with thoughts of food. Suddenly all sense of the importance of competing with the nymphets has disappeared. What I want is an apple strudel. No, scones with jam and cream. Maybe even . . . I spy a packet of oatcakes and scour the writing on the back to ascertain the calorie content. 100 g yields? One biscuit therefore . . . I'm too hungry to do sums. Cake decorations. Dreams of riding through marshmallow on a banana split.

First day's filming:
Woke at 6am and dragged myself across London to the health club where we are filming. Cold in cellar. Lots of gawkers. I do feel silly. And someone stole my knickers from the dressing room! Worst thing? Not being finished and having to diet for another week. So – no binge-up tonight.

Day Two:
I spent the morning in bed with Michael Parkinson. He was a great sport about it. Lying there, getting soaked by twenty gallons of freezing water which spurted from the mattress on a given cue. We corpsed quite a lot during the rehearsal – probably releasing nervous tension. It wasn't that it was embarrassing exactly, it's just that,

well, what do you say to a famous person you scarcely know who happens to be in bed with you in full view of a large crowd of onlookers? Love to the wife?

Day Three:
Spoof tampon commercial. Diet again. White swimsuit. Extras all younger, attractive. Press photographers turn up. Freezing pool, gawkers. Next day, front page – reported as 'Sexy Swim'.

Day Four:
Wonder Woman sketch, then Shirley Williams sketch on street. Hundreds of onlookers. Loads of people wanting to meet me but disappointed to meet only 'the face that wrecked Brixton'. But I remember meeting Shirley Williams and very charming she was too. Someone says, 'It's that awful woman from the SDP.' A barrow guy: 'No it ain't. It's Billy Connolly's bird!' Cringe cringe.

Although that series didn't take off, I started to be even more in demand for movies. Richard Lester invited me to be in *Superman III*, which involved shooting at Pinewood Studios and in Calgary, Canada. I had not enjoyed making most of the movies I'd done before *Not The Nine O'Clock News*, probably because they were stinkers. But this was different. Richard Lester was a delightful, enormously bright man, and I also got to work with a hilarious comic who had set himself on fire and lived to tell the tale – Richard Pryor. Richard was my kind of man: funny, childlike and dangerous.

You used that word again – 'dangerous'. Such men really appeal to you, do they not?

Frankly, yes. We had lunch together every day and I adored him. He reminded me of Billy – vulnerable and insecure, yet also strong and primitive. He had nearly died after igniting himself while free-basing cocaine and drinking 151-proof rum at the same time. Now that takes multi-tasking to a whole new level. Apparently he actually ran down the street on fire – until he was caught by the police. He later joked that the explosion was caused by dunking cookies into a glass containing a volatile mixture of low fat and pasteurized milk. But the accident was a terrible assault on his body – he had sustained burns over more than half of it, and had to wear special, soft cloth-ing against his skin because it was still painfully sensitive.

Chris Reeve was charming, too, and it was fun playing a crazy, bad girl who seduces Superman. Yes, I 'did it' with Superman – and it's still a badge of honour! But there was something so surreal about the whole experience – if that word can actually be applied to six months of turning up every morning to play an archetypal siren in an American blockbuster based on the most famous cartoon character of all time! The whole thing was wonderfully over-the-top. They created the Grand Canyon AND the Statue of Liberty inside the studio for God's sake!

Next, I did another movie called *Scandalous* with John Gielgud and Robert Hays. I was under a lot of stress at the time, because I was also playing Mabel in Joe Papp's production of the Gilbert and Sullivan operetta *Pirates of Penzance* at Drury Lane Theatre. That role was very difficult for me. I had never sung professionally before, if you discount parodies and a truly dreadful pop record I once made (what is WRONG with me?).

I have to agree with you about that . . .

Hah! Anyway, my voice was largely untrained, so although I was a natural soprano I had spent a gruelling rehearsal period with the brilliant Marge Rivington, who coached Bette Midler and Linda Ronstadt. Marge actually helped me to add nearly an octave to the top of my vocal range, and vastly improved the quality. Critics were lukewarm about my London singing debut, but once I settled in and controlled my nerves I was pretty good. And I really enjoyed it – the cast, the music, singing with a huge orchestra. I spent a whole year performing in that very popular show, and loved having such consistency. Not everyone takes to long runs, though. At the beginning of the second act, George Cole, who played my father the Major, had to carry a sopping wet handkerchief onstage with him, which I would later take from him when he cried, and squeeze it onto the trumpeter's head. As the run wore on, I gather this became a bit tedious for George, who finally said to me when we were waiting in the dark to go on, 'You know Pamela, whenever I think of you, I think of a handful of wet.'

There were breaks in filming from time to time and, on one occasion, I asked Chris Reeve if he could recommend a nice, quiet beach haven where I could have a rest. See, I was becoming aware of the effect doing two movies and a stage show at the same time, plus my new life in the public eye – and my relationship with Billy – was having. I wrote in my diary:

I admitted to myself that I'm suffering the effects of cumulative stress from the past year, so I bought 200 dollars' worth of books from a somewhat pretentious 'alternative' LA bookshop and proceeded to engage in much stressful activity carrying the damn things halfway across the world. But I discovered a questionnaire compiled by a Doctor Holmes from the University of Washington School of Medicine, which tells you that if you score over 300 you're in trouble (Princess Di recently scored 417). Well at this point I have a total of 1245, and it was that realization that's made me a basket case.

See? Although I was joking around, I was totally into psychology way before I entered the field. Anyway, thankfully, I recognized my need to rest. Chris Reeve told me about this place in the Bahamas, a tiny Cay where the local people were unimpressed by celebrities and the snorkelling was ace. I managed to meet Billy there for a short spell – in fact, he only had one day there in between his own touring commitments. I taught him to snorkel, which he absolutely loved. But it was then I realized just how uncomfortable he was in the sea. He didn't seem to understand basic safety considerations. Well, it was hardly his customary environment. At one point I noticed he was swimming awfully close to stinging fire coral, while a large barracuda had taken an interest in him and was following close behind. Not wanting to alarm Billy, but needing to move out of danger, I waved gaily at him, signalling him towards me. He completely misinterpreted my semaphore and waved back a happy greeting – which immediately turned to fear and panic as his right hand hit the fire coral and his head turned just enough to clock the big, toothy fish. 'He's just inquisitive,' I explained. 'He likes you!' But Billy wouldn't buy a word of it.

Another new experience I provided for Billy was a fortieth birthday party . . .

Sounds like you partly see your role as being responsible for his entertainment . . . ?

Yeah, well, at times that's pretty close to the truth! But apparently no one had really bothered to give him a birthday party in the past, so I decided he should have an exciting fortieth bash. For some reason I dressed as a schoolgirl. A lot of wonderful friends came, and Elvis Patel, a Pakistani Elvis impersonator, performed. So did a man who had an act where he saved the world from Armageddon using Wonderloaf bread. As the finale, I got a pope lookalike, a Welsh man called Mr Meredith, to jump out of a cake. Even the fact that I could not sleep that night because some very famous rock stars had secretly been snorting cocaine on our bed did not detract from the fun of the evening. And finally having a birthday cake – even though a man resembling his nemesis emerged from it and blessed the crowd – meant a great deal to my howling, ex-Catholic hubby.

By the time *Superman III* premiered, I was pregnant with Daisy. Billy accompanied me to the red carpet event in London and Zandra Rhodes lent me a lovely dress, which I mistakenly wore back to front. Told you I was a fashion idiot. Billy and I had been having a bit of fun – crazy nights partying at Tramp, the famous members-only nightclub in Jermyn Street run by Johnny Gold, or at Legends nightclub with people like Julian Lennon and some of the New Romantic bands that were around at the time, such as Duran Duran, Ultravox, Spandau Ballet, Culture Club. I even remember, erm, removing some of my clothing under the table at Legends in the presence of a paparazzo. What was I thinking? At least I got some comedy out of it: 'People have the wrong idea about me,' I complained. 'The other day I was having a meal in a restaurant and the waitress said "Would you like the wine before or after you undress?"'

When we were out and about in public, Billy and I used to play a game. If someone asked us both for an autograph we would subtly fight to grab the page and write far more than necessary – 'Love and cuddles, and may the bluebird of happiness shit all over your birthday cake' – and in such large letters that the other could barely find space on the paper, and had to squash his or her name in between 'best' and 'wishes'. If only one of us was recognized, the other would crow openly, to the embarrassment of the other – and the fan. Once someone approached me before Billy, but I discovered my little song of triumph was premature. 'I was just wondering,' said the woman, 'what's Sting like?'

When interviewers asked: 'Do you and Billy help each other with work?' I'd answer: 'Hinder, actually. We either steal jokes from each other, or sell lines in return for sexual favours.' Oh yes, I was deliberately provocative, probably trying to control the situation in a paradoxical fashion. 'You appear to seek publicity . . .' they'd say. 'No,' I'd reply, 'I never do anything deliberately for publicity. I went out the other night and was met in the foyer by a barrage of photographers. Now, I didn't mind, but it really startled my tiger.' I'd follow that up with: 'No seriously, I like being in the papers. It saves writing home.' Yeah, I know . . . Billy's a lot funnier.

But I behaved defensively because I was really finding it very uncomfortable to be so much in the public eye. The press interest was unbearable at this point. I didn't know how to handle it. I was probably making a lot of mistakes, but it was painful to be misunderstood, misrepresented and attacked. I hated meeting new people because I always felt they'd already formed an opinion of me that was shaped by the tabloids. The final straw was a photo of me looking very pregnant with a story about how this once beautiful young woman was now a big lump. I was incensed. It wasn't just insulting to me, it disrespected all women. My developing maternal instincts were telling me I needed to protect not only myself, but especially my future child from this kind of life. Billy seemed to be handling it just fine, but I felt like we needed to run away. Our lives simply had to change, because we were about to be parents.

Now it was serious.

Chapter Nine

BLUE HOLE TO BABIES

It was all Jacques Cousteau's fault. The great diver concocted a list of his favourite dive sites in the world – many of which he himself had discovered – and obliged divers to seek them out for ever after. That is why I found myself, in 2008, with five other advanced divers on an inflatable rubber boat, poised above a bottomless sea chimney off the coast of Belize. The Blue Hole of Belize was Cousteau's second favourite dive in the world, but it was one of my scariest. 'This will be a negative entry,' announced our guide, meaning that we should deflate our dive jackets so we could plummet fast the second we hit the water. 'You must descend to one hundred and thirty feet as quickly as you possibly can.' The sooner we reached the famous, deep caves in this eerie chasm, the longer we'd have to explore them. Even so, because of the depth and the need to ascend very slowly, the most we'd have down there would be around four minutes.

I checked my equipment and nodded to my dive buddy. 'One, two, three . . .' We synchronized our flip into the foaming sea and forced ourselves downwards as fast as our breathing cavities would allow. This was no time to delay at the surface and equalization had to be rapid. Oh God, it was murky. Visibility was far worse than I had imagined, and once we reached a hundred feet I became aware of being 'showered on' by weird white particles. Even with my powerful underwater flashlight I could barely see the massive stalactites and stalagmites the ancient caverns were known for. I remember thinking, 'Cousteau actually loved THIS?'

That's the same question I was just about to ask you . . .

Hmmm, well, actually, yes. It was rather like visiting Stonehenge – an ancient and curious monument that cannot entirely be explained (although geologists think the hole was part of an underwater cave system whose ceiling collapsed). Part of its allure is the fact that the site has become a part of diving folklore as a weird and wonderful Mecca for extreme divers. I suppose you have to be a diver to understand . . . but let's cut to the end of the dive. The four minute warning was upon me. I could barely see my trusty dive computer, but it was beeping like crazy to prompt immediate action. And there were thumbs up signs all around me that had only one meaning: time to ascend. We began slowly. Having descended so deep, our climb had to be painfully slow. Did everyone have enough air to get to the surface? It's easy to lose concentration or get panicky and expend more air than expected at that depth. 'Must stay calm and alert,' I had told myself.

I more or less managed that until I saw the first bull shark. Oh no! Not only did I have to ascend extremely slowly, but I'd be surrounded by these mothers (literally – they all seemed to be pregnant) the entire way. I love being in the water with most sharks, and feel safe with them because I know they are unlikely to attack. But bulls are an exception. 'I don't trust them,' our guide had warned.

'Breathe,' I told myself. 'You cannot afford to panic.' Just then I caught sight of my buddy who was so wigged by the bulls his breathing had become dangerously shallow. I swam closer and took his hand. 'OK?' I made the universal divers' sign. He returned it, tentatively, then as an afterthought wobbled his other hand to sign that he was shaky. I watched our bubbles; there are two sizes, and one must never ascend faster than the smaller ones. My main concern was our safety stop – a necessary, five-minute stationary period at fifteen feet. My buddy was not going to like that. Desperate to get to the safety of the boat, he looked decidedly antsy when the group stopped ascending and began to count down. Now there was nothing to do but hang about there, trying to maintain the same depth and, at the same time, avoid becoming a shark's lunch.

Suddenly I remembered that, a couple of nights before, my buddy and I had tried salsa dancing in a mainland bar. I grinned cheekily at him (well, as far as one can grin with a face full of breathing equipment), faced him, and took his right hand. I began to shake my shoulders, then used his arm to complete a slow turn, ducking under it salsa-style. He got the idea and pulled me towards him, rocking me backwards and forwards then turning me again. Now he was starting to relax. Eventually, the rest of the group was at it too, ducking and weaving while the bull sharks eyed us with benign curiosity.

It did the trick; it took our minds off a perceived danger about which we could do nothing, and relaxed us so there was less danger anyway. Experts say sharks are sensitive to human mood changes, or more accurately, the changes in the water's ph levels that occur when our mood is altered – and it's best to stay very calm. Yeah, like I said, 'Dancing saves lives.' But, thinking back, I'm not really sure why those circling bulls seemed annoyed at first. Perhaps this was just a bad time to be around them, with little ones on the way; after my own three pregnancies, I know just how they felt.

I mostly loved being pregnant. For a start, it was a licence to eat.

Feeling fantastically free from the pressure of maintaining a 'TV weight', I ate and ate and ate – not realizing I was bingeing excessively and putting myself at risk of pregnancy complications. I grew absolutely enormous, but I was happy.

It's a terrible idea to have a baby with a comedy god. At a time when the focus ought to be on you and the urgency of your caesarean ('watermelon-removal'), there was Billy sucking up all the attention and causing mirth among people who, ideally, needed to keep their hands nice and steady. That behaviour of his was on top of his shocking announcement, just days before my due date, that at birth he himself had been nearly ten pounds. Yowie! I called my obstetrician forthwith and pleaded for a Caesarean. Fortunately, he had already decided I'd have one, because Daisy was both enormous and upside down. Whew! At that time, the usual Glaswegian paternal behaviour would have been to disappear to the pub when the first labour pains struck, but Billy's devotion – and probably his curiosity – led him to be at my side throughout the process.

'I've seen your bladder,' he announced later, in a smug, slightly creepy, sort of way. Apparently there was a rather dodgy moment during the operation, when he came close to passing out and had to be helped from the surgery but, all in all, he did rather well – well, if you discount the fact that, cradling our newborn child, he followed the surgical team to their changing room and did twenty minutes of comedy for them while I waited furiously, lying captive on a gurney in a corridor.

I was terribly worried about leaving hospital. There was a whole posse of photographers waiting outside. Would my baby be in danger? The men might crowd us, chase us. I had already felt physically threatened by the 'pack' on many occasions. Or would Billy lose his temper with them again and retaliate violently? I needn't have worried. A few flashes and well-wishes, and we were on our way home.

As new parents, we were in heaven. Welcoming Daisy into the

world was thrilling, and my intense maternal feelings of love and care for her were soon flooding through me. Given the ambiguity about mothering I'd picked up though my childhood experiences, I had worried about whether I'd ever be a good mum . . .

Well, that's understandable, given your relationship with your own mother . . .

Yes, but actually I bonded very quickly with my new little person. And Billy was an attentive father – taking his turn at nappy-changing and helping me to get the rest I needed. He sang Daisy to sleep – usually to Ry Cooder's 'Little Sister' – and invented something called 'Sleepy-toes', a kind of improvised poem that has never failed to transport a baby into the Land of Nod.

You seem surprised . . .

Well, Billy already had two children, Jamie and Cara, who were still living with their mother in Scotland. I met them fairly early in my relationship with Billy. They were delightful, shy, Scottish children; although, naturally, they were troubled by their parents' divorce. I met them outside Drury Lane Theatre when I was in *Pirates of Penzance*. Billy had brought them to a matinee and I can't imagine what they thought of me at the time. I remember that my hair was short and spiky (chopped for a cover of *Cosmopolitan* magazine) and I seem to remember I was wearing leopard-print stretch trousers and a T-shirt that said 'Fuck Art – Let's Dance!' Perhaps it was not the best introduction to a future stepmother but I can't be sure because, to this day, I have not managed to get anything concrete out of Jamie and Cara about what impression I made. But I quickly came to adore them both, although I was very concerned about all the upheaval in their lives – some of it due to me.

You have feelings of guilt?

Well, yes. I mean, it was all pretty messy. And public. And, unfortunately, the children were dealing with a number of other, significant problems, although it took me and Billy a while to discover exactly what those were. Jamie, it turned out, had not attended school for nearly a year, and Cara was miserable for a multitude of reasons connected with the fact that Billy's ex-wife Iris was struggling herself. Challenged by alcohol addiction, depression and a hoarding disorder, she was unable to care for herself properly, let alone her children. Just before Daisy was born, Billy and I decided to seek custody of Cara and Jamie, a process that was enormously stressful for all concerned – and, again, not the smoothest when it involves a comedy god. At one point, a court reporter was detailed to sit in our house, watch our family interaction, and interview everyone. There was a heart-stopping moment when Cara, questioned about her father's style of disciplining, mischievously repeated his jokey line: 'He always says he'll thrash me within an inch of my miserable life!' See what I mean? If you can help it, stay away from comedians. They just cause endless trouble.

But, fortunately, the official had a sense of humour, and recommended that Billy be granted custody, with regular visits granted to their mother. I felt terribly sorry for Iris, and did my best to get her some help. She entered treatment for a very short period, but failed to improve. The children saw her only sporadically after that. She eventually moved to Spain, became estranged from her children, and struggled greatly with her psychological problems right up until her death in 2010.

Her children, though, thrived in new schools in London. We had bought a converted fish factory in Fulham, and they moved in. Pink and green striped couches, red spiral staircase, wacky pottery everywhere – that became our sanctuary and we tried to create normality for them. Normality? Who am I trying to kid? Well, it was a crazy kind of 'normal'. At least they had a routine and attended school. In summer we had picnics in the enclosed courtyard, drove to Cornwall for minibreaks, and gazed at shooting stars on Hampstead Heath . . . More or less ordinary? Well, if you discount things like the fact that our answerphone always contained hate messages because I'd done a greeting that was a perfect Margaret Thatcher voice: 'I'd like to take this opportunity to tell you all that we're not at home . . . Do kindly call back later. And if that's you, Denis, please pick up a tart on the way home – preferably a little Spanish one . . . You like those swarthy temptresses don't you?'

Right from the start, I really adored Jamie and Cara, but I was conscious that I was a rather wacky stepmum. I do know I was caring and nurturing, though – they really brought out that side of me, as did Billy. And Daisy, of course. But notes would go to school teachers on my stationery, which contained a cartoon of a couple sitting at home in their living room. The woman says to the man: 'Shouldn't you be out having your name linked with Pamela Stephenson?'

Then there was the pretty constant doorstepping by freelance journalists and others. Billy had developed all kinds of anti-pap strategies, none of them very successful. He once thumped one with a long French loaf he was bringing home for tea, although after that we didn't really feel like eating it. But that did put a whole new spin on the club sandwich.

Instead of edible weaponry, I preferred to use wigs and costumes to disguise myself as, say, an elderly lady. I enjoyed walking right past packs of newshounds without arousing any suspicion whatso-ever. Once or twice we both donned Arab robes to be anonymous while attending a public event – the Alternative Miss World for example. We really craved privacy, especially early on, because we didn't want Cara and Jamie to be confronted with pictures of us together that might have unkind captions attached. After Billy and

I both appeared in the Secret Policeman's Ball comedy concert, I attempted to put the paparazzi off the scent by exiting the theatre with Eric Clapton, but that didn't work and they were soon badgering Billy for a picture. It's never wise to confront a Glaswegian. 'You better put some Vaseline on that camera,' Billy warned one photographer, ''cos it's going up your arse.' Another time he smashed a man's camera and there was a subsequent court case and the forking out of cash to replace the broken equipment. Things got to the point where I had to have a conversation with Billy about trying to be calm and avoid conflict. But, understandably, he became particularly incensed by press intrusion when the children were present. We both particularly resented the fact that Cara and Jamie had been accosted by journalists while walking around their village in Scotland.

When Daisy arrived, Cara and Jamie cooed over her too, and my concerns about whether I was up to creating a happy 'blended family' began to evaporate. Billy and I were finally starting to settle down – as far as that was possible for two comedians. Frankly, being a two-comedian family was a lot less useful than having matching Hondas. But Cara and Jamie travelled with one or both of us whenever necessary, and they particularly seemed to love coming to New York when I was engaged for a season as a cast member on *Saturday Night Live*. Now I was trying to be a good mum, while at the same time about to do the toughest job of my entire career. *Saturday Night Live*, or *SNL* as it's known, was the most famous and popular TV sketch comedy show in the United States at that time. It was a little like *Not The Nine O'Clock News*, except that it was broadcast live by NBC in front of a studio audience in Studio 8H on floors 8 and 9 of '30 Rock' – the GE Building at 30 Rockefeller Plaza in Manhattan. It had – and still has – a kind of cult following; if having thirty-six million viewers per week could ever be considered cultish. When I joined the show in 1984 it had already been on air for ten years and had produced major film stars, such as Bill Murray, Dan Aykroyd, Chevy Chase and John Belushi. Back then, the show was already legendary, but it's still popular and has now spanned three decades.

Each episode is hosted by a famous guest (during my season these included Jesse Jackson, Tina Turner, Ringo Starr and Eddie Murphy) and a major band. Yet *SNL* has struggled to stay on the air for so long – it's had a volatile history of producer, writer and cast changes. When I came on the scene, its creator Lorne Michaels had departed, and the show had been sliding downhill to terrible reviews under Jean Doumanian. She was fired after a performer (Charles Rocket) said 'Fuck' on live TV, and Dick Ebersol took over. For the new season, he brought in some established stars: Billy Crystal and Martin Short joined Christopher Guest, Harry Shearer, Julia Louis-Dreyfus, Mary Gross, Jim Belushi, Rich Hall, Gary Kroeger and me, and we did our best to turn the show into a hit once more. We were successful.

But with the pressure of a live show every week, very little time to prepare and rehearse, we were all under enormous stress. Each cast member was given an office on the 17th floor. Mine was a lovely corner one that I put to good use as a feeding station for Daisy. I needed a refuge. In those days, *SNL* had a drug culture. In light of this, the late John Belushi's untimely demise became very understandable to me. Mood-altering substances came up to the 17th floor in pizza boxes, then doors would be closed to anyone who was not part of the 'inner sanctum'. Yet again, I was an outsider, and not only because I didn't take drugs. Being female was not the issue – Julia and Mary were also in the cast, and America already had a strong legacy of funny women. No, I was culturally an outsider. I knew little about American society and history – at that time I felt I barely spoke the same language. One of the most humiliating early moments was being cast as an electoral officer during the presidential elections and having to post coloured flags on different states as they were called out. Where on earth was Arkansas, and why was it pronounced as if it had a 'w' on the end? If only I'd taken Geography at school instead of Latin!

This was not a team as *NTNON* had been, with producers working hard to create cohesion. Rather, people seemed to be deliberately pitted against each other. Just being a cast member did not mean one automatically made it into the show each week. If you did not find a place in a sketch – or write one yourself – you could be going home after the first readthrough. The competition was intense – and not just between performers. Writers were jostling to place their sketches, too, and they favoured writing for the established American stars because they were less likely to be bumped. I began to write as much as possible, but realized that firstly, I was ill-equipped to come up with American satire, and secondly, I was damned if I did and damned if I didn't. If I wrote a sketch that made it into the show, that might be perceived as an affront to the writing team, who might then fail to write for me the following week. If I did not write for myself, others might not either and I'd be out of the show. It was brutal.

Again, you found yourself in a situation where not only were you an outsider, but you were risking rejection in a very intense manner . . .

No kidding. And, there was no rest. As a mother of a new baby, I found that particularly difficult. I mean, I was actually relieved to be away from the UK – in a place where I was not so well known – but it was a bit like 'out of the frying pan, into the fire'. As soon as Saturday's show was over, we had to start trying to come up with material for the coming week. By the end of Tuesday, all written work was supposed to be in, and there was a terrifying readthrough for around fifty people on Wednesdays. Then selected sketches were rehearsed and blocked. After Saturday's dress rehearsal nearly half the planned sketches were cut, and then the live show kicked off at 11pm with what was known as a 'cold opening', where one of the performers would break character in the middle of the first sketch and announce into camera: 'Live from New York, it's *Saturday Night!*'

I remember being absolutely bewildered, terrified, frantic and desperate during that season, and I'm not even sure how I survived it. Especially without Billy being around. I remember looking down at the street from my office window on the 17th floor and thinking, 'I understand why stressed Manhattan executives often decide to jump.'

You became . . . suicidal?

I thought about it. But Daisy always grounded me. I had to stay strong for her. I decided that the only way I could survive – professionally – was to find a niche for myself into which no one else could fit. That niche turned out to be rock parodies. I took on Madonna, Cyndi Lauper, Billy Idol – thankfully, my efforts were so well received I remember the co-producer saying to me, 'So, you gonna put another nail in rock 'n' roll's coffin again this week?'

I created a toothy, unintelligible British character with red hair and buck teeth that Americans found hilarious because it supported their impression of weird Britishness, and I played a huge range of American characters, from Lauren Bacall to Nancy Reagan, but the process of the show always seemed unwieldy and terrifyingly haphazard. There was really no time to learn lines – most people read them off cue cards on the night – which seemed amateurish to me. How I missed having a decent rehearsal period – not to mention the far superior BBC makeup and costume department!

I even managed to do some of my more outrageous material on

American television, such as a series of sketches wearing giant, moving breasts . . .

Breasts yet again . . . ?

I know, I know, but these were funny. In the first sketch, I spoke directly to the camera and introduced the men of America to my chest, pointing out the various features. Since this was American television, I had to refer to my nipples as the 'twiddly bits on the end'; although Billy Crystal, in the same episode, was allowed to say 'nipples' in his opening monologue. Different rules for boys and girls? Ahhh! (I spent a considerable amount of time negotiating with the censors at various points during that run.) But, anyway, in that first sketch I introduced my body and attested to my normality but soon, my left fake breast began to move up and down. People shrieked. Then it started jiggling fast and, eventually, it took control of me, whirling me round and finally flipping me right over my desk. It was a nice piece of physical comedy that was well received and lead to follow-up sketches. In fact, I was shocked to learn that, many years later, Britney Spears did something very similar when she hosted the show – probably wearing my 'moving tit contraption' that I'd left behind in the wardrobe department (you can see her bit on YouTube). Or perhaps hers were digitally animated, which sadly wasn't an option in my day!

Pamela I'm sorry to be so . . . Freudian, but I can't help pointing out that breasts – the shape, size, deflation, humour and baring of them – is an omnipresent theme in your life. Put that together with your deeply troubling mother issues and, well, you know where I'm going with this . . . ?

Once again, doctor, your brilliance astounds me. If breasts represent my relationship with my mother, my *SNL* tits sketch was a dynamic re-enactment of maternal control. OMG – what about that time I held a seance with them? Was I unconsciously harbouring thoughts of matricide?

Probably . . .

Oh man. And I made such a big deal of it when Billy had his nipples pierced on Father's Day!

Saturday Night Live became a hit show again, and that was gratifying for everyone who worked on it. But it was shockingly stressful and, as a new mother, my focus really had to be on Daisy and the rest of my family. I lived between Rockefeller Plaza and my small apartment on 71st Street. Billy commuted between London and New York, and Jamie and Cara flew out whenever school breaks allowed it. Everyone was relieved when the season ended and we settled back to life in London.

Amy was born in July 1986, and Scarlett turned up two years later. It was a happy time. To my surprise, I discovered that I really loved being a mum. It was as if I now had the opportunity to be the kind of mother I would have wanted for myself.

Billy and I enjoyed entertaining and loved getting together with pals, first at the Fish Factory, then in Bray, and finally in Winkfield, after we moved out of London. It was good to have a place where the kids had more room to roam around the garden. We painted the walls in mad colours and filled the place with rock 'n' roll art. We had front gates designed to look like the Sydney Harbour Bridge, and the walls of our dining room were painted to resemble the grassy stripes of a freshly mowed lawn. We even had a bed with a built-in alarm clock that triggered small aeroplanes zooming round it to the tune of 'Those Magnificent Men'. Oh yes, we were a zany duo.

But it was lovely to be able to spy a fox out of our bedroom window and have picnics on the lawn. Once novelist Kathy Lette turned up and we all had high tea dressed up in crazy frocks I'd worn for various performing events – frothy ball gowns in funky prints, marrying leopard with tartan and lace. Strangely enough, that look recently came into fashion, but back then it was an affront. It appealed to the fashion disaster in me.

When it comes to appropriate dressing, I so rarely get it right. My excuse is, I never gleaned a sense of style early on. Or rather, the sense of style I acquired in the Australian 'sticks' was decidedly drip-dry. I remember the first time I received an outfit that I really liked. It was not one of my mother's pretty home-made creations that matched my sisters', but something I actually chose. It was a mauve-and-white gingham check skirt-and-blouse ensemble with a little frill around the arm hole. I was given a white cardigan to match, and I simply could not believe I'd been allowed to have pearly white shoes with a tiny high heel. I must have been just fourteen. This outfit was for some special occasion – I can't remember what, but it was probably a school or church fellowship outing, or possibly a football match. I remember that the night before I was so excited I couldn't sleep. I had hung the outfit on my door with the shoes lying beneath it, so I could gaze at it from my bed.

We didn't have money for nice clothes then but, as soon as I began to earn my own money – first at the Boronia Park petrol garage on Saturday mornings and eventually in the restaurants, bars and nightclubs in town – I began to invest a large portion of my earnings on acquiring pretty things to wear. It was cheap, high-street stuff but I noticed it gave me confidence. Many years later, when I met Joanna Lumley on the set of *The New Avengers*, she and I began chatting about clothing. 'I often buy ordinary, cheap clothes,' she said, 'saying to myself, "I know I can make that look good."' This really impressed me. Now I realize she knew a lot about fashion because she'd been a model, and she could recognize high-street items that were barely discernible from designer clothes and put them together so they looked chic. But, at the time, I was mystified. 'What does that mean?' I wondered. 'Isn't it enough just to buy something off the peg in High Street Kensington and wear it? How would you go about doing something special to it to make it "look good"?'

Frankly, I don't think I'll ever figure out how to be chic. I do buy some designer clothes and I love many of the fashion gods, but somehow there's always something missing. Various stylists have tried to mould me but I'm pretty much a lost cause. And I've made some truly memorable fashion *faux pas* – like the time I wore that gorgeous Zandra Rhodes creation back to front. Zandra had been so kind to lend me the frock; I had no idea I'd worn it incorrectly until years later. And she never chided me.

Probably my worst costume error was when Sarah Ferguson invited me to a big dance before her wedding. 'Wear your best frock,' she said. But what did that mean? I had not been raised as a woman who attended fancy dinner-dances, and I had no idea that everyone would be dressed to the nines in long ball gowns. I had just given birth to our second daughter, Amy, so my body was dreadfully lumpy at the time. I finally threw on a short, baggy cocktail dress and took off with Billy for Elton John's house. We had planned to meet him and his then-wife Renata and travel together to the dance, then stay the night at their house. Renata opened the door in the most exquisite, flouncy ball gown, with her hair elaborately coiffed and perfect make-up. She was carrying a kind of spring flower basket that matched her dress, and I just gaped at her. 'Come in!' she said, looking me up and down in absolute horror. Out of extreme kindness, she tactfully tried to persuade me to change into one of her spare ball dresses, but I was too embarrassed to accept. Elton shot out of the car ahead of us when we arrived – I

suppose he wisely did not want to be seen with such a fashion disaster. I was shocked to see how the women were turned out: absolutely stunningly gowned and dripping with incredible, real jewellery. I tried to make the best of it but I was mortified. No one spoke
much to me, and the next day there were nasty pieces in the paper
– diary quotes from 'unnamed sources' who said I was the worst-
dressed woman in the room. Correct.

You still have a lot of feelings about that, don't you? Your 'outsider'
issues were really at core, weren't they? A painful reawakening . . .

Mmm. Then there was Sarah's wedding, and I absolutely cringe
when I see photos of myself that day. My outfit wasn't that bad for
the eighties – black and white silk print frock and white jacket – but
my hair! I was having a bad hair day – no, an entire bad hair decade!
And so my 'chic' outfit was topped by a spiky, white-blonde bouf-
fant with a black-and-white fascinator perched on top. What is
WRONG with me? That day was pretty stressful for a nursing mum.
We ran in to take our places in Westminster Abbey while our car
circled with nanny and Amy in the back. But the ceremony was so
long I had to sneak out, leaking breast milk all over my dress, and
try to find them. And there was such a huge crowd that we got stuck
trying to drive home; I remember trying to breastfeed while Billy,
who had been spotted by fans, drew even more attention to us. See,
we'd run into Jackie Stewart who'd eyed him in his suit and said,
'Today, your street cred goes out the window!' So, in the car, Billy
waved to the crowds like the Queen and leaned out, shouting – in
his idea of an upper-class accent – 'Get back to your fucking work!'
   It's amazing I was ever invited back to a Royal do, but apparently
I was kind of forgiven – or maybe just pitied. Subsequently, I did try
– but rarely managed – to get it right. I remember once wearing an
impossibly tight fishtail dress, attempting to negotiate a staircase

with Princess Diana clucking sympathetically beside me: 'Yes it's
sooo difficult to walk downstairs in that style . . .' Oh yes, and at
that do I made the mistake of asking Billy to fetch my powder
compact from my evening purse. He was away for ages, so I went
back to check on him and to my horror caught him looking through
every evening purse lying on a Palace sofa! It was perfectly innocent
– he simply couldn't remember which was mine – but anyone else
observing him might have thought he was up to no good. An absolute *deus ex machina* moment. Another time I wore a Vivienne
Westwood ball dress with a large train that was equally difficult to
manage. That was also a post-baby moment and I had tried to whit-
tle down my waist with a cruel corset undergarment which was so
tight it made me feel faint. In fact, halfway through the evening I
had to remove it and dump it in one of the Queen's wastepaper
baskets. God knows how our illustrious hosts ever put up with me;
it really speaks volumes about their kindness and tolerance.

The final *coup de grâce* came when Billy and I were in Scotland
and we were invited to visit Balmoral. This was just after Billy had
appeared in *Mrs Brown*, and the Duke of Edinburgh was going to
take him to see where John Brown had lived and worked. I remember being on the phone to Prince Andrew when he was setting up
arrangements for our coming to tea. 'What are we supposed to
wear?' I asked gingerly. To my horror, I heard Andrew relay my
question to his mother. 'She wants to know what to wear,' he
laughed. 'Ordinary!' said a ridiculously familiar voice. I had no
problem with deciding what to wear on Sarah's hen night, however.
I had discovered a few days earlier that Prince Andrew and a few of
his cronies – including Billy – were gathering for a stag dinner, but
that nothing had been planned for Sarah. 'Let's do something!' I
insisted. 'I'll take care of it!' I hired some police women's uniforms
from Berman's and Nathan's under a pseudonym, threw a few of
my stage wigs and spectacles in the back of my Range Rover, and

took off to meet the 'girls' – Sarah, Princess Diana, Renata John and Julia Dodd-Noble. We all dressed in the uniforms – well, except for Julia, who was to play a 'tart' we were arresting. I was worried about our going out in public like that, and tried to get Diana and Sarah to wear the wigs I'd brought to avoid recognition, but Diana resisted. Sarah wore the wig I normally wore as Mrs Runcie, the wife of the then-Archbishop of Canterbury. In the spirit of having a girls' lark we escaped the protection police and piled uncomfortably into my Range Rover, with Diana squeezed into the baby seat.

Just as I was about to pull away from the kerb, a large, angry man reached into the car and put an arresting hand on my steering wheel. It was one of the Royal policeman, who told me in no uncertain terms that I was doing something I shouldn't. At that point I realized that, as the driver, I was responsible for the safety of the future Queen and her sister-in-law to be, and I'd better not screw up. We negotiated terms. I drove carefully and slowly, and the police followed. Eventually, we piled into the back of a police van and made our way to Berkeley Square. Diana jumped out and began directing traffic (yes, a considerable amount of champagne had been imbibed at this point). We then ducked into Annabel's nightclub in Berkeley Square, where a bunch of *Daily Mail* journalists were having a party. Ironically, they didn't recognize us, but the manager of the club thought we were a bunch of strip-o-gram girls and tried to chuck us out. We raced off to Buckingham Palace. Poor Sarah got stuck trying to climb through a barrier and we had to pull her out. Then Diana and Sarah started taunting the guards on duty by dangling their world-famous engagement rings (Diana's was diamond and sapphire, Sarah's a large ruby) under their noses and chanting, 'Guess who we are!' Good times. I suppose we were just like any other British gals out on a hen night, with, well, a couple of rather important differences.

The drama increased when Prince Andrew came racing towards

the Palace gates in his Jaguar. We continued to play policewomen –
well, we tried to be calm and authoritative and refuse him entry –
but Diana was so excited she kept laughing and bouncing up and
down. Finally he realized something was up and roared off in the
other direction. 'You know how I knew?' he said later. 'I recognized
Diana's jump.'

The next day all hell broke loose because the papers got wind of
it. They had no pictures, but they just montaged some anyway.
Diana was hauled on the carpet to explain things to her mother-in-
law, but apparently it was considered . . . amusing. Well, it was. It
was a thoroughly splendid wheeze.

I've had a lot of fun over the years with my pal Sarah. When our
children were young they used to play together. In fact, Sarah and I
were in the Portland Hospital together having Scarlett and Beatrice,
so they're the same age. Sarah was always kind enough to invite us
to her kids' birthday parties and they usually had a theme. One year
it was Dragons and Urchins, and the idea was that the kids' mothers
or nannies should be the dragons and the children were to come
dressed as scruffy Oliver Twist types. Martine was – and still is – our
beloved helper. An endlessly kind and highly talented woman from
the Scottish island of Islay, she joined our family when Amy was a
baby, and has now worked for us for twenty-six years. 'I was very
surprised when I met you,' she said to me recently. 'I had just seen
you on the *Bob Monkhouse Show*, and I was expecting a very different person.' 'One who set fire to things, perhaps?' I teased her. 'No,'
she blushed, 'you were a very dedicated mother . . . Although you
did wear a lot of crazy jewellery.'

Martine has always managed to design and make highly creative
costumes for our children for various events, and for this particular
birthday party she made some adorable urchin outfits for them,
and hired a bright red furry dragon suit for herself, with a separate
headdress. But unfortunately, that headdress completely covered

her head and restricted her vision. This dragon suit also had large floppy feet that made it difficult for her to walk but, entering into the spirit of the event, she did her best to move in it.

We arrived a little late. The police instructed us to park the car in a paddock at the bottom of the large hilly garden. We struggled out of the car. I had the three girls with me because Martine was so restricted in trying to walk in her dragon suit. We could see that a lot of people were gathered at the top of the hill and, as we got nearer, we realized that the judging of the fancy dress competition had already started. Worst of all, the judge of the dragon competition was Her Majesty Queen Elizabeth herself. She was standing in the middle of a parading circle of dragons, staring down at Martine looking very displeased. Martine, of course, could barely see, so she was oblivious to this. But everyone was now waiting for her, including the Queen. I was horrified, but utterly helpless to prevent the unfolding events.

The monarch of our realm spoke to a policeman, who immediately raised his megaphone and called to Martine. 'Would the red dragon climbing the hill please hurry up and make her way immediately to the circle!' But Martine didn't hear this. She was oblivious to all the attention that was now focused on her. There she was, just taking her time and struggling with her enormous dragon feet. I had lagged behind with Daisy and Amy. I called to Martine but the headdress covered her ears and she couldn't hear. Now everyone had stopped what they were doing and were watching Martine clomp her way up the hill. I was in two minds about whether to pretend I wasn't with her. She eventually got to the top, quite exhausted, and joined the circle. I had the sense that people were aghast at her apparent lack of interest in joining her Majesty's pleasure. And the Queen had had enough. She marched over to Martine and knocked twice on her papier mâché headdress. 'Who's in there?' she inquired curtly. Martine flung her arms up in an annoyed fashion. 'Och, for Pete's sake!' she wrestled off her headdress and found herself face to face with our Gracious Leader. 'Aggghhh!' she screamed in terror. It could not have been worse. 'Did you really have to scream?' I chided her afterwards. 'Well,' she protested, 'I mean, she's on all the stamps . . .'

Billy and I enjoyed being in London together. We tried to see theatre events and rock concerts as often as possible – even the ballet. I was nervous about introducing Billy to *Swan Lake* but he absolutely loved it. And opera – he really got a taste for it. We even went to Glyndebourne once, and Billy found the whole experience terribly funny, especially when a rather snooty woman farted loudly right in front of him.

I'm beginning to understand that you and Billy bonded partly on the basis of your BOTH being outsiders . . .

Mmm. It did feel like 'us versus them' a lot of the time. And, as you'd expect from two comedians, we shared a lot of private mirth about things we noticed around us. Once we went to see Liz Taylor in a West End production of *Little Foxes*. We probably should have known better than to attend a mega-diva's theatrical swan song, but it seemed so camp it was unmissable. At one point in that dreadful, self-consciously 'starry' performance, Miss Taylor walked towards a window. At the exact moment she peered out, someone backstage flipped a switch and a light went on – presumably to enhance her cheekbones from that angle. It was the kind of celebrity-driven stage feature that should never, ever happen, but it probably seemed like a Good Idea to keep the diva happy. But Billy and I just lost it. Not only was the visual effect highly noticeable and distracting, but what made it particularly amusing for us was that the gay couple behind us made sounds like the alien tune in Spielberg's *Close Encounters*: 'Do de do dee doooo . . .'

Billy and I barely recovered for the rest of the evening. A little later we met Liz Taylor, at a dinner given for her by John Reid (who managed Elton John and Billy at the time). John had set up a photography studio at his house, so guests could have their photos taken with her. Of course everyone wanted to be photographed with Liz – she was the stars' star. When it was my turn I asked her to put on a red nose because Comic Relief had just ended and I happened to have one with me. I love the photo of her wearing it. She was a good sport and the red nose reminded her of an incident that is an incredible insight into what it must have been like to be as famous as she was. 'I was asked to be a clown for a charity venture in LA,' she said. 'Some make-up artists and costume people created an elaborate clown appearance for me. Every part of me was disguised – I had full clown white face make-up, my eyebrows were arched, my eyes were crosses, my mouth completely altered to a huge downturn. I wore a purple bubble wig, and had a baggy, spotted romper suit, fully padded, and very long, funny shoes. The other performers and I walked anonymously down a street in Beverly Hills, which was such a novel experience for me. I was just saying to someone, "This is wonderful – being able to walk down the street and not be recognized by a soul – how freeing!" When all of a sudden, I heard a passing woman say to her husband: "Hey, Chuck, look at that! It's Elizabeth Taylor dressed like a clown!"'

It had already become clear to me that really famous people had to work very hard to protect not only their privacy but their sanity as well. One day, Livvy and George Harrison invited Billy and I to their house for lunch. Oh, come on! This is my last name-drop in this chapter. Anyway, we were very taken with Friar Park – a huge and rambling mansion that George had rescued and Olivia had lovingly restored. This was their haven (well, until they were viciously attacked inside that 'haven' some years later). But that day, George was wonderfully relaxed. He took us in a little boat through a secret waterway into an underground grotto. It was a charming, unexpected feature of their wonderfully unique home. A few months later, when I was about to give birth to Scarlett, they invited us to a concert at Friar Park where Ravi Shankar played such incredible, rousing evening ragas I could feel Scarlett dancing in my womb, and within forty-eight hours she was out in the world. Another time Billy, George, percussionist Ray Cooper and I went for dinner at a Chinese restaurant. During the meal, a man approached our table and asked Billy and I for our autographs but completely ignored George. It was bizarre. The man must have seen our smirks because he finally asked, 'Is there . . . anyone else who's famous?' 'Yeah,' said Billy. 'There's a Chinese waiter over there who used to play for Celtic.'

But I was now a mother of five, and still just about managing my career as a comedian. I'm not going to pretend it was easy. I remember running into Ringo Starr's wife Barbara Bach in town one day when I was struggling to shop for groceries with three small children. She told me later she thought to herself 'I can't leave her alone with all those kids!' so I must have appeared completely overwhelmed. But you do what you have to do, don't you? Every woman who has had three or more children under five at some point will wince at the same memories. What a learning curve that was! And who knew the double pram – which seemed to be such a good idea when I bought it – would not fit through doors, down aisles . . . many essential places. Hats off to all fellow working mothers.

I had developed one-woman shows, which meant I had to go on tour. In particular, I had markets in the UK, Australia, New Zealand and the Middle East. Not many mothers tour the world with their babies AND a snake. The snake – whose name was Fred – was a real problem. He was a large python with whom I performed an 'Eve'-type sketch, but I dunno – maybe it was something I said? Fred did not want to co-operate with me. For a start, snakes hibernate in winter, so whenever I was in a cooler region he would become terribly sleepy and I'd have to drape him near my dressing-room lights to wake him up. I had to feed Fred a quarter of a sheep every month (yes, really!) and, after he had just eaten, he would be particularly unsociable. He would pee and fart on stage, making a huge puddle and loud noises. And, let me tell you, if you're on stage with a snake and the snake farts, no one in the audience thinks it was the snake.

I remember the searing heat of that tour, being driven through the desert with Martine and the kids . . . Abu Dhabi, Dubai, Bahrain. And then there was the concern over my material, which was – to say the least – edgy for that part of the world. In fact, the promoter came backstage after my first show and said: 'Pamela, I'm afraid there's not one thing in your show that's actually legal in the Emirates . . . Well, maybe it would be for a man . . .' But I was play-ing to expat audiences so it turned out to be fine. We also spent three months in Australia and New Zealand, touring around doing my one-woman, one-snake, two-dwarves show and— Oh, didn't I tell you about Melanie and Tony? Very talented little people who played various roles in my show (for example, in a sketch satirizing the Catholic stance on birth control, I sawed a pope look-alike in half and out came Melanie and Tony as two mini popes). I was rather worried about them, though. They were very young and hadn't travelled much, and I was afraid for them, especially in the Middle East, because there were all kinds of scare stories about how people could be kidnapped and sold into a harem. Actually, the idea intrigued me. There were probably times when I wondered, 'Maybe I could be kidnapped for a harem! Yeah, fuck this comedy thing for a game of soldiers. Wouldn't it be rather nice to lie around in silk robes, having my toenails painted by eunuchs, while I waited for some nice handsome sheik to have his way with me . . .?' Kidding . . . I think.

Hmm. I suspect the pressures of being a mother AND having the responsibility of doing a solo comedy show every night on tour – let alone trying to manage the snake – must have been enormous. No wonder your fantasies might have led you to crave being pampered and taken care of – even as some kind of odalisque . . .

It's true that the work seemed to be getting harder. I continued to appear in movies, but they were all pretty terrible. I did enjoy working with Barry 'Dame Edna Everage' Humphries in Australia, though. What a human work of art he is! It was just after Amy was born. Cara was there and Martine cared for her, Daisy and Amy in my trailer while I was on set. I was still breastfeeding and it was really hot. Not great for the kids, and I was exhausted. But I took them for trips – we visited Rottnest and Magnetic Island. In New Zealand, I broke my wrist while playing Nancy Reagan. I was doing a promotional TV performance when I fell off a table – yes, really – and felt terrible pain as I hit the ground. My promoter, Ian, took me to the doctor, who turned out to be a *Not The Nine O'Clock News* fan. 'Just wait there,' he said, not realizing I was in agony. 'I'm just ducking home to get my *Hedgehog Sandwich* album for you to sign.' I was close to passing out by the time he returned.

When the babies were small and portable, it was relatively easy to go on tour in foreign countries, but eventually it became impossible. I was definitely struggling with the demands of being both mother and comedian, but something else had occurred: I just wasn't as excited about comedy as I once had been. Although I still enjoyed performing live in my solo shows, I'd really achieved everything I ever wanted in the field, and now I was getting bored. I was no longer interested in movies; I found them tedious and time-consuming, with very little opportunity to have any creative control. And I had already starred in the two best TV comedy shows in the world. What else was there for me to do? Where was the next challenge? I finally realized it might lie beyond my current profession.

In 1991 American producers Michael Elias and Rich Eustis asked Billy to take over the leading role in the prime-time American hit TV comedy show *Head of the Class* on NBC. He was to play Billy MacGregor, a teacher providing 'enrichment' for gifted children, replacing Howard Hesseman who had been in the show for five years. This was an incredible opportunity for Billy, and one that eventually helped solidify his career in the United States; however, it created considerable upheaval in our lives.

Warner Brothers wanted a four-year contract, so we decided to move everyone to Los Angeles. But, before we did so, I insisted Billy make an honest woman of me. Yes, it was I who proposed, although I didn't exactly get down on one knee. 'Look Billy,' I said, not terribly romantically, 'it would be sensible for us to get married before we settle in the States. Americans aren't as relaxed as the British about marital status, and I think it could be very important for the kids.' Billy resisted this idea like crazy. 'I made a mess of it last time around,' he demurred. 'We don't need a piece of paper . . .' But I stood my ground.

In 1989 we got married in Fiji. Billy wore a kilt made of painted paper bark (*siapo*) and the rest of us wore sarongs. Barry Humphries gave me away, and the small island we chose was taken over by various intrepid friends. Two real Scottish bagpipers led me along the beach to a strangely nervous Glaswegian, and we made our vows in the water, to a wet but kindly Fijian minister. In accordance with local custom, the whole marriage actually took three days, with a surfeit of feasting on local ferns, reef fish and even sea snake. On the first day, I was told I had to take to the sea and prove I could provide for Billy by catching a bag of fish with a spear. This I did, but I have a strange feeling someone was pulling my leg.

There was a bit of drama. For a start, Billy didn't really want to marry me. I guess he felt once was enough, and we had the most enormous row the night before we gave our vows. Everyone on the island must have heard him shouting at me. I'm just glad I was smart enough to have him captive on a Fijian island; no way he could do a runner. But the next day he made up for his opposition by being so moved he cried real tears when I approached him from the other end of the beach.

Fred was not the only ornery snake in my life. Our wedding island was well populated with highly venomous, banded sea snakes that liked to come on shore, especially at night. Being revered by the local people, they had to be treated with respect and could not be disposed of, or even corralled, so getting back to one's *bure* (Fijian hut) after dinner was quite an adventure. Unfortunately, Ringo's wife Barbara Bach suffered from a snake phobia. One evening they left their windows open at dusk and returned in time to see a pile of writhing reptiles taking over the floor space. Damn! If I'd only been a psychologist back then I might have loudly claimed they shared an unconscious fear of large penises. But even as it was there was quite a to-do.

There were only about thirty guests. The wedding invitation had been painted on silk sarongs that everyone wore. I had a lovely tropical garland in my hair and an exotic gold necklace given to me by Shakira Caine (Michael Caine's wife) from her personally designed jewellery collection. Despite the sea-snake threat we were all barefooted. Jamie and Barry Humphries' boys, Oscar and Rupert, helped our girls along the beach, shading them with umbrellas made of giant leaves. Everyone looked very pretty and the photos from that day are wonderful. I suppose my parents were miffed that they were not invited, but it was actually a huge relief for Billy and I to be away from family pressures. When my mother saw my wedding photos she did let me know how amusing she thought it was that I was such an old bride, being given away by a not-exactly-youthful surrogate in the shape of Barry Humphries. Jesus, I was only thirty-eight, but I guess for her generation we were positively ancient to be wedding party protagonists. I wish we still had the video of the wedding ceremony – shot by our good friend the director Richard Lester – but it disappeared within months of our return to the UK.

We arrived in Los Angeles in 1990 and searched for a house in a number of different suburbs – Santa Monica, Beverly Hills, Hollywood. Nothing appealed until our estate agent was just about to give up on us. She finally sighed, and said: 'There's one last possibility, but it's really weird . . .' Billy and I looked at each other with a knowing smile. The man took us to a ranch house in the Hollywood Hills that had been converted into a high-walled studio by an Italian artist, Alexander Burri. The man had even painted his trees red. It was perfection. 'We'll take it,' smiled Billy.

Billy complains that when he saw the place he liked it the way it was, whereas I saw 'potential'. It's true. I set to work knocking down walls, upgrading the kitchen, installing a swimming pool . . . Well, duh! It was California, after all. Our street was an enclave of interesting people – Quentin Tarantino on the corner, David Hockney down the road, Eric Idle in the next-street-but-one. Dan Aykroyd, Bridget Fonda and Dwight Yoakam were nearby – it was a fun place we'd just happened upon. And there I go again, name-dropping. Do you care? I don't. It's just a bit of fun and, coming from where I started in life, it just tickled me. And they – most of the people in Hollywood – are the same; escapees from all kinds of ordinary, boring, upsetting or even dangerous places they couldn't wait to leave behind.

The human menu in the Hollywood Hills was one thing, but the physical landscape was challenging. You know, I now realize I was never able to feel entirely comfortable in California. Perhaps the aridity of the place just reminded me too much of Boronia Park. And there was always the weird unreality of it; even the trees were force-grown, using water from elsewhere, in what was essentially a desert. When I think of the sounds of California now, it's always the slush slush slush of the sprinklers. There are sprinklers everywhere, on the lawns, on the sidewalks – run on timers, and always waiting to soak you without warning.

But that wasn't the only way to be ambushed in Los Angeles. The movie industry was brutal, on every level. It didn't matter who you were, what you'd done, everyone was vulnerable. We witnessed terrible cruelty perpetrated by powerful movie industry people onto less powerful others, a hideous jostling for parts and position, and that was truly ugly to behold. But while they raised hairs on the back of our necks, the ordinary folk we came across were well meaning and hospitable . . . 'Have a nice day!'

We settled the three youngest children into schools. Billy started work on *Head of the Class* (he eventually made a total of twenty-two episodes, then followed that with a series of his own). At first, it was hard to get used to him playing a real leading man – with short hair, eye make-up, plucked eyebrows and tinted pancake foundation. 'Potato-face!' he would exclaim into the mirror at his beardless self.

But Billy became an American star. I was enormously proud of his achievement and, even though he wrestled with the fact that such work wasn't really 'him', he seemed to enjoy it for what it was. I applied for the Green Card lottery and was successful and, as a result, we all became permanent residents of the USA. But what were our prospects as performers there? Our combined profile in the UK had been substantial, but now we were swimming in an even bigger pond. Could we keep afloat in California? We were about to find out.

Chapter Ten

LA LA LAND

It was a hazy, humid dawn. From my vantage point aboard a converted fishing boat just off South Australia's Neptune Islands, I watched Darwin's theory of the survival of the fittest acted out in all its gory detail, right before my eyes. Mug of coffee in hand, I had climbed on deck to enjoy what I had thought would be a delightful first-light display of Australian sea lions playing around in the white caps. But they were not the only creatures enjoying a spot of break-fast fishing. Every now and then the soppy smile on my face would be replaced by a horrified gasp, as yet another cute, furry creature was savagely snapped into oblivion by the gigantic jaws of a Great White shark, breaking the surface at a terrifying pace.

Eventually I could stand it no more, and climbed down to the aft deck to don my diving gear. At this time of year, the water was surprisingly cold. I added a layer or two, and a thick hood, and joined my dive buddy in the steel cage that would hopefully shield us from faring the same fate as those sorry sea lions. My buddy was grinning in anticipation of some serious jaw-snapping. As we began to descend in the cage, he held up a large tuna and began to slice it with a knife. The blood seeped into the salt water all around us, seeped out between the bars of the cage and beyond into the blue. At 65 feet we made the divers' 'OK' sign to each other, but I knew his meant more than that: 'That smell ought to bring the sharks up close and personal . . .' Dark shapes began to loom in the distance, advancing towards us at speed. Then I noticed the physical reality – there was just one thin cable between us and the boat.

Perhaps the Great Whites were no longer hungry. They had been taunted with tuna bait on the surface to draw them closer to the non-divers on the boat, and many of them had managed to grab the chum. And that was on top of their 5am sea-lion hors d'oevres. But I was really surprised that it was so hard to lure them towards our cage. And frustrating – I was dying to get a stunning snap of a massive pair of open jaws.

But the Great Whites would not co-operate. Were they camera shy? They swam gracefully around us at a respectful distance, behaving just like, well, ordinary fellow undersea creatures going about their business. My brain found this hard to comprehend; it was contrary to everything I had heard or believed about the greatest predators in the sea. All it would take, I thought, would be a few drops of blood and they'd swoop on you in an instant (as a teenager I had been careful to never swim in the sea if I had a cut or was menstruating – just in case). Yet here we were, carving up a giant tuna, with gallons of blood already swirling around us, and yet these top food-chain critters stayed far off. I began to take some photographs but, annoyed by the bars of the cage, I unlatched the door and swam outside. Now I'd got my buddy's attention. He raised his tuna knife to shrug his shoulders and stared at me in alarm. 'What the hell are you doing out there?' His eyes were bulging behind his mask. 'Take it easy,' I casually returned his semaphore, then turned my back on him and inched closer to the nearest toothy beauty to get a better shot.

Within seconds, a strong, insistent pair of hands was dragging me back inside the cage. 'Are you crazy?' He was glaring at me, with one finger circling his ear. Dive buddies rely on each other underwater, and it is certainly wise to caution another diver who might be taking unnecessary risks. But for me, being within feet of creatures that are considered to be the most dangerous in the world without a barrier was profoundly moving, illuminating and life-affirming. These gigantic killing machines were truly the stuff of nightmares – the terrifying nemeses in Spielberg's *Jaws* – a movie that tragically led to a huge escalation in the slaughtering of sharks generally. And they weren't even interested in me. Phooogh. A girl could feel quite rejected.

Rejection, of course, is a common experience in the centre of the movie industry. In Los Angeles one risks rejection on so many counts; for being too plump, too old (guilty as charged), too light, too dark, too worldly, too naïve, too poor, too different, too bold, too timid, too bright, too dim, too honest, too sly. The only things you could never be criticized for were being too rich or too thin. Even my husband was at risk for being considered too rude, too volatile, too Glaswegian . . .

What about you? You provided strong support for your husband, but what was it like for you to undergo such a massive relocation, such an enormous change?

Well, it wasn't easy, but I really didn't mind. Los Angeles always tickled me. I loved the craziness of it, the laidbackness of it, and even its stupidity. I remember being struck by the amazing vehicles – bright pink stretch limos and even cars that were turned into works of art by a self-promoting actor called Dennis Woodruff. I was curious about the unusual people one would see on the streets: a man in a long, brown robe carrying a cross (people called him 'Jesus on Sunset') and, of course, the many movie stars who were just going about their business doing everyday things. Some of the more bizarre sightings I remember were Monica Lewinsky out shopping in Fred Segal, Cher in a diner, and the time when I accidentally got my heel trapped inside a man's shoe as I took my seat beside him at a film premiere; then realized it was Jeff Bridges. Ouch – for both of us!

But we already had some happily memorable moments from an earlier time when Billy and I had first visited the town together; when the first *Star Wars* movie came out and Roger Taylor from Queen took us to see it at what was then known as Mann's Chinese Theatre. I had never been in such a loud cinema before – I guess it was early 'surround sound' – and I remember the place was knee-deep in popcorn. But it was enormously exciting. I could never have imagined that I would one day interview the girl with the weird plaits over her ears on a psychology TV programme called *Shrink Rap*. But, back then, who knew – outside the Hollywood Inner Circle – that Carrie Fisher was, well, Carrie Fisher; a brilliantly funny and bright writer struggling with bipolar disorder, hiding behind a cute smile and a button nose?

Everything in Los Angeles at that time seemed extreme. There were a lot of very thin people, who lived on diet coke (and often recreational coke as well) and had all the money, and a lot of very fat people who lived on burgers and hot dogs and just waddled around the theme parks. No one seemed to be of medium weight. I used to joke that they don't let you into Beverly Hills if your thighs wobble but it was sort of true; it took me precisely four months of living there to decide I needed a personal trainer.

So . . . your weight issues really came to the fore in that environment?

Yes. I remember becoming extremely body-conscious, comparing myself to other women to an extent to which I'd not done in the past. It was the first time I'd lived in a place where people really prioritized youth and beauty over intelligence. Wealth was important for a man, but a woman had to be gorgeous and appear young, or she was ignored. Almost all the women I knew were blonde; it seemed to me you had to emulate the California-girl style, even if you were, say, Jewish or African. And it was a complete no-no to look your age, which meant an enormous amount of cosmetic tweaking all round. See, the Californian climate dries out your skin and actually promotes wrinkles, so the beauticians, masseurs, personal trainers, hairdressers, personal shoppers and plastic surgeons all do big business in attempting to reverse the signs of ageing. I began to consider procedures and treatments I'd never heard of before – liposuction, laser skin resurfacing, human growth hormone injections. At one point I was pulled aside by one society woman and chastised for telling my true age. 'Honey, if you're gonna tell people you're forty-two, no one's gonna believe I'm thirty-five. Zip it!'

In those days the unofficial social king and queen of Beverly Hills were Marvin and Barbara Davis. Marvin, who died a few years ago (leaving the kids to have monumental and public squabbles about the money), was a street-smart business man of Irish descent, while his wife was a glamorous blonde from a Jewish family from Dallas, Texas. Marvin had run 20th Century Fox studios and, among other properties, owned the exclusive Pebble Beach golf resort as well as Aspen ski resort. The Davises were the power couple above all other power couples; you had only to watch huge Hollywood stars kowtow to them to be certain of that. They held an annual charity event called the Carousel of Hope Ball that would be attended by princes, presidents and the biggest stars in sports and the performing arts; and every year they had a major Christmas party that provided the benchmark for a person's success the previous year – an invitation to it was a decided thumbs up. One would arrive in evening dress and be greeted in the drive by carol singers dressed in Victorian costumes, while elves hurled fake snow from the mansion's ramparts.

Walking in you'd probably find every one of your silver screen and music heroes – and a few TV stars, writers and politicians thrown in. Sidney Poitier and his wife Joanna, Frank and Barbara Sinatra, Berry Gordy, Don Rickles, Bette Midler, Sean and Micheline Connery, Clint Eastwood, David Niven Junior, Yvette Mimieux and her husband Howard Ruby were just a few of the people who attended each year. Someone incredibly famous would get up and sing; one year it was Barbra Streisand, then Stevie Wonder sang 'White Christmas'. David Foster usually played the piano. As we left we were always plied with large wooden nutcrackers, music boxes and hot chocolate. One evening I walked in ahead of Billy and Frank Sinatra stood eyeing me up from one side of the hallway. 'You look so purty!' he winked. I've kept the dress I was wearing that night – purple crushed velvet with gold trim made by Antony Price. I wish it still fitted me.

It was Michael Caine who introduced Billy and me to the Davis family, and we were grateful because not only did we find them charming and highly amusing, but they were kind enough to include us at all kinds of fantastic gatherings. The Davises hosted EVERYBODY. Sometimes we'd go to one of their weekly movie nights, held in their own cinema. They'd rent a first-run movie and we'd all sit munching popcorn in large, reclining armchairs. The Davises were incredibly generous to all their guests, but it was terribly discombobulating to look around the room and see people you'd idolized for years tucking into their thin-crust, smoked salmon and crème fraîche pizzas (a speciality of celebrity chef Wolfgang Puck who usually catered).

Our kids were also subjected to fame-fest parties, although

fortunately they were relatively unaware of it all. One day our middle daughter Amy – then around eight years old – was invited to attend a children's birthday party in a Hollywood mansion. When she returned she was wide-eyed with excitement. 'They had a petting zoo!' she exclaimed. 'And there were peacocks walking around. And a funny old man in a dressing gown.' We finally worked out that the latter was Hugh Heffner (at the time when he was married with children), and that she'd actually been partying at the Playboy Mansion! OMG. Another time we were invited to Berry Gordy's place for an Easter egg hunt. Now our kids may have complained that the boys from Michael Jackson's extended family were super-fast and took all the eggs, but Billy and I just thought it was a hoot.

There were many 'OMG!' moments during those early years in LA. After a while we became pathetically blasé about hanging out with our heroes but early on it was shocking. You'd be invited for dinner and discover that the house you were approaching up a stunningly impressive drive was the mansion from the TV show *The Beverly Hillbillies*. It was not unusual to be treated, after dinner, to a performance by someone amazing. Once it was an incredible Motown group, another time it was the fabulous Natalie Cole. Once at the Davises' Christmas party, the New York Rockettes high-kicked up and down their grand spiral staircase, and when a large soul choir sang after dinner, Sean Connery got up and danced spiritedly in an impromptu attempt to recover his African roots. Or something like that; I believe alcohol was involved. But I adore Sean. He's a really wonderful human being who doesn't care a jot about Hollywood rules.

The carpool lane at school was often a celebrity parade, although there was something quite stressful about feeling you had to be in full make-up just to pick up the kids. Careers, I was told, were made and lost in the supermarket aisles; you didn't want to be caught under that harsh lighting by any prospective movie director. And the beach was even worse. An industry town takes no prisoners; no wonder I was already thinking about moving on from show business. But I came to understand how an Inner Circle works. No outsiders, no gossip to outsiders – although there was plenty of gossip within the group. Everyone seemed to know exactly how much people made. Billy was often called upon to be funny after dinner, and he was always brilliant, but it made him very nervous to be expected to entertain such illustrious people and eventually he began to dread it. Unlike Don Rickles, who simply stood up and roasted everyone mercilessly. 'Bob Hope couldn't be here tonight. He's looking for a war.' (To Sinatra): 'Frank, I know you won't like to hear this but your career's over.' Billy usually talked about something topical, which made me very nervous, because most people there were Republican, and an ex-President or two were usually present – perhaps Ronald Reagan. Looking very gaga, poor man.

In the world of rock 'n' roll, wives and girlfriends are a necessary evil. I probably should have realized long ago that an invitation to Billy from a pop star does not necessarily include me. Well, excuse my feminism. When David Bowie invited Billy to hang out with him at his hotel in LA, I should have taken the hint, but I didn't. David, of course, is enormously bright and interesting. He loves contemporary dance, and introduced us to the brilliant dance group La La La Human Steps, which features strong women lifting men and even throwing them around the stage. I loved seeing that. I mean, I don't know how they could have done that without juicing themselves up with testosterone to increase their upper body strength, but what's a moustache or two between friends?

Anyway, just an hour or so into our evening with David at his hotel – in keeping with my usual ability to make a terrible *faux pas* – I suddenly said, 'Oh my God, David – you've got one brown eye and one blue one!' David gave me a sideways look. Of course, almost everyone in the world knew that he has mismatched eyes. (What is WRONG with me?) David then embarked on a talkathon, that is, he and Billy 'rapped' for almost eight hours non-stop. I have no idea what they talked about – I was just desperate to leave and find my bed. I was so tired I could barely stay upright, but my brain kept going, 'It's DAVID BOWIE! I've GOT to stay awake.'

Then there was that party at Gail Zappa's house where porn mogul Larry Flint arrived in a wheelchair disguised as a gold throne pushed by burly Men in Black – it was for Moon Unit Zappa's karaoke wedding at which even the priest did a number (well, one of the priests – I think it was the Christian one. The other person officiating at the wedding was a chubby woman who 'worked with crystals'). But I think everyone's energy was well-UNbalanced by the end of that evening. I'll never forget Rose McGowan, a very pretty soap star who was going out with Ahmet Zappa at the time, doing an amazing rendition of a heavy metal number in a frothy summer frock – wonderfully bizarre. And, after the newly-weds retreated up the aisle, they returned in terrycloth dressing gowns with towels round their necks à la rock 'n' roll and sang a number. Crazy, enormous fun. I love the Zappa family, especially Diva who likes to knit (a thoroughly rebellious act for one of Frank's daughters) and Dweezil who's just so goddamn cute. And Gail keeps dropping bombshells like: 'We lived next door to Charlie Manson and his "family". I used to see their comings and goings through my kitchen window . . . !'

One of our favourite couples to hang out with in LA was Sidney and Joanna Poitier. Wonderful people, and I especially loved to see Sidney go from elder statesman to giggling Bahamian kid in a nanosecond – usually when Billy pushed his funny bone. The Poitiers kindly helped us place Scarlett and Amy in the same school their own children had attended. Later, I enrolled Amy at the same school the Zappa kids had attended, and Scarlett joined her a couple of years later. Once it was a kind of hippyish school, but now it's also highly academic. 'Yeah, I went to your school,' Moon said to Amy. 'We went barefooted if we wanted, and the vending machines only contained apples.' Nowadays pupils still call the teachers by their first names, and there's no uniform. I really like that style of education; lessons are conducted in semi-nar form with everyone arguing the point, and the kids are really taught to think for themselves and question everything. Yes, the cult of the individual is alive and well in such schools; although it did make 'answering back' to one's parents a virtue. I just had to put up with that.

But the heady LA scene has its limitations. I could see that, if left unchecked, I could end up scoring high on the 'vacant' scale. I could turn into one of those blonde women – too thin to be healthy (if only!) – focused on charity events, perfecting the art of understated dressing to impress, regular nip 'n' tucking, and sleeping with one's personal trainer. Not my idea of a fulfilled life. After I caught myself doing ridiculous things, such as purchasing two Labradors at a charity ball, I thought, 'Pamela, you're losing it!' and promptly decided to go back to school.

Of course, it wasn't just finding myself seduced by LA's charmed life that made me want to switch careers. I finally managed to own up to the fact that I was bored with comedy. And show business in general. If you count my childhood shows, I had been performing for thirty-five years. I still loved the actual work, but most of the periphery stuff – touring, always having to try to look good, dealing with various quirky (actually, that's being very kind!) agents and managers, press intrusion – it was all getting very old. So, what could I do? Appear in movies again? I was bored and annoyed with that kind of work – especially the auditioning process.

In 1984 I had a new agent at Creative Artists Agency (CAA). Rick Nicita had been recommended to me by Richard Lester and we got on pretty well, at least he seemed to understand my sensibility. But I wasn't really like other women who would go to auditions and be very accommodating. I didn't know how to behave. For example, I once went to see a casting agent about being in a movie with Molly Ringwald. They flew me to New York because they were serious about casting me but, halfway through my reading, I stopped and said, 'Listen, why don't you get Cher to do this? She'd be perfect.' Agghh! You're not supposed to do things like that . . . What is WRONG with me?!

Anyway, in Los Angeles, I was sent me to meet the well-respected movie-making brothers David and Jerry Zucker, who had written and directed *Airplane!* and were now looking for a comic actress to appear in their new spoof comedy *Top Secret*. The movie was set during World War II and the character I read for was that of a French woman involved in the French Resistance. She would lead the central male character into a wacky espionage scheme. I read a scene in my best French accent, and got on well with the Zucker brothers, so I thought I had a chance. But the message went back to my agent: 'We're looking for a REAL French woman.' Well, I was fuming. 'That's ridiculous,' I said. 'I'm an actress, I can be totally French . . . *N'est pas?*'

Then I hatched a mad caper. I asked Todd Smith from CAA to call the casting agent. 'Tell her you have a new French actress on your books who has just arrived in California. Tell them she doesn't speak much English but you feel she could be perfect for the role . . .' Todd complied, and I donned a complete disguise. As Danielle Bergeronette, a dark-haired beauty from Perpignan who had just made a comedy with French pop star Johnny Hallyday, I flounced back to the studios where I behaved coquettishly towards the Zuckers . . . and a little erratically. At one point, when they were telling me the story of the film, I even pretended to get upset. 'You joke about Le Resistance?' I pouted, '*Ce n'est pas amusant . . .*' 'Well,' said Jerry, hurriedly trying to cover his tracks, 'It's just a movie . . .'

Oh, I enjoyed myself. At the end of the meeting I left the room, then whipped off my wig and returned to tease the brothers. We all had a jolly good laugh, but I still didn't get the part. 'Yes, it's true we want a real French woman,' explained Jerry. 'But not THAT one!' In the end, the role went to Lucy Gutteridge, a non-French actress who had appeared in *Airplane!* Yes, I never liked feeling powerless to create my own destiny; and that, unfortunately, is the lot of most Hollywood actresses.

Even beyond the humiliation of auditioning, I hated the whole process of movie-making – sitting alone in one's trailer for hours and hours in full make-up, having to stay so incredibly thin (or at least that's what I believed was necessary for me), travelling to far-away locations to film and never being sure when it would all end. And anyway, since I was now in my forties, and the cult of youth was alive and well – especially when applied to woman – I knew things would only get a lot harder.

I'd already achieved everything I ever wanted in comedy, and now I would just be repeating myself. I longed to do something with less focus on external appearance and behaviour, and more focus on my brain and internal self. I also recognized that it would be better for the children and family as a whole if I was firmly rooted in one place.

Most importantly, I sensed this would be the most important step in my personal evolution. The mysteries of the mind – especially my own and Billy's – had been drawing me towards a formal investigation of them for many years. Rather than being just 'an option', deciding to become a psychologist was probably the most vital step in my destiny thus far – and not just for me, but for the whole family. I had been leading up to it since my teenage curiosity about, well, poetry really. I had never heard of the 'mythopoetic centre' back then, but yet I understood that human beings held within them a reservoir of acute feeling, longing and passion that could not be articulated through ordinary conversation.

Yes, aside from the sheer intellectual curiosity I held for the workings of the mind, the desire to be a psychologist seemed to emanate from the part of me that cradled my own aching and harboured enormous empathy for people like me. And now I'm grateful for the people and circumstances that frustrated my performing career, because they helped pitch me towards what I was truly meant to do.

But at the same time, it was downright scary to imagine doing something else, being someone else . . .

What exactly was that like for you?

Oh, I guess I actually underwent a massive existential crisis. I was having daily intrusive thoughts and images of a giant crack appearing in my universe, through which I was gingerly trying to step into another world. 'On that other side,' I thought, 'No one will know who I am.' The image was powerful; I would almost say it was a hallucination. I had come to identify so strongly with myself as a performer I just couldn't imagine letting go of that, no matter how ready I was for a new career. It was a rather obvious psychological image, but the feeling that went with it was one of genuine, extreme fear.

I had to persuade my timid self, to proceed slowly – with baby steps. Feeling very insecure, I took myself off to Antioch University for a beginner psychology course, just to see how it felt. I absolutely loved it, and adored my professor, Dr Joy Turek. Joy advised me about the field of Psychology and the life of a professional psychologist, and I eventually enrolled in the doctoral programme at the California Graduate Institute – one of the best clinical programmes around.

I was ready to use my mind in a different way. This may seem strange, but psychology is not that different from comedy. Both involve the examination of human behaviour. I had been interested in the subject since I was a teenager. Eric Berne's *Games People Play* was very popular in the seventies – one of the many 'pop psychology' offerings. I gravitated to *Primal Scream* by Arthur Janov which, for the first time, exposed me to the notion of healing catharsis, in this case taking off to the woods to have a good scream and let your demons out. I began to understand that we were all creatures who held important truths below the surface of our conscious minds, and that notion truly intrigued me.

I was also drawn to Luke Rhinehart's *The Dice Man* because it was utterly anarchic and proposed breaking all the social rules I'd come to obey; it was shocking to consider any other way of being in the world, but I longed for such freedom. I was re-evaluating everything in those days – and a good thing, too. I felt I had to re-educate myself in what really mattered – the antithesis of what I'd already been taught. And I searched for people from whom I could learn. Oh, I was on a mission. I regularly consulted the Chinese oracle, the *I Ching*, that had been providing guidance in symbolic, often cryptic, form to people for thousands of years, and I learned that it could be trusted. When it had told me, just before I left Australia, that 'It would be of great benefit to cross the wide water in a large boat', I paid attention.

You were desperately searching for guidance, weren't you?

Yes, since I was a teenager, really. But in California, I finally found my way to a wonderful therapist, Lu, who provided the solid psychotherapy I really needed. And she eventually guided me into her field. She completely changed the way I fitted in the world, helped me make sense of my life. After I began working with her I came to have a far better understanding about the things that continued to upset and sadden me. I mourned things that had happened to me early in life and began to recognize how my psyche had buried trauma-inspired thoughts and feelings that subtly influenced my behaviour and choices in an unhealthy way. My initial healing took several years and, as you know, it's ongoing; but at least I learned to be hopeful that one day I can be truly, deeply happy . . .

Pamela, what do you imagine happiness is actually like?

For most of my life I would have settled for the absence of pain. Instead, I settled into an academic life and found that I adored studying. At first it was terrifying to have to take exams again, but I soon got used to that. I admired most of my tutors, and found them encouraging. The California Graduate Institute was not the most highly accredited establishment in the USA, but swisher universities, like the University of California, Los Angeles, only offered research programmes in psychology. Anyway, at my age I wasn't going to be snooty about where I got my degree; the clinical programme at CGI was excellent and nicely set up to accommodate 'mature students' or people who were also working and needed to progress through the course at their own pace. I love that about America; it's easy to find learning programmes that work for you at any stage in your life. And my fellow students at CGI boasted a wonderfully wide range of ages, races, ethnicities and backgrounds.

Billy was hugely supportive. In fact, he was thrilled that I was doing something that brought, as he described it, 'an atmosphere of studiousness into the household'. But, naturally, being me, I pushed myself terribly hard and put extreme pressure on myself to get As in every course (anything less would wound me). What is WRONG with me?

Pamela, in this instance, you already know the answer to that question . . .

Hah, yes. I do.

Articulate it, if you please . . .

I had unconsciously internalized my parents' expectations and addressed them to myself.

Precisely. But the workings of the unconscious are mysterious so you didn't figure it out at that time. But frankly, getting Bs – and being content with them – would have been fine and even more appropriate for a busy wife and mother.

Yes, and I didn't really have to steam through my PhD faster than anyone else had ever done it . . . And yet, that's what I made myself do. But I did really enjoy the process immensely. I loved all the material – well, except the higher-level statistics, which I found ridiculously challenging. But I especially loved the psychodynamic courses about childhood trauma, learning about personality and mood disorders, my hypnosis courses, and my studies in human sexuality. Actually, CGI provided a particularly good sex therapy training, and it was there that I first formed an idea that I might specialize in that field. It's always a good idea for a practitioner to have a speciality and, after a couple of years, sex therapy seemed an obvious choice – along with hypnosis, trauma work and mood disorders, which also came to the fore as possible specialty areas.

I was fascinated by the field of sexuality and the psychology of sex. It seemed to me that it was a far less well-trodden path than many other areas of my studies – probably because many professionals were scared of it. It wasn't easy to learn to talk comfortably with patients about their sexual problems, to put them at their ease and be helpful. First you had to be very comfortable with your own sexuality and get rid of your prejudices. In order to be a skilled sex therapist one has to be non-judgmental and, since most of us have been brought up in a society with negative attitudes towards sexuality, people usually enter adulthood with an enormous number of hang-ups. I was no exception (well, just look at my history!), but I worked hard and, after a good deal of extra training through professional bodies such as the American Association of Sexuality Educators, Counselors and Therapists, it was very gratifying to emerge as a well-trained sexuality professional.

But in your personal life – even before you began formal psychology training – you had already been learning about aspects of the brain and psyche, hadn't you?

Yes . . . well Billy, of course, is a very unique individual and I was very interested to find out how he ticked . . . More importantly, there were a lot of day-to-day issues we both faced due to his learning difference and I wanted to know how to help him. I knew he was very easily distracted, and had some severe problems with short-term memory. For example, he loves to cook and, at that time, he particularly loved to follow Madhur Jaffrey's Indian recipes. So he'd stand at the kitchen table and write himself a shopping list, then take off for the shops. The special places where you can buy fresh Indian spices were some distance away, but he'd get there and realize he'd left the list behind. That was in the days when he refused to carry a mobile ('You take a wild beast somewhere on the Serengeti Plain and tag it, then set it free again . . . Only it's no longer free, is it? It's got a fucking tag on it!'– that's how he viewed mobile phones). And I'd be there at home unable to study because I'd found the list and was worrying about when he would realize he'd left it behind, and how upset he'd be. And I'd be furious all over again that I couldn't get him to carry a mobile (nowadays he's the one complaining that he can never get me on the phone, and I grit my teeth and try to avoid saying, 'Hah! Now you're getting some of your own medicine.').

So I started studying learning disabilities and Attention Deficit Disorder, and began to understand how the trauma Billy sustained as a child affected his present life, and the relationship between alcohol/substance abuse and both trauma and ADD. It was a revelation, although I had to tread very carefully and avoid appearing to diagnose him. That, of course, would not have been appropriate; although most psychology students find themselves looking at the people around them in a new light! I observed him and thought a lot about his unique challenges, and it honestly made me even more impressed with him, knowing more about what he had overcome. But if I ever said anything that sounded dangerously close to the mark, Billy's immediate retort would – understandably – be: 'Quit the psychobabble!'

But Billy finally decided to seek therapy for himself! This was triggered when he happened upon an American TV programme in which the well-known psychotherapist and author John Bradshaw was talking with a small audience about childhood trauma. When I caught Billy crying by the TV set, I knew he was ready to heal. A great therapist then helped him come to terms with the abuse he experienced as a child.

I had to face the reality of with my own psychological shortcomings. I finally understood that I'd had an eating disorder for more than twenty years, although now that I no longer needed to diet for filming, it seemed to be in remission. I had begun to go to the gym regularly . . . and was still reaping the benefit of erm, my first face lift. Inspired by the pressure to look good beside the thin, athletic, youthful-seeming blondes who inhabited my new town, I had sought out a plastic surgeon shortly after arriving in LA. He had also replaced my old silicone implants with more natural-looking saline ones, and performed some liposuction on my thighs. But that was before I began my psychological studies; otherwise, I might not have bothered.

Through my psychology course I learned to be a better parent, acquiring new skills and a better understanding of child development. I was already acutely aware of the mistakes my parents had made in putting too much pressure on me, for example, and not being warm. I tried to be as loving and tactile as possible, and did my best to see my children as individuals and love them for who they truly were . . .

And Daisy . . . she turned out to be a truly unique individual, didn't she? Like Billy in so many ways . . .

Mmm. Daisy is a truly adorable creature – bright, funny and quirky. Nowadays she is very outgoing socially and just loves to tease me mercilessly. She adores small children and works as a nursery school assistant. I don't usually talk about her publicly – or any of the children, really – but Daisy has . . . certain challenges and developmental delays in various areas – learning, eye-tracking and large motor skills. When she was around four we began to notice she did not achieve certain developmental milestones, but it was really only once we settled in LA that we found someone who could figure out exactly how to help her. We found her an excellent school for kids with special needs.

You're downplaying all the worry and anxiety you and Billy had about her . . . all the time you spent searching for the right treatment, school placement . . .

I suppose . . . yes, I am. It's never easy for parents to figure out how to help any of their children, and when you have a child with special needs there's the added challenge of being an advocate for her, finding your way to services and the right treatment protocol. Of course, my psychology course was enormously helpful. I often joke that I needed to get a PhD in psychology just to understand myself and the unique people in my family . . . but it's more or less true!

Now, our middle child Amy – there's a natural born actress! She has not entered the field of show business but, honestly, she was a proper diva at three years old! She was sweet-natured, loving and kind, too, and she was a very placid baby, for which I was very grateful, since a lot of my energy had to be focused on Daisy. That's one of the hardest things about having a child with special needs in the family – finding the balance of focus with the other siblings. That truth was brought home to me loud and clear by one of my patients, a woman who had a brother with severe special needs. She felt she had suffered greatly in a family where he had unwittingly sucked up an unfair share of available parental attention. 'If he's "special",' she said to me, 'then what does that make me? *Not* special?'

But Amy has a beautiful spirit and continues to be a very caring person. She, too, had some challenges with focusing that made academic learning harder than it is for most others, but she has gone on to achieve excellence in higher learning – just shows you, doesn't it, that people who struggle at school can be the ones who shine in tertiary education.

As for Scarlett – a chubby-cheeked, exuberant bubba who grew into a poised, teenaged ballerina. She is sweet and loving, with a sensitive nature and is a gifted artist. I encouraged Amy and her to attend ballet lessons in LA. Not only did it make their bodies strong with grace and good posture, but the discipline it once imbued in me was something I wanted for them. It was a good choice, I think. On weekends, when other youngsters were sulking around the city's malls, they were rehearsing for performances with the American Youth Ballet – and loving it. OMG I just realized something. Do you know I actually dressed my three girls rather alike from time to time? Never exactly alike, but close enough! How could I have repeated that mistake? I must ask them if they resented it. What is WRONG with me?

Unfortunately, we all naturally parent by rote, and have to work really hard to avoid unwittingly making our own parents' mistakes . . .

Anyway, well before we went to the USA, Cara had chosen to attend full-time boarding school in England. After leaving, she lived with us briefly in LA, then attended Glasgow Art School and emerged with a Fine Arts degree in Photography. After school, James toured with Elton John and other bands, then eventually settled in LA where he began to work in the film industry – in the props department. Unfortunately, like Billy, he struggled with one of the issues that commonly runs in families – substance abuse. In the early nineties I took him to the airport and told him: 'Jamie, we're going on a plane to a place called Hazelden. You won't be back for many months but you're going to get the best possible help.' He did, and he has been sober ever since. He's a gentle soul, whose mantra is: 'I'd rather be fishing!'

Boy, there was such a lot going on within your family, wasn't there? And after the first two years in LA, Billy was away a great deal, either touring or making movies. Can't have been easy . . .

Yes, but it was nice to have the support you get from being in one place for a while. I made good friends among my academic pals and, being more home-bound at that early time in Los Angeles, I gradually got to know our neighbours. That was a new experience for me; in the past, I'd always been travelling too much for that. And what fantastic neighbours we had! I already name-dropped some of them. David Hockney invited us to his house and studio – just a hop, skip and a jump from us – and there it was: THE swimming pool! The one in all those amazing paintings! He was finishing a large picture of the Grand Canyon that was on its way to an exhibition in Paris. It was painted on many squares of canvas that I suppose made transportation easier. He told us he was sending the 'canyon' separately from the 'sky' – which wasn't quite dry; Billy and I found that practical detail very amusing.

David was also into painting his 'sausage dogs', as I call them, although I believe they were dachshunds. He loved those dogs, and even had special car seatbelts made especially for them. His hearing was deteriorating but he didn't want to wear hearing aids in what he called 'old ladies' knickers pink' so he had the company make them in better colours – one red and one green. What an amazing man. Such purity of vision, and an utterly enviable artistic life. David had designed the sets for a production of the opera *Turandot*, and he had a full model in his studio. He played the music of one of the acts and moved the scenery and lighting around by hand to show us what it would be like. Someone told me he had devised a drive along Mulholland Drive all the way to the beach, with music that matched the view and mood at every point – what a brilliant idea! I longed to be invited on that ride.

Dwight Yoakam also lived nearby. Billy and I both really admire him as an actor. We found him to be delightful and intense. I am intrigued by people who are unafraid to let their dark side be seen in their art, like painters Francis Bacon and Lucien Freud, and actors Kevin Spacey, Chris Cooper and Steve Buscemi. Some of the characters Dwight has played have been downright scary and I love that. And he seemed so . . . multifaceted. One day there was a power cut up where we lived, which meant that our electric gates were stuck shut and I couldn't get out. Dwight came wandering past when I was trying to force them open, and I asked him to assist by climbing over and helping me to push from the inside. 'Sorry,' he said in his southern drawl, 'I can't do that. I'm on my way to see my agent.' I was a bit taken aback, but it wasn't personal. He was wearing pale blue suede cowboy boots that would definitely have been ruined by that climb. The boots were set off by the skinniest jeans you've ever seen (they would probably have ripped), a pale blue shirt and matching, pristine cowboy hat. Oh yes, definitely not Mr Fixit attire.

Eric Idle and his wife Tania were our closest friends in the area. They are great hosts and continue to have wonderful dinner parties in their sprawling Spanish mansion. And Billy and I also adored getting to know Steve Martin; an extremely bright, cultured man whose writing I very much admire. He's also an excellent banjo player, just like my husband. Unfortunately, I have never warmed to that instrument; in fact, it thoroughly irritates me. And I can be pretty scathing about it. What do you call a gorgeous blonde on the arm of a banjo player? A tattoo.

Since Billy refused to carry a cell phone, in those LA days I felt I never knew where he was; although it was usually at the cigar store on Ventura Boulevard or at McCabe's Guitar Shop where there were musical concerts by people like Loudon Wainwright. Confession time: when I first met Billy, I pretended to like folk music more than I actually do. Heavens, I used to sing it myself and play the guitar, but all that mopey wailing has limited appeal. Billy, on the other hand, made no bones about the fact that he hated jazz – which I quite like – and is unimpressed by most pop music. I prefer the more lyrical rock music, so we both enjoy Eric Clapton, Elton John, The Beatles, Bob Dylan, Phil Collins, David Bowie, Queen, Foreigner and Travis, but when it came to my favourites (mainly lots of female vocalists like Beyoncé, Mariah Carey and J.Lo), Billy was scathing. Chick music, that's what I'm into. Toni Braxton's 'Unbreak My Heart', for example. I still play that on our kitchen jukebox in Scotland and have a moody dance all by myself. Oh, and Andrea Bocelli . . . Fabulous!

Oh God, I sound such a dork, don't I? I also like the Black Eyed Peas and lots of more edgy bands only I, erm, can't actually think of them just now . . . Hmmm.

As I was hearing you talk about your friends in LA and the music that has been the background to your life, you sound far more positive. It's as if, after you settled in LA – well, especially after you began psychotherapy treatment – even though you had quite a few serious family challenges, you came out of your depression and began to enjoy family, studies, people . . .

It's true. I sometimes wonder what my life would be like if we had not moved to LA. For a start, I'm not sure I would have sought treatment in the UK, or trained as a therapist. Also, getting some help for Daisy was crucial – I don't think learning differences were as well understood in the UK at that time. But to go back to music for a moment, I have often wondered about the people who were the muses for some of the famous love songs I adore and was utterly gobsmacked when I met two of those muses – Ann Jones, for whom Mick Jones from Foreigner wrote that amazing song 'I Want To Know What Love Is', and also Pattie Boyd, who inspired Eric Clapton to write 'Layla' and for whom he wrote 'Wonderful Tonight'. I wonder what it must be like to be adored and honoured in such a public way! Lucky cows.

My husband certainly goes public on many aspects of me, but they are usually in the interests of summoning public mirth! Like telling the world about my beauty preparations, my 'angry' looks, my fashion mistakes, and my penchant for knocking down 'perfectly good' partition walls.

But I'm really not complaining. Surely it's just as much of an honour to be the butt of a comedy god's joke? Not quite so personally satisfying, of course. Yes, that's it: if only my husband would write a song about me ... Oh wait, since he specializes in black humour versions of the country-and-western ballad it would probably be along the lines of the Lynn and Conway song 'You're The Reason Our Kids Are Ugly'.

No, Billy's just not the romantic type. He once told me his definition of everlasting love was Ray Charles and Stevie Wonder playing tennis. Oh, but he did write me a ditty for Valentine's Day:

Roses are red
Cardigans are beige
Stop all this romantic stuff
And act your age.

Ho hum.

Chapter Eleven

SHAKE, SHAKE, RATTLE AND SHAKE / FEAR AND LOATHING IN LOS ANGELES

In April 1992, there was a bad feeling in town, a spot of tarnish on the tinsel. We'd been following a trial on TV that begged all kinds of questions about racism within the Los Angeles Police Department and, after a jury acquitted three white and one Hispanic police officers, accused in the videotaped beating of black motorist Rodney King following a high-speed pursuit, thousands of people began rioting. The Los Angeles Riots lasted for six days. Widespread looting, assault, arson and murder occurred, and property damages topped roughly a billion dollars. In all, fifty-three people died during those riots and thousands more were injured. Most of the insurgence occurred in a part of town I – and most people I knew – had never visited, so there was an uncomfortable sense of being disconnected from something that was undeniably important to us all. We could see the smoke from burning businesses and homes that had been deliberately torched by the rioters, though, and violent scenes commandeered our TVs. There was word it was all advancing closer and would soon be on Sunset Boulevard – unthinkable! I've never been sure whether I was a woman with a decent social conscience òr an incurable 'bleeding heart'.

Pamela, that judgment would be in the eye of the beholder . . .

Mmm it's true, and I've been called both. I remember having lunch with a friend by the swimming pool of a hotel on the Sunset strip and feeling terribly guilty that we were enjoying ourselves in such luxurious surroundings while awful things were happening in South Central LA. Did one turn one's chair to avoid seeing the smoke clouds to the south, or face the indigestible truth? My white face often troubles me, especially in times when I am faced with the realities of black/white antipathy. Though you'd never know it to look at me, I too am a child of colour. Well, that's a nice way of putting it. You know that term used as a slur for someone perceived to be black on the outside and white on the inside – 'choc ice'? Well, what's the opposite of that, white outside and black inside – Liquorice Allsort? Yeah. That's kind of what I am. Except if you called me that I wouldn't be offended.

Issues of race and colour are always complex, but it seems for you there's an added personal ambivalence . . .

In countries that were colonized by Europeans you hear a lot about 'white man's guilt' and, uncomfortable though it is to admit, I probably have it more abundantly than people whose whiteness goes back for more generations than mine does. I'm angry that the truth about my Maori heritage was kept from me for so long. I mean, there I was pursuing a career in the UK without much contact with relatives in New Zealand for quite a few years – and identifying as an Australian, of course, because that was my citizenship – then all of a sudden I learned that certain NZ cousins were embracing their Maori-ness, speaking the language, producing incredible Maori carvings, and claiming Maori land. Seriously? I admired them enormously, but I was also left wondering 'How the hell did that happen?', 'Why didn't I know about this before?' and 'What does that say about me? I'm the same generation as them . . . do I have ANY idea who I really am?' It was a shocking revelation.

The truth about your heritage was always there beneath the surface, as a sort of unconscious 'elephant in the room' amongst your folks. At some level you probably knew things you could not have articulated . . .

Yes, but for all I know, it may have been openly discussed among family members in New Zealand; perhaps it was just that we Australians were a bit out of the loop. But I still don't understand why neither of my parents ever mentioned our Maori heritage. Did they not think it was important? Were they uncomfortable about it? I wonder if it was my mother who wanted it swept under the carpet – after all, she had lived in a real 'us and the natives' colonial set-up in Fiji.

But once I knew that my great, great grandmother was Hira Moewaka, a woman caught in the middle of the wars that raged between her people and her white husband's, it was as though a large piece of a jigsaw I didn't even know I was working on got slotted into place. Some of the mysterious feelings I'd had when confronted with issues of race and colour at various points in my life made more sense. For example, after we immigrated to Australia we learned about the people who lived there before Europeans arrived, but my Australian history lessons at school barely touched on the genocide that had been perpetrated on aboriginal people throughout Australasia. And no one ever spoke the atrocious truth about how aboriginal children were removed from their families to be brought up in hostels as 'good Christian children'. I never met Aboriginal people until I was in my twenties, but adults described them in disparaging terms, providing all kind of ethnocentric rationales for their treatment at the hands of white people. I felt enormously uneasy whenever I heard such things – over and above the natural empathy any decent person would feel – yet I couldn't really explain it.

When I began to travel the world, I found myself in all kind of situations that pushed my 'half-white-guilt buttons'. I was acutely upset to be called 'pork' in Jamaica (that's a sexualizing term for a white woman), and recently, in Papua New Guinea, it was painful to be 'locked down' at night behind barbed wire fences designed to protect white people from the locals. And 'fuller-blooded' Maori or Polynesian people have often hurt me by being unaccepting. Yes, when a black or brown person assumes I'm 'one of the enemy' – descended from the white perpetrators of slavery, injustice and colonialism – that is particularly painful for me because it's only half true. I always want to scream, 'Don't look at me like that! I'm far more like you than you think!' But as a wise African-American friend once taught me, 'I don't need to respond to all the ignorance that comes my way.'

So, during the LA riots you were more disturbed by the ethical issues than the safety ones?

That's commonly my greater concern in such situations. In most of the hostile environments I've been in, I've found that, yes, I might have been afraid of being physically attacked, but far more upsetting was always the question, 'Why exactly are these people a threat? What has been done to them that makes them act like this?'

How did you handle being with small children in the midst of civil unrest?

Quite a few people I knew in LA – even those I considered liberal – let it be known that they had acquired firearms to protect their

The start of my bad hair decade.

Daisy's first birthday – with Cara in a party mask.

'Tiger in a tankini' – Jamie and Scarlett in Fiji.

Our Fiji wedding.

I thought he should be shirtless . . .

'The spider and the gadfly' –
Daisy and me at Halloween, 1991.

'Hag and bones' – with
Scarlett age five.

'Puppy love' – with
Scarlett (*left*) and
Amy, 1995.

'Fearless symmetry' – Cara, the year she came to live with us.

California kids (l–r): Amy, Daisy, Scarlett, 1991.

'Snap freeze' – Deer Valley, Utah, in 1998.

'Girls Just Wanna Have Fun' –
my forty-fifth birthday party.

One too many piña coladas
– with Sharon in Hawaii.

The Royal Waikoloan
Hawaii 1995

A Cool Yule: Christmas 2006, at Grand
Central Station, NYC. With (*l–r*)
Amy, Daisy, Scarlett, Billy and Jamie.

'Feeling kilty' – at Dad's
funeral.

The Graduate.

'Mortally bored' – the new doctor's brood after a long graduation ceremony.

Sunset Crew – Maui, 1996.

Jelly baby – Palau, 2011.

'But I didn't get you anything!'
Papua New Guinea, 2012.

'Did someone forget to brush her teeth?' James and me doing the Viennese Waltz during the *Strictly* tour.

homesteads (I had always thought of a homestead as something you found in *Little House on the Prairie* and wondered whether a mansion, say, in Bel Air, with a swimming pool, gym, tennis courts, cinema and seven-car garage actually qualified as a homestead?). The topic of having guns in the house was hotly debated and, to be honest, I did consider it. Well, it was impossible to avoid playing out threatening scenarios in our minds. Many people upgraded their security and some even took Armageddon-type steps, such as creating bunkers or 'safe rooms', but I felt this promoted a 'them and us' sensibility and undermined due sympathy for the people who'd been wronged. After all, the essential issue was really one of racial discrimination and injustice, and shouldn't we all fight against that? With a sick feeling in the pit of my stomach, I took the girls out of town to Santa Barbara for a few days, just in case. But, eventually, the civil unrest subsided and passions cooled.

Once we were back in LA and schools reopened, there were appeals on the radio for people to come down to South Central, where the worst of the rioting had occurred, and help with the clean-up. 'Bring a broom and trash bags' was the request. Next morning I drove to an utterly foreign neighbourhood. I would not normally have risked taking my car down there (carjackings were common, even a couple of miles from Beverly Hills) but as I drove further and further south, I noticed a very unusual sight. I was not the only one heading downtown in a smart car with a broom in the back. People from all walks of life had joined the clean-up force. It was unheard of. There were Porsches headed that way, alongside family Fords, chic BMWs, clapped-out Volkswagens and Ford pick-ups.

South Central was completely broken and burnt. Distraught residents tried to welcome us, but their tears took over. I spent a bit of my time trying to comfort people in crisis, and I was proud of the united effort of Los Angeleans who would normally remain segregated into groups according to economic status; from what I had seen of the town, this was an absolute first. I once accompanied the wife of a film industry mogul – with her security team – to an address in east LA. As we left what's known as 'the golden triangle' (Bel Air to Beverly Hills to Pacific Palisades) and approached West Hollywood, she asked 'Is this the same time zone as Beverly Hills?' She was only half-joking. Strangely enough, being just one of the many whose city was in crisis made me feel more at home in the place. We had all been through something together. All right, people were polarized in their opinions about the riots and the events that instigated them, but it was more like a massive family furore than a national rumpus.

Perhaps your empathy for people who react violently to oppression is particularly engaged because the tendency to lash out defiantly as a defensive measure has been a feature of your own behaviour . . .?

Undoubtedly. When I feel painfully threatened to my core I do feel inspired to go on the attack.

Mmm, well, it's the natural response for people like you who grew up believing that the only time they're loveable is when they're not being themselves . . .

Well, either that or I withdraw. Someone once observed that in repose, my face often looks thunderous, as if I'm plotting.

And are you?

Yeah, sometimes. But I may be feeling shy. Out of my depth. It frightens me, not being sure of my next move. There's a point where I feel I have to come up with a quick and savage display of bravado to disguise it.

It's occurred to me that perhaps the external upheaval in Los Angeles at that time may have served to deflect temporarily your focus from your internal chaos . . .

Yeah, well, there was plenty of that. My psychology course really pointed it up. I started expressing myself on paper, and reading it back helped me to see my life more clearly. I became more aware of the way I internally processed things, and how much I was dealing with in trying to manage my family as wife and mother when I could barely manage myself . . . It was hard, you know. And, on top of my own, long-term issues, just like every parent of a child with a disability, I felt guilty and overwhelmed by Daisy's challenges. But the most difficult and worrying thing was realizing that I myself was an absolute infant, psychologically speaking. I had so much to learn about myself. And having made this switch from a performing career – well, it was definitely the right move, but I was lost all over again.

Where did you find comfort?

Well, it was a day-to-day sturggle. I focused on trying to be the best parent I could be, while still attending to my studies . . . and I found my way to Jean-Paul Sartre, who, I suppose, helped me to recognize my own experience in the way he described his existential crisis in *Nausea*:

> Something has happened to me, I can't doubt it any more. It came as an illness does . . . cunningly, little by little; I felt a little strange, a little put out, that's all. Once established it never moved, it stayed quiet, and I was able to persuade myself that nothing was the matter with me, that it was a false alarm. And now, it's blossoming . . .

My passion was dead. For years it had rolled over and submerged me; now I felt empty . . .

If I am not mistaken, if all the signs which have been amassed are precursors of a new overthrow in my life, well then I am terrified . . . I'm afraid of what will be born and take possession of me – and drag me – where? I would like to see the truth clearly before it is too late.

Classic existential angst . . .

All very well for you to say. It may not seem that bad to you, but it was really a horrible, horrible feeling. My feet didn't seem to be properly on the ground. Later on, I learned that I was actually experiencing a pre-psychotic state.

Derealization? A perception that things going on around you in the world are not quite real?

That's it. Really nasty sensation. Bit like the time I tried magic mushrooms in Bali, only, back then, it was deliberate and there was added vomiting. I even experienced a couple of full-blown panic attacks – terrifying! I didn't realize what was happening to me, and thought it might have been a heart attack, until I recorded my symptoms later and looked them up:

> **Portrait of a Panic Attack**
> *Butterflies in stomach*
> *Worthlessness – sense of*
> *Despair*
> *No power*
> *Panicky*

Numb
Glazed
Sick (nauseous)
Short of breath
Lethargic
Unable to move much
Stunned
Fundamentally arrested

Hmmm. If you'd recognized your symptoms while you were experiencing them, it would have helped assuage them; that's the first step in the treatment for panic attacks – helping the sufferer recognize exactly what's occurring . . .

Yes! As it was, I thought I was dying! Afterwards, though, at least I vaguely knew I was at the beginning of a terribly painful healing process. I clung to the belief that eventually I would feel better; if I'd not had that hope, I don't know how I would have kept going.

Aside from the therapy you were receiving, did you manage to find some method of soothing yourself?

Well, meditation, poetry, prose . . . and I started painting. Oh, and this was so weird, I became obsessed with quarks – you know, the basic building blocks of sub-atomic particles? I painted abstract impressions of them. Now, that may seem way off-centre but, in fact, it made a lot of sense. See, scientists had named some of those quarks, but they didn't really understand their attributes so they gave them names that suggested kinds of – well, they used the term 'flavours', such as 'charmed' and 'beauty'. But here's the kicker – the quark that had been named 'truth' was still waiting to be discovered! In other words, they knew it existed, but just couldn't find it!

I didn't understand the connection at the time, but now it makes perfect sense that I should have become so interested in those particles, it was a metaphor for what I thought I needed most at that time – to discover the elusive truth about myself.

Pamela, were you aware that quarks are associated with strong nuclear forces?

Hmmm, well, I certainly felt I could explode at any moment. It must have been rather difficult for Billy to deal with my considerable unrest at that time. He couldn't possibly have understood it, and probably felt quite threatened by what I was going through. I was undergoing massive change and was not emotionally available to focus on him as much as I had in the past. In those days, it wasn't so good to be the King. He did his best to show appropriate empathy: 'Hey Sugar Tits, I suppose a fuck's out of the question?'

I became very interested in dream work, too, and took a DreamTending course at a Jungian Institute in Santa Barbara. Around that time I dreamed I was in a huge living room – rather like our one in LA. In this room there was a fascinating woman, Vigdis Finnbogadóttir, who was the Icelandic president from 1980, and the first woman in the world to be elected as head of state in a democratic election. I introduced her to Billy. She had a beautiful, spirited, white horse with her, who I was told was married. I wondered what that meant for a horse. Suddenly it started rearing up and the task of taking it outside to the beautiful, green, rolling hills we could see through the large windows fell to me. I tried to hold its reins but it resisted and reared up violently, jerking its head sideways. I completely lost control of it just before I woke up.

What are your thoughts about the meaning of that dream?

I think I was struggling with a personal metamorphosis within the context of my marriage. I had spent so many years focusing on my husband – all the abuse he'd had to deal with in his own family of origin, and his subsequent issues – alcoholism, self-destructiveness, his own sense of unworthiness – but now I was desperately searching for meaning and peace in my own life.

I found inspiration in unusual places, unlikely people ... For example, on a trip to New York I visited the Matisse exhibition at the Museum of Modern Art and was profoundly moved by the painter's life and work. They had designed the exhibition so his art was displayed in chronological order, and so at first I wandered past his early work – canvases he had painted from his parents' house – finding it dark, repressed, almost sinister. But, as I walked on, more colour began to appear. The paintings were still naïve, with an unfinished quality, yet they had a kind of raw confidence about them. Soon after, I noticed the influence of other artists such as Turner and Cezanne, and the impact that fauvism, cubism and even Persian miniatures had had on the young Matisse. I found myself emotionally drawn to the man and his work. His frustration was palpable; his struggle to find himself – as a man and as an artist – spoke to me. I became aware of some of his personal issues – including his marital ones. His painting 'The Conversation' really got to me, with him in his pyjamas and his wife in a robe – him standing, her sitting – clearly more of a confrontation than a gentle chat. Oh yes, Billy and I had been there. Then Lorette, Matisse's muse and mistress, appeared in many different guises and I became more and more intrigued about what was really going on in his life, and how on earth he had managed to keep those women from ripping each other's eyes out.

The landscapes from Couleur, France, rendered during Matisse's fauvist phase, held my attention less strongly, and the same was true of his New York paintings and those with a Moroccan influence, but when I came across 'Dance (I)' and 'Dance (II)' my heart began to leap. I found them joyful, alive and free, even though they're unfinished.

Now there's an unconscious subtext there – a strong connection with the role of dancing in your own life . . .

Wow, yes! Didn't realize that before. But, anyway, eventually I reached the room that contained the really famous works like that one of the woman with the guitar. Anyway, all the ones I recognized were hanging there. But I was shocked to learn that, at that point, Matisse was pretty much bed-ridden. He was painting with an elongated brush on canvasses attached to his bedroom walls. Incredible – the pinnacle of his work as a painter achieved under such challenging conditions! Reluctantly, I turned the corner to the last galleries, expecting to see the sad, fading work of a dying, eight-four-year-old with a physical disability – but instead I was met with 'Jazz'! For me, that was a moment of epiphany. I burst into tears. Instead of what I was expecting – decline and death – here were Matisse's most vibrant, most daring, most colourful and most exciting works. Aged eighty-four and while bed-ridden the man had found cut-outs – his best medium. He could barely hold his scissors! I cried for hours. There is hope, I realized. Even at the end of one's life. If all else fails, at least it wasn't too late to achieve what I fundamentally needed – an understanding of myself, and a way out of all my pain. I wrote in my diary:

I am *devastated, grateful, humble.*

Now that I was imbued with renewed hope, my ambition for happiness became utterly unrealistic. Yes, as my Christmas wish list at the end of December 1992 reveals, I was greedy for a tad more than a pair of high-heeled Manolos:

Passion, Freedom, Truth, Love, Joy, and Grace.

Was that really too much to ask? At New Year we went skiing in Aspen, Colorado, as guests of the Davises. Well, the kids and I were skiing; Billy was standing by the skating rink, giggling at everyone who fell over. Aspen is hedonistic, crowded and ritzy; I found the place did not match my focus on spiritual and psychological growth, as my 'New Year' poem illustrates:

Plunging down the ice-mountains
I forgot to count the weeks,
Or inquire if coloured feather-masks
And sequin-chested women
Could hold off flash-flood fury.

Then, drowning in shock-waves from shattered treaties,
I stripped the gingerbread house;
And, comforted by loathing,
Joined the conga-line of corpses
Hallowing the strut.

Yet remembering today the touch of concrete
How can I now beat my drum?
Or crush the impossible sadness
Of a very long time from now?

Oh yes, I was still in big trouble – and I don't just mean because my poetry was crap. 'Take control,' I wrote in my diary. TAKE

CONTROL . . . TAKE CONTROL! Another five months of therapy later, I was still desperate and questioning everything:

So what is it? Is this truly the beginning of my taking control of my life? Of beginning to 'tell' as Sartre put it? Is indeed 'adventure' even possible the way my life is structured now? How did I manage to get to this point? I ask myself this so often now. How did I manage to sleep-walk for so many years? Chakrapani [a Vedic healer I consulted] mentioned 'self-deception'? How exactly am I deceiving myself? It could have meant many things. Whatever it is, it is cruel, and it inflicts the brightest pain, the most pathetic need. Look, at the end of the day, I'm only a little teenager who never got anything like the love and support she needed – and I'm not really big enough to take care of all these other people – WHAT THE FUCK EVER MADE ME THINK I COULD??

But after another three months, I was beginning to turn a corner:

Well, it's over. I feel it. It has to be. Talked again about 'duality'. Thank God I understand that now. Apparently I can cope with it. It makes a lot of sense. Question: balance – could I ever achieve that?

I'm excited about what's happening internally. Suddenly I feel . . . released . . . so there's the possibility my mind and psyche can develop without guilt or self-doubt . . .

And, finally, on 4th October,1993, I wrote the following:

I woke up this morning and this was my first thought (I looked at my painting of the previous night – the most joyful I've made):

'I've been sad for many years. No blame. A state of my own making – self-delusion and so on – but now it feels as if I've been set free – spiritually, mentally, physically.'

Then I noticed how loudly and happily the bird was singing outside my window . . .

Thanks to the brilliant help I had received – and my own perseverance – I was a different woman from the one who had first arrived in LA. Not yet in optimum psychological health, but a million times better. Over the next year I continued to work in therapy – in parallel to my academic studies of psychology. And I tried other forms of healing, other courses – including empowering physical exercise like Tae Bo – different types of meditation, the Avatar 'creative living' Course, Buddhist retreats, tantra (it's not just about sex!), Qigong, shamanic healing, motivational speakers like Marianne Williamson, Ayurvedic massage, self-hypnosis, acupuncture and Vedic Healing. Fuck me, I was turning into the cliché of a card-carrying, classic 'me-generation' Californian!

Yes, but it seems to me as if you may have been trying to rework the teenage developmental stage that, due to your trauma, you failed to finish . . . Trying various styles and self-definitions in an effort to find out who you really were . . .

Mmm . . . I even went back to church, albeit to a kind of all-inclusive place of worship that welcomes everyone from Sufis to Satanists. I know it all sounds pretty weird, but I don't believe it's ever a bad thing to be a seeker, open to all kinds of learning. And my approach to all those different disciplines was simply to take what was useful and discard the rest. But, truthfully, while those things were interesting adjuncts to my healing, it was the long, hard work of undergoing psychotherapy that most effectively led me out of my malaise.

Thankfully, I finally reached the point where I was not only resolved in my own mind, but ready to be of proper help to others. What I'd been through myself helped me understand others – their pain, their despair, their anxiety, their struggles with relationships – and I felt confident about my ability as a psychotherapist.

But in California in 1994 there was more turmoil to come – if not in my psyche, at least in my physical environment. While driving along the wide, palm-lined Santa Monica Boulevard one January afternoon, I felt a sudden urge to turn into the parking lot of a store I'd rarely patronized. It was a hardware store, one that sells everything from energy-saving light bulbs to barbecue sets. In a bit of a daze, I wandered inside. I was not consciously looking for anything in particular, but something drew me towards certain products. For example, there was a display of battery-powered torches and some emergency kits that all Californians are advised to keep in their homes in case of natural disasters. I already had one of them at home somewhere, but I imagined it was out of date so I picked up another – just in case. And some torches – one for each bedroom – as well as spare batteries and a set of emergency house lighting that I installed the minute I got home. Well, you never knew. Former host of *The Tonight Show* Johnny Carson once famously quipped: 'Things are looking up in California – the mudslides have put out the forest fires.' It was a bit like that.

Where we lived in the Hollywood Hills, high above Universal Studios, the whole of the San Fernando Valley was stretched out below us. We could see the yellow smog line (I fancied we were above it, but I'm not entirely sure) and, in the summer, dark smoke from the forest fires sometimes blackened the sky. It never seemed like a particularly healthy place to live, but the line, 'The air quality today could be hazardous to your health' was usually delivered by such a pretty news anchor, with such a bright smile, it was easy to ignore the threat to one's lungs. Jesus, what would we hear next? 'The water's toxic'? 'There's vipers in your mailbox'? 'The zombies are coming'? 'But have a nice day!' Some people actually did keep axes in their cars in case of a zombie invasion . . . Or was it to ward off the junkies who tried to clean your windscreen at traffic lights? Who knows? LA's a crazy, unpredictable town. And it enjoys a kind off perpetual summer, so driving the kids to school on a rare wet day was always hazardous. The oil build-up on the roads could easily send you into a skid, while rocks – even large boulders – were liable to topple on to the road. And there was a novel way to rub shoulders with your neighbours: whole houses had been known to slip down a hill.

On 14th January 1994, on my way home from that hardware store, I suddenly decided to telephone my best friend from the car (in those days you were allowed to dial and drive). 'Hi Sharon! I was thinking . . . You know, I think we ought to . . . um . . . get out of town this weekend.' 'Dunno honey, I'm kinda busy . . .' Billy and Jamie were away, and so was Sharon's husband Dennis. 'C'mon! I'll put the girls in the car and pick you and Kelly up around ten,' I insisted. 'We can drive up to Big Bear and see if there's any snow. I'll book a place. Bye!'

I'd never done such a thing before. Why then? In the deepest recesses of my intuition, had I known something shocking was about to happen? Probably. Three days later, at 4.31am on Sunday morning, the beds in our Big Bear hotel started shaking violently. I immediately knew what it was – the dull rumbling and shaking of earth tremors were fairly frequent occurrences in LA – but this was different, far more powerful than I'd ever experienced. We all woke in great alarm. When the girls began to whimper, I clutched them tight and we all hung on for dear life. 'When will it end?' I remember thinking, 'Is the building about to collapse? Should we try to sprint to the doorway?' But we were being pitched about so precariously it was impossible to move off the bed. The shaking lasted nearly twenty seconds. I know that doesn't sound like a long time, but when you're on one of nature's most challenging roller-coasters it seems like forever.

Once the shaking stopped, we turned on the TV and discovered that what became known as the Northridge earthquake had just occurred. Its epicentre was not far away, in Reseda, a city below us in the San Fernando Valley. Thankfully, in Big Bear we were far above the valley. The earthquake was given a 'moment magnitude rating' of 6.7, which was disappointing, in a ghoulish way. As Californians we had become pretty *au fait* with earthquake ratings and could usually guess pretty accurately what level we'd just experienced. 'I bet this is a three!' the kids would say as we crouched under a table ('Drop, Cover and Hold' was the rule). We would have predicted an eight for the Northridge quake but we learned later that it just seemed that high because the ground acceleration was one of the highest ever recorded in an urban area in North America, measuring 1.7g. The effects were felt as far away as Las Vegas, more than 220 miles from the epicentre. Fifty-seven people died, nearly 9,000 were injured, and the damage bill came to twenty billion dollars. There were endless, nerve-wracking aftershocks – I remember one particularly nasty one when the kids and I were watching a show in a Santa Monica theatre – and an outbreak of potentially lethal Valley fever, a respiratory disease caused by inhaling airborne spores that are carried in large clouds of dust created by seismically triggered landslides.

But if we were nearly thrown out of bed in Big Bear, can you imagine what it would have been like if we'd stayed in LA? Thank God I installed the emergency lighting, because Jamie came back to the house unexpectedly and needed it when all the power went out and the windows shattered. Had I unconsciously predicted the quake? I suppose, I said to Sharon, if animals can do it, why not a sloth of a psychologist? For years after that she and other people around me got uneasy whenever I felt the urge to leave town.

At that point in my psychological career I fully understood post-traumatic reactions, and most people seemed to be suffering from them – including me and the kids. The aftershocks were frequent, strong and terrifying, and since the main quake had weakened many buildings and structures, we were always afraid that subsequent trem-ors would cause them to collapse completely. Freeways had already crumbled and we didn't feel safe on the road or at home. If a truck drove by you'd think it was another quake rolling in – they sound rather similar, with that low, ominous rumbling. Heavens, even a Joe Cocker track would make us 'Drop, Cover and Hold'.

Several friends lost their homes in the quake, and our house was a shelter for waifs and strays for several months. In particular, my friends Michele and John moved in with their two children. Michele was a primary school teacher and a fantastic mother, so that turned out to be a wonderful chance for me to observe her interaction with her children up close and learn from her advanced skills. See, I just never had the maternal confidence I should have had. My heart was in the right place and I worked hard at being a good mother, but I was always second-guessing myself. People who've been parented well can ask themselves in any given situation: 'Now, what would my mother have done?' But, in my case, it wasn't good enough simply to avoid emulating mine. No, I needed practical advice and good modelling, and Michele – as well as Martine, of course – certainly provided that.

I just can't imagine how it must have felt for Michele and her family when their entire apartment building collapsed in the middle of the night. In the aftermath of the main quake, many local buildings were condemned, while lots of people voluntarily moved out of their homes and camped in open spaces (in Beverly Hills they set up tents on their tennis courts!). The fear of being killed by your own home collapsing on top of you while you slept – even from an aftershock – was omnipresent.

So, you would say you and your children were all suffering from post-traumatic effects?

No question. We were hypervigilant – alert to the possibility of another shock – and very on edge generally. It was hard to sleep and we all had nightmares. I didn't want to leave the children even for a minute but I had to work. My therapy office became flooded with people needing trauma treatment.

I had been practising psychotherapy – at first under supervision – since I gained my Master's degree in 1992, but at that point I was still quite a way from being fully qualified. If you're going to seek help from a psychologist, it really has to be someone you can trust – right? You want to be sure he or she will be consistently competent, provide exactly the type of treatment you need, and not tell your secrets to their manicurist. Fortunately, the State of California shares that point of view. People think of California as a laid back, 'anything goes' type of place – and in certain fields that may be the case – but not so in psychology. The State has rigid and highly demanding legal and ethical requirements for psychologists, and tough criteria for licensing – including incredibly challenging exams. In the UK the rules are not so stringent but, in order for me to become a licensed professional in California, I had to jump through many, many hoops. Once I obtained my PhD in 1994, by passing all my exams plus writing and defending my doctoral dissertation on 'The Intrapsychic Experience of Fame' (what happens in the mind when a person comes to public attention), I had to start studying all over again for the licensing exam. The latter was in two parts: firstly you had to receive a high score in a written exam that covered every branch of psychology – clinical, industrial, research, statistics, social, and so on; and then there was an oral exam, in which highly experienced psychologists grilled you face to face on your ability to assess, diagnose and treat a patient. And, on top of all that, I had to complete 3,000 hours of supervised clinical practice, which takes most people between three to five years.

Frankly, it's a good thing that these requirements must be met; having legal and ethical rules (such as guarding patient confidentiality and never having sexual contact with a patient) written into law – with jail punishments for non-compliance – is an excellent way to protect the public. Nevertheless, it took me six years or so to complete my studies and receive my licensing qualifications; and that was considered fast. It was such a relief when it was all over. I felt enormously proud and grateful.

Billy and many other people in my life – including my children – congratulated me and seemed genuinely pleased about my achievement. On the other hand, my mother was very snooty about the fact that I had attended a graduate institution rather than an Ivy League university, while my father once snorted that he thought psychology was a 'soft science'. Oh, Lordy, Lordy, Lord.

But Dad never knew I graduated. Six months before I finished my PhD he suffered a massive heart attack – his second. The first more minor one had occurred in the eighties, when my father was getting into a boat on the beach in Rio de Janeiro. Perhaps the sight of all those near-naked, butt-shaking women was more than he could handle.

But this second attack was serious. My mother telephoned me to say he was on life-support in the UK (where they were now living) and I'd better jump on the next plane. I knew what she meant – obviously he was not likely to survive – but my psyche kept forming a rebellious question: why? Why should I jump on the next plane? To do what? Say what?

Within two hours of torment over what to do, I had developed a severe toothache.

Surely a psychosomatic response? When a person cannot use words to describe how she is feeling, the body will often act for her . . .

Yes, I suppose so. Isn't it amazing how the body can do that? My dentist informed me that I urgently needed a root canal and began the process. 'Of course, you must not fly,' he warned me. Hah!

Interesting – and what torturous ambivalence you must have felt . . .

'I wish I could be there,' I lied to my mother, 'but my dentist has forbidden me to travel. It could be dangerous – and very painful.' 'You're going to miss seeing him alive,' she said. 'We can't keep him on life support forever. We're going to have to switch him off.' The full meaning of this sunk in slowly, but the immediate harshness was shocking. 'OK,' I said, 'but, well, I'm really stuck here. Billy is in the UK, though. I'll get him to come.' I felt bad for offering Billy as the scapegoat, but it turned out he didn't mind at all. Actually, he has a strange fascination with death and will travel half-way around the world to attend the funeral of someone he hardly knows.

Next time I called, Billy was ensconced by my father's bedside. 'You should speak to him before he goes,' he said, sounding just a little reproachful. 'He's barely conscious but he may hear you. Have a go. I'll hold the phone up to his ear.' Before I had a chance to protest, there was a terrible silence, except for the irregular, pressured breathing of a seventy-eight-year-old man to whom I was being forced to say goodbye. 'Bye, then, Dad,' I said awkwardly. 'And thanks for ... um ... thanks for ...' I couldn't think of anything much so I just said, 'for the great education.' That was it. I was numb. Baffled. Hurrah for Sharon, who was beside me explaining I didn't have to feel guilty about not being at his side, not caring, not anything.

What a very difficult time for you ...

They turned him off shortly afterwards. My father passed away on 21 July, with the rest of the immediate family – and Billy – at his side. Of course, once he had died, my tooth stopped hurting and settled down enough for me to travel.

Well, that was to be expected ...

Yes. Billy met me at Heathrow and took me to the hospital. 'I watched him fight for his life,' he said reproachfully. 'It was awful sad. He's in there.' He pointed to a door off the chapel and I entered alone. The corpse of an old man I once knew was lying in the bed with his eyes closed. This ... THIS was ... my father? I gazed at him for a long time, expecting to feel something. But nothing came. Oh, I had lots of questions. 'Why didn't you love me?' was the first one. 'Instead of kicking me out, why didn't you help me?' and 'Why didn't you ever tell me I was Maori?' But it was all too late. His face seemed softer in repose. He was greyish, and I began to notice small details – his large ears with hair growing out of them, his brown nose, his fat, furry cheeks. He looked ... oh my God, I never noticed this before ... but he looked exactly like ... a wombat!

All of a sudden, I began to shake. Just a little at first, in waves, but eventually those waves all joined up and my whole body vibrated with frightening power. Then sounds began to come out and at first I didn't recognize them. The feeling I was having was so unexpected, so alien in this situation, I couldn't have labelled it at first. I hope you'll understand this, but it wasn't sadness. And it wasn't tears. It wasn't shock. It was mirth. Yes, it's terrible to admit, but I started laughing. Uncontrolled, all-consuming hysteria overtook me. I became louder and louder – to the point where I was afraid Billy and other people outside would hear me – but I couldn't stop. I was aching, doubled over, powerless to stem the continued vibrations in my body. Tears squirted from my eyes more plentifully than if I'd been crying. It was so wrong, so bizarre, so . . . incredibly satisfying.

Grief takes many forms . . .

Oh, but was I grieving? I'm not sure. I had no conscious sadness. I finally left the room with a smug, secret knowledge. Once again, I had been dreadfully bad; I had performed the ultimate, disrespectful act in the presence of my own dead father. But, unlike our first painful 'goodbye', this time it was I who was in control. I set the tone. I walked away of my own accord. At last, he was powerless to accept or abandon, to love or hate me. I was free.

So. Go on. Now tell me I'm nice . . .

Chapter Twelve

IT'S NEVER TOO LATE TO
HAVE A HAPPY CHILDHOOD

It was one of those moments when my fragile but essentially trusting self suddenly became engulfed and silenced through the eye-expanding treachery of a deliberate ambush. I have been trained to be ready when another human being physically attacks me, but only under proper hostile conditions – not verbally, in the comfort of a BBC couch, before a live studio audience on *The Graham Norton Show*. In November 2011, I had been asked to appear to promote *Strictly*, and dutifully prepared a short comedic act in which I would instruct the affable host in a couple of rumba steps. The plan was simple: I would wiggle a short routine, Graham would mince obligingly, and the audience would fall about – job done.

But first, I had to sit on the couch while a man who was the star of another BBC programme – a reality thing called *The Apprentice*, in which people got fired – came on to promote it. I had previously seen the American version with Donald Trump, but I learned that my fellow guest – a man called Lord Sugar – was his UK counterpart. I soon discovered how inappropriate his name truly is. Having pretended to be friendly before we went on air, this man suddenly launched a vicious, public attack on me for being a psychologist. He not only denigrated me and my profession, but he also spoke disparagingly about 'middle-aged women' who return to studying – especially psychology – belittling my achievements by saying that psychologists bought their degrees at Sears. I really don't know what was eating him, but I was so shocked by his vitriol that I could barely respond.

His attack complete, Sugar departed, leaving me stunned and speechless, with an acute sense of failure, fury and regret – thinking of all the brilliant things I should have said. Fortunately, the next guest was James Blunt, a man whose sweetness, sensitivity and talent makes him the very antithesis of Lord Sugar. Graham began chatting to him, and made a nudge-nudge-wink-wink reference to the use of James's surname in Cockney rhyming slang. At that point, James turned to me and said, 'By the way, I thought Lord Sugar was a real James Blunt to you!' Bless that man. But I was left with a sick, shameful feeling of having been publically abused without properly standing up for myself. And I still don't understand why . . .

Pamela, when Lord Sugar was saying disparaging things about psychology, whose voice were you hearing?

Ahhh. Yes. Projection. In that moment he became my critical, rejecting father.

Correct . . .

OK. I hear you. But he was still a right James Blunt.

Pamela, I'm wondering . . . What happened in the aftermath of your father's passing?

The children flew over with Martine and attended his funeral. Over the years, I hadn't been keen for them to spend much time with my parents, fearing that it would not be healthy for them. I had seen some signs that justified this, for example, when my father came to see Daisy and noticed that she was walking – albeit a little later than most children do – and he exclaimed, 'Ah! Progress! That's what I've come to see!' That comment alone led me to ensure such cold, unloving expectations were never perpetrated on my children again.

My mother and sisters were a tad frosty with me, to say the least. Well, it was understandable. But I felt strangely comfortable taking my rightful place as the Black Sheep Bad Girl Alien the Bane of My Parents' Lives. It would not have been authentic for me to have been anything else. But the star turn of the funeral was Billy, who had been asked to speak a passage in Maori tongue, for Pete's sake! He was now my mother's Golden Boy, I suppose because he had turned up at the crucial moment and done what was supposed to be my duty. I was almost annoyed at the irreverent King of Comedy. Would I have been able to be so nice at his father's funeral? No. But it was difficult to explain to my husband that I would have happily turned my back on the whole Stephenson affair. I had to show Billy gratitude, because he had sweetly and lovingly really tried to do the right thing by me and my family; but, in reality, I found the whole charade quite irksome. And if you've never heard a Glaswegian haranguing a dead body in the Maori language, well, I just wish you could have been there!

Had you ever told your husband about your family history, how you really felt about your parents?

Yes – but fairly sketchily, I'm afraid, and I regret that now. Anyway, back in LA, I pitched myself into facing my final round of study, and eventually became licensed as a psychologist. I set up my own private practice (previously I had been doing therapy within a colleague's practice) and continued to help individual adults, children and teenagers, as well as couples and families, heal from mental health problems and make sense of their lives. I thoroughly enjoyed the work. Certainly, I often found it very difficult, heart-rending and stressful, but it was always rewarding to witness the resilience of the human spirit and watch people heal.

Now you're sounding like a grown-up – perhaps for the first time since we began. Did you feel in some ways at this point in your life – especially now your father had passed away – that you'd finally reached full adulthood, or at least psychological maturity, yourself?

Let's hope so! Nice to finally come of age at forty-five! My father's death cleared a lot of gremlins from my psyche – so much so that I almost began to miss them. In fact, six months afterwards I wrote:

Now that all that pain has gone, I find myself searching for it. It was my friend; I lost myself in it – at least I was <u>feeling</u>. Now I'm trying to recapture it . . . through memories, music . . . any trigger back to that dark place . . .

It is common for healing to be experienced paradoxically as loss . . .

Mmm, it took me some time to be able to celebrate my recovery. But at least my own healing immediately informed my ability to heal others – and, in turn, I felt I very often learned from my patients.

We all do . . .

Yes. Powerful work. Strangely enough, I also found doing psychotherapy to be very … creative. After all, you're in a room with another human being, with all their preconceptions and resistances, designing an approach that will help lead them out of all that pain they're in. I sometimes feel it's not such a switch from comedy. Human observation and interaction, but without the laughs. Strangely enough, I eventually came to realize that comedy itself can be enormously healing for an audience – especially when it's performed at my husband's high level. He's always getting letters from people who say he has helped them recover physically, psychologically, or both. Well, he also gets letters that start: 'Dear Mr Connolly, I'd like to assist you in mounting a ballistic missile platform on your car so we can take over the world . . .' but that's a whole other matter.

Did you miss any aspect of working in comedy yourself?

No. Well, I suppose, I still do miss actually performing – such a very quick route to a natural 'high'. But that brief euphoria was replaced by the more gentle, longer-term sense of satisfaction at being able to help people, of seeing their lives change for the better. And I was so often enormously moved and inspired by my patients, witnessing what they faced in their lives, their courage. For example, when I first started practising I was afraid of seeing people with terminal illnesses. I was worried about having to watch them die and how that would make me feel. But, from the very first time I saw someone 'to the door', I realized how incredibly rewarding such work could be. Human resilience – what an amazing thing that is!

You yourself had worked hard to achieve peace and psychological health, so you knew it was possible. That placed you in an excellent position to lead others to a similar place . . .

Mmm . . .

And even just making a career change – that's something many people would like for themselves but are afraid – you were now in a position to guide them . . .

Oh, but there was something about that . . . When I began to practise, I was concerned that patients might either know or learn about my performing background and mistrust me. What if they looked around on the internet and caught me performing some of my more outrageous antics? Well, wouldn't you be a tad worried if you saw your therapist doing the American Express sketch? But eventually I realized I didn't have to be enxious about that. In fact, since many of the people I saw in therapy were in show business, they appreciated that I had a comprehensive, insider's knowledge of the field. I found it rewarding to help a person negotiate the psychological pitfalls of such a precarious career. People in certain cities in the USA are more comfortable than many British people would be to seek therapy. Some of them even regard it as a smart business necessity, to seek advice on how to handle the stresses of such a pressured industry, and deal effectively with some of the difficult personalities who populate it. I developed a new theory about the nature of fame and how to handle it, and that was an extremely useful therapeutic tool.

I equally enjoyed doing sex therapy – being able to help people overcome sexual disorders, correct sexual problems between couples, and manage that ubiquitous 'Am I normal?' question. Again, I felt inspired by people I worked with, some of whom faced enormous physical challenges – such as disability and serious illness – yet still wanted to maintain their sex lives against the odds. And I found myself becoming a champion for a greater societal acceptance of sexuality in older – or, as I prefer to call them, 'chronologically advantaged' – citizens. I also worked in the area of pain relief . . .

Another metaphor?

Hmmm. Well, hypnosis was one of the therapeutic tools I used to treat mood or eating disorders, trauma and problems with self-esteem, but I began to be in demand by dentists also, as a hypno-therapist for pain. Lots of people can't tolerate anaesthetic, so if such a person needed, say, a root canal, I would facilitate a trance state in which they could have the dental surgery without feeling pain, yet be awake enough to follow instructions. I found that kind of work fascinating – and so did the dentists, who were usually non-believers until they actually worked on a patient without medication support for the first time. I used to enjoy seeing them shake their heads incredulously. I'd smile and say, 'You see, Dr X . . . There are more things in Heaven and on Earth than a shot of Fentanyl . . .'

My practice was going well – in fact the whole family was flourishing in California. But unfortunately, after sitting on my butt so much, I was approaching the size of that flying Disney elephant. Yes, my body had expanded along with my mind. A British newspaper carried a story about how I'd gained weight, printing a horribly unflattering photo snapped outside my office. Worse, just as my clinical psychotherapy work was beginning to flourish, a British tabloid journalist invaded the privacy of my practice by posing as a patient to try to get a story. I felt outraged, violated. My new career, everything I had worked so hard for, was threatened because it seemed I could not protect either my own privacy or, more importantly, that of my patients. This was an extremely serious situation for which I was ethically required to seek consultation from a professional review panel. Would my past life as a performer make it impossible for me to maintain a confidential psychotherapy practice? I stepped up security, but yet again, my anxiety was soaring. Would there ever be safety?

I can understand your anger, as well as your despair . . .

Eventually things settled down again. After a couple of years out on my own, Dr Marvin Koven from CGI invited me to teach at my Alma Mater. I joined the Psychology Faculty as an Associate Professor and taught Human Sexuality, Sex Therapy, Advanced Sex Therapy, Clinical Practicum and Hypnosis courses for six years. I really enjoyed teaching. I loved our lively classroom debates and watching my students develop into mature professionals. And I was pleased to discover they were taking their learning home. At graduation, spouses, partners and boyfriends of new graduates would often sidle up to me and say something like, 'Thanks, Professor Connolly – I really enjoyed your sex classes!'

Ever since I was a student, I had been involved with AASECT, the American Association for Sex Educators, Counselors and Therapists and, in the late nineties, I became Secretary of that organization and co-chaired a couple of Annual Conferences.

Oh, and I'd begun to do research – mainly on transgendered people in non-Western societies – and I presented my findings at various professional gatherings. I was particularly interested in biological males who felt they were female, and biological females who felt they were male. Their sense of being 'trapped in the wrong body' was fascinating to me. At the time I was studying the psychological formation of gender, and was treating American transgendered people who, I felt, had nothing wrong with them. Yes, they were different, but it seemed to me their main problem was that they were misunderstood. While doing this work I remembered that, when I was in my teens, one of my New Zealand cousins had told me that Maori parents who have too many boys sometimes raise the youngest one as a girl. He said that they thought this necessary if the family already had enough boys to go fishing for food, and needed more help in the house. When I heard this same story about another Pacific group, the Samoan people,

I felt inspired to visit that island and investigate. Of course, the phenomenon my cousin had described actually turned out to be a culturally acceptable way of dealing with the arrival of a differently gendered person in the family. But it occurred to me that a cross-cultural study of transgendered people could inform Western people's understanding of how to be more accepting of gender differences, so I embarked on a major research project.

First I set off for Samoa with a group of CGI students. It was strange how I immediately felt at home on that lovely island. I experienced a curiously powerful feeling of belonging. But it was particularly riveting to get to know the community of transgendered people there (better to call them 'gender liminal' since they tend to change genders back and forth even during the course of one day). The *fa'afafine* ('like a woman'), as they are known, taught me a great deal. In Samoa, gender is defined as much by the work one does as by one's appearance, and the *fa'afafine* were proud that they could do the work of both men and women. Western influence in Samoa – especially Christianity – has altered the full appreciation that gender liminal people once enjoyed; however, unlike in the UK and America, the *fa'afafine* were able to be highly visible and enjoyed acceptance throughout most of Samoan society.

I conducted interviews with many of them, and also with their female-to-male counterparts, the *fa'atama*, and I made a teaching documentary about them. Over the next few years I travelled to Samoa a few more times, always feeling inexorably drawn back there – not just for my study, but because the place spoke to me. It was hard to explain but, for one thing, the people there felt like cousins – presumably because of my own Polynesian roots.

Eventually I conducted similar studies in Tonga, and took a trip to India to study the *hijra* – the transgendered people there who enjoyed almost deity-like puissance in the court of the Moguls but who have now been demoted to begging on the streets. That fall from grace occurred upon the arrival of the British Raj, who made it illegal to 'impersonate' a woman if one possessed a male body. The plight of the *hijra* stirred enormous compassion in me, and I was also appalled to learn of their self-castration methods. Many undergo these dangerous attempts to become 'real women', and a significant number die during the process. It's shocking, heart-wrenching and stomach-churning. Trained medical doctors sometimes carried out the procedure, but it was often a ritual ceremony in the jungle involving a rusty knife, hot oil, and turmeric powder. Yeah, sorry guys, I guess I just made your eyes water.

While I was pursuing my psychology career, my husband Billy, who prefers to use turmeric in his delicious curries, was following his own, new path – being gathered into the bosoms of the American people. They decided they loved him, despite what they referred to as his 'potty-mouth'. He followed *Head of the Class* with his own TV series *Billy* (a comedy show about a man who marries a friend to obtain a green card), after which he returned to doing more stand-up concerts and acting in movies. The fact that he loves film acting is baffling to me. I wouldn't have thought he would possess the level of tolerance for all the things I found onerous about the process. But then, in a way, it's an ideal life for him. Someone picks him up in the morning in a big comfy car (Pete Townsend, Billy told me, used to walk out on to the street, pout and say, 'Where's my pram?'). Then he is transported to the set and ensconced in a make-up chair where a nice, mummy-type person fusses over him for an hour or so, then a nice daddy-type person gets him dressed. Then it's off to his trailer where he will probably sit strumming his banjo until he's called briefly to do a scene or two. Meals on tap, cups of tea a-plenty, then home in his pram and repeat the next day – perfect! Oh dear, it sounds like I'm belittling what my husband and other actors do in the movie industry, when in fact the work can be extremely arduous, challenging and uncomfortable in many ways.

Perhaps you're slightly envious of his movie success . . .

I'm more envious of his remarkable ability to tolerate all the crap that goes with it! I could never manage that. And I'm really proud of him – how could I not be? Billy has done amazingly well to become a world-class film star – especially since he did it without any formal training. I just wish he would stay alive throughout all his movies; it was so difficult to find the right explanation when the children kept complaining, 'Oh no, Mummy, Daddy's died AGAIN!' Billy even croaked in a Muppet movie – the only person ever to do so! Now, that had to be traumatic for the kids . . .

Bringing up children in Los Angeles had many good points, but it was not always easy. Oh dear, and now my past really caught up with me! For example, when our kids first went to school there was a roster for car-pooling so parents who lived close to each other took it in turns to do the school run. A couple of years earlier, when I was a cast member on *Saturday Night Live*, I had made quite a comedy meal out of impersonating pop singer Billy Idol, turning his number 'Eyes Without A Face' into 'Wrong Voice For The Face', so imagine my embarrassment when we ended up car-pooling for each other's children. Yeah, in a situation like that, 'Hah hah, I didn't really mean it' doesn't quite cover it.

Culturally, LA is very different from the UK, so in all kinds of ways it was a fast learning curve. I really like the way individuality is encouraged in American children, though, and at Amy and Scarlett's school, the kids were taught to think for themselves and solve problems without being spoon-fed. Their classrooms were places of lively debate. Rather than being lectured at, they were expected to challenge their teachers. This was such a novel concept for Billy and me, who'd had such different schooling. But we both agreed with the school's policy that teaching the children to be self-assertive and comfortable with public speaking should be a priority. Every week the school held a 'Town Meeting' in which people lined up for a turn on the microphone, to make an announcement, tell a joke, or complain about the latest Presidential candidate; I came to marvel at my daughter's self-confidence. Daisy, too, in a school for young people who work better in small groups, came to understand and compensate for some of her particular, unique challenges. With the special help she received she became an excellent self-advocate.

I was worried about drugs, because there is no school in Los Angeles without them, but at least there was an excellent anti-drug education programme at my children's schools. In any case, Amy and Scarlett put my mind more-or-less at ease: 'Oh, Mom, don't worry. We know which kids take drugs, which ones are the dealers, and they're all just losers.'

Like every parent, I was also worried about my girls' physical safety and so I arranged for us all to do special courses in personal protection and self-defence. Those lessons, with San Francisco-based trainer Andre Salvage, were fantastic. Andre listens carefully to each person's fears and evaluates their day-to-day risks. Then he designs individual programmes to teach them to pay attention to their intuition, in order to avoid getting into danger in the first place. He also teaches children and adults exactly how to fend off attackers physically – even those carrying weapons. It was shocking to watch my children fighting 'to the death' against large men in padded suits – kicking them hard in the knees and crotch, gouging their eyes and screaming blue murder – but it was also a relief to know that if anyone tried to hurt them they'd know what to do.

I was thrilled to watch my youngest daughters grow into strong young women who were unafraid to stand up for themselves and express their points of view. I'm not sure that was always easy for Billy, being put on the defensive by bright young girls talking about political and social issues. And his political incorrectness – for example, 'The best way to solve playground arguments is a good smack in the mouth!' – caused a lot of eye-rolling. But the more I understood what he had overcome to achieve the success he now enjoyed, the more admiring of him I became.

Cara, too, was making her own way in the world quite brilliantly. After she finished school she attended the Glasgow School of Art and began a Fine Arts degree focusing on photography. With a unique and dedicated approach to her work, it was clear she would do well. And Jamie inherited a solid work ethic from his father – as well as a gentle, caring nature – that meant he was thoroughly liked and appreciated in his rock 'n' roll world. And he inherited Billy's directness. 'I love you, Pamsy,' he once said to me when my newly lasered face was covered in yellow ointment and gauze, 'but right now you're seriously scary.'

But Billy and I had such different childhoods from our children. I think Billy found it particularly difficult to watch Daisy struggling with her learning and focusing issues. He had experienced something similar – but minus all the help and understanding she received. When Billy was a child people knew little about such issues, but his teachers seem to have been particularly lacking in patience and understanding, so he grew up believing he was stupid. That was cruel, unfair and untrue. By contrast, Daisy knows she is bright but challenged in certain specific ways. She has been taught coping strategies and is unafraid to ask for help when she needs it. As every parent of a child with a disability knows, you really struggle with even simple things, such as finding ways to help her tie her shoelaces, brush her hair and play appropriately with a friend. But I was able to find great therapists and teachers for her, and the awareness and respect for people with differences that largely seemed to prevail in California meant that Daisy was comfortable and accepted in a drama group, with a martial arts class, and at her church social group. You had to monitor everything consistently – but the opportunities were there if you had the time and energy to seek them out.

And Billy has always been extremely protective of Daisy – and, indeed, of all his children. They in turn were always tolerant of his quirkiness. After all, not every father responds to: 'Dad, is that mayonnaise on your face?' with: 'The question is not whether I have mayonnaise on my face. The question is: do I suit it?'

For me, those years in LA when the children were at school provided an opportunity to experience vicariously a fun childhood. Since it didn't come naturally for me, I copied parents I met who really knew how to play with their children. I learned to be silly with my girls, and planned outings to theme parks, shows, museums, concerts and movies – things my sisters and I almost never did as kids. I absolutely loved Disneyland – still do – and had the challenge of avoiding the queues and packing in as many rides as possible in one day down to a fine art. In our shorts and bum bags (yes, seriously!), we charged round from 'Peter Pan' to 'Space Mountain' to 'Pirates of the Caribbean' (the latter was always right after lunch) and ended the day watching Tinkerbell fly across Cinderella's castle before the fireworks display and evening electrical parade. My favoruite Disneyland experience was the time the Duchess of York came to LA and the Americans closed the freeway so she, our kids and I could travel to the theme park. Naturally we got on all the rides without queuing, and I have a photo of us all together in one giant, whirling teacup – surrounded by 'men in black' with earpieces, whirling in all the other teacups. Hilarious. As my therapist at the time used to say: 'It's never too late to have a happy childhood.'

I sought out the wacky styles of entertainment Los Angeles had to offer, like Sushi On Tap, a Japanese restaurant where, right in the middle of your California Roll, the music would suddenly change to 'Puttin' on the Ritz' and the Japanese waiters and kitchen staff would trot out grinning and do a tap dance number. Halloween was always great fun. My costumes were an eclectic mix – a fortune-teller, Queen Elizabeth, a pirate with a hook, a ninja warrior, Dracula's bride, and Marilyn Manson's mother. The girls particularly enjoyed St Patrick's Day, when they would wake and find that leprechauns had sneaked into the house overnight and got up to all kinds of mischief – furniture would be overturned and there would be green footprints and glitter everywhere. Even their morning toast would be an unappetizing shade of green. Less exciting, apparently, was my own prank – turning up in their classrooms wearing long, green, curled-up elf shoes ('Mom! Did you have to?!'). Oh yes, aided and abetted by the equally fun-loving Martine, I was a playful mum. Well, thank God, I'd finally acquired some *joie de vivre*.

We went roller-skating and biking down in Venice Beach, dressed in red, white and blue for beach barbeques in Malibu on the Fourth of July, and attended Superbowl parties, even though we knew nothing about American football. We went on road trips to some of the fantastic outdoorsy-type places that America has to offer – Yosemite, Red Rock Country in Arizona, and Lake Powell. I was never quite able to bring myself to camp in the woods like other Californians, though – Billy was never available to accompany us, I didn't trust myself to manage the tent and, well, two words will suffice: grizzly bears! I heard those beasts can behead you with one swipe from OUTSIDE your tent! Once I agreed to go on a family camping trip arranged by the school, but my children were mortified when I brought along a portable loo. Talk about being prepared. I really would have been a superb girl scout.

Most people we knew in LA really went to town throwing birthday parties for their children. This was new for me and Billy – his birthday was barely celebrated and I never had a party until I was an adult, so I suppose I tended to go a bit overboard when it came to my own children, too. And there is a huge Jewish population in LA, so when the children became teenagers there seemed to be a bar mitzvah or bat mitzvah every weekend. I was absolutely amazed by those events – and terribly envious. I simply could not imagine being so appreciated and celebrated for coming of age. In the synagogue I was always so moved it was impossible not to cry.

California has amazing and varied resources. When I bought two utterly wayward Labrador puppies for the children, it was a no-brainer to call the dog trainer. But I remained absolutely hopeless at managing those animals and my kids were not much better. The animals were draining my energy and straining my benevolence. 'I recommend Prozac,' said the trainer. 'Well,' I replied, a little surprised, 'my therapist and I have discussed that possibility but, well, we decided against it for now.' 'Oh, not for you,' the trainer said quickly, 'for the puppies.'

Occasionally, my mother visited us in LA, and I was usually quite nervous about her arrival. But I was glad for the chance to learn more about my relationship with her – always hoping it would improve. In some ways it had; my feelings were relatively benign towards her at this point. But I guess I held on to a crazy longing that things between us could eventually become warm and fuzzy.

A part of you still believed that could happen?

Yeah. Fat chance. Once I even took her to Las Vegas with Cara (what was I thinking?), and it was truly weird to see her loping along the Strip past hookers, touts and drag queens. She didn't say much. All right. It was probably my dark side that dragged her there. I took her to some show at Caesar's Palace – I can't remember what it was, but I like to imagine it involved gyrating male strippers and a woman smoking with her fanny. No – I wouldn't dare; it was probably . . . I don't know . . . Celine Dion. Cara, at least, thought it was all a hoot. She's such an original young woman, with a fine sense of irony.

I was impressed, though, by the way my mother became so independent after my father died. In 1997 she published a book about Fijian history after Western contact – told through post-cards that had been sent home over many years, mainly to the UK. She called it *Fiji's Past on Picture Postcards* and, as one would expect from my intelligent and focused mother, it's an excellent and thoroughly researched book. My sister Claire and I accompanied her to Suva for the launch, which was held at the museum. This was a novel experience. We'd never done anything together like that before. Thankfully, my wonderfully pragmatic sister played her usual role of buffer against any flare-ups. I seem to remember that they laughed at me rather a lot, especially when I tried to drive the rental car – it had been many years since I was confronted with a stick shift – and I found myself growing emotionally younger and younger. I remember asking for jelly and ice cream for dessert and thinking, 'What am I, five again?' But Mum without Dad was interesting to observe. She seemed to have gained strength of self-determination – and an increased level of stubbornness. Yes, she was formidable. But I respected her achievement – the book was a labour of love for her, although one I'd had no idea she was undertaking. I should mention that it was around this time that she said one remarkably heartfelt thing to me – the only comment of its kind I ever remember her saying my whole life. It was in Los Angeles and came out of nowhere – and there was a little choke on the end of the sentence. She said: 'I'm sorry for being such . . . a . . . bad mother.'

It is possible that she knew then that she was dying of cancer. I had arranged for her to see my doctor, ostensibly for a 'general check-up', and she may have learned something she did not wish to divulge. Apparently, she had once worked in a laboratory next to a man who chain-smoked strong Turkish cigarettes, and she was convinced that was how she contracted lung cancer. I never knew she was ill until much later; in fact the only time she directly referred to it was when I happened to be at her house in Epsom and noticed she had a bulk order of toilet rolls sitting in the garage. 'Why on earth . . .' I asked without thinking, and she answered with the driest, funniest line I'd ever heard emerge from her mouth. 'Well, Pamela,' she replied acidly, 'I wasn't expecting to have such a truncated life.' There were several mysteries to Mum's life since Dad died. For one, she seemed to have become a type of counsellor. To this day, I'm not even sure exactly what she did, but she was a kind of lay Christian guidance counsellor for clergy and people who were following some kind of spiritual path. Her work was based on St Ignatius's teachings. Strange that a couple of years later she died on that saint's own Feast Day.

This new path of my mother's – as a nurturer of other people – only fuelled my sadness and sense of mystery about our relationship. From time to time – in public, usually at a book-signing or something – strangers approach me with words along the lines of: 'I knew your mother. She was a truly wonderful woman. She guided me when I was seeking help at a crucial time in my spiritual journey.' I look at them and nod blankly, suddenly imbued with a mixture of envy and pain. Well, what am I supposed to say? 'Bully for you!'

Pamela, of course it takes as long as it takes, but you have held on to your bitterness towards your mother for such a long time – do you ever think about what it would be like for you to let go of that?

If only I could! If only I could have more compassion for her. Even the realization – after she went sneakily through all the drawers in my LA house and neatly labelled and alphabetized everything – that she suffered from obsessive compulsive disorder, did not soften my feelings towards her. That's when I took her to Universal and stuck her on the Jurassic Park ride – 'It's a gentle, sightseeing tour . . .' I lied. 'There'll just be a few fake dinosaurs.' A fast-cornering, neck-whipping roller-coaster ride later – ending in a stomach-in-mouth plunge into cold water that soaked the front-seat passengers (I had made sure she was one of those) – she turned to me with a wry, defiant smile. 'Thank you for that, Pamela,' was all she said. Oh, yes, my shadow side was well and truly out that day. And I have no remorse. To be honest, it still makes me chuckle.

'Pay me more, lady, or I'll make the camel dance . . .'

Ah! Wow, I never thought of that. Hmm. It was a replay, I suppose. In Egypt all those years ago, I learned that to control my mother physically was the ultimate payback . . .

So, do you like me now?

Chapter Thirteen

FROWN LINES, FARTING AND FRECKLES

It was a horrid, horrid thought: Sharon and I were about to turn fifty. Quite a milestone for anyone. In the El Torrito Mexican restaurant in Beverly Hills, where we frequently solved the problems of the world, we looked at each other resignedly over large strawberry daiquiris and plotted. 'We're going to have to decide,' said Sharon, half-serious, half-mischievous, 'on where we're going to put our energy. Over the next decade, are we gonna work on becoming smarter or cuter?' 'Agreed,' I said. 'There's just no time to do both.' 'I vote for cuter,' we both said, simultaneously. That was it.

We planned beauty appointments, make-up advisory services, a spot of surgery and a jolly shopping trip to Neiman Marcus, a Beverly Hills department store we all preferred to call 'Needless Mark-up'. I was definitely feeling like I was approaching a very unpleasant threshold, and that's putting it mildly. To be honest, I was panicking. I was about to become invisible, unwanted, on the dumpster. From now on it would just be frown lines, farting and brown spots. Call the latter 'freckles', if you will, but, either way, if you want them gone in the interests of youthfulness, they require

laser skin therapy from a machine called Fraxel that inflicts a ridiculously high level of pain. I'm talking serious torture.

Anyway, to cheer me up, Sharon suggested we go to a lovely resort
in Sedona, Arizona, for my birthday and take all our kids. Billy was
on the road, touring. That's the reality of a comedian's life, especially a successful one – and thank God he falls into that category.
Anyway, the idea was to explore the Sedona region, which is known
for a kind of New Age spiritualism. It's also thought to be a place
with an unusual kind of 'energy' and I was curious about it. I
respected Native American shamans – many of whom lived in this
region – and I was hoping for a kind of philosophical or spiritual
insight. And the fact that UFO sightings are believed to be common
in the Sedona environment only made the place more intriguing. Oh
stop it. No, I don't really believe in alien abductions, crop circles, past
lives regression, or any of that woo-woo stuff, but it's fun to imagine!
Perhaps some benevolent alien creature could beam me up to the
planet of everlasting youth . . . Wait, wasn't that a *Star Trek* episode?

Anyway, my first experience in Sedona was of a more corporeal
nature. On my dreaded birthday, 4 December, I booked a Swedish
massage. In fact, several of us did – Jamie, who had been driving the
minibus we'd hired for our road trip, needed a Shiatsu work over so
he went before me. I sat in the waiting room for a couple of minutes
before my appointed hour arrived, feeling old and unattractive.
Suddenly, the inner door opened and an absolute love-god peeked
out. 'Dr Connolly?' he said. 'I'm your masseur. Follow me, please.'
This hunk led me into a darkened massage room, then instructed
me to remove my clothing and lie down. He didn't have to ask twice.

I hadn't requested a male massage therapist, but I certainly had
no objection. I sneaked a look at him. He was gorgeous. 'I think I
just massaged your brother,' he said, looking at my name in the
book. I was about to correct him, when I stopped myself. 'Ah,
yes . . .' I murmured, thinking, 'Sweet! He actually thinks Jamie was

my brother! I wonder how old he thinks I am . . .' I closed my eyes and felt his warm, practised hands roaming soothingly all over my back. Perhaps I drifted off, luxuriating in the sensuality of his touch. It felt a little . . . naughty, dangerous, but I didn't care. Pretty soon he was asking me to turn over so my naked front was exposed. I complied and was dozing again when something entered my mind, a little . . . question.

Now he was massaging my arm. He had extended it out towards his body and, it was strange, but the back of my hand seemed to be making contact with something. Something warm and hard . . . Something inside his clothing. 'Don't panic, Pamela,' I told myself. 'Think very, very carefully about your next move.' Being the curious, adventurous person I am, I considered going along with it – but then he made a move to touch me in places he shouldn't. Oh, stop it! Men have relief massages – why shouldn't a woman have a 'Happy Ending', as well? But it was a little too sleazy and, anyway, I wasn't that desperate. 'Sharon put you up to this, didn't she?' I giggled. 'Who?' he asked. 'Listen, beautiful, can I come to your room tonight?'

Of course that was the last I saw of him, but it was a powerful and timely affirmation that I wasn't entirely 'over the hill'. I never asked Sharon if she set it up or not. It's the kind of thing she's capable of but, actually, I don't want to know. I'm lucky to have such a wonderful BF.

That story about the masseur was just a prelude to the most important thing that happened while we were in Arizona. The area is considered to have special vortices and portals and, I have to admit, I did feel a kind of 'special energy' there. Some have explained the vortex as a 'magnetic energy field' and warn visitors that they might experience the phenomenon known as *déjà vu*. Others go out on a limb and say it's the Headquarters for Earth-based Command, and that – even by day – it's common to

spot so-called 'lenticular cloudships' and other alien craft playing a game of cat and mouse with the US military fighter jets.
Alrighty then.

But since Sedona is a New Age Mecca, it seemed fun to explore
that side of things, so Sharon, the kids and I took off in a jeep with
a Native American guide and headed for the Red Rock mountain
tops. The whole place was magnificent, especially Bell Rock,
Cathedral Rock and Boynton Canyon. I felt very uplifted, although
I couldn't understand why. Perhaps it was the masseur – or my new
Neimans bra. Anyway, at one point, we were near a high cliff and I
mentioned to our guide that I didn't like looking over the edge.
'Come,' he smiled, walking towards a sheer drop. I shook my head.
The rest of the gang encouraged me to follow him ('Don't be a
"fraidy-cat", Mom!') so I took a few, tentative steps. He walked back
to me and said, 'Close your eyes.' Now, everything inside me wanted
to scream: 'Not on your Nellie!' But, for some reason, I obeyed. His
voice was calm, authoritative, kind. Cradling my shoulders from
behind, he gently pushed me forward. Under his guidance, I took a
couple of steps, then one or two more. The rest of our group fell
silent. 'Stretch your arms out to the side,' he instructed me. I did,
and then very slowly I took six or seven more steps.

My heart was beating terribly fast, yet there was an inner calm.
'Open your eyes,' he said.

What I saw before me was the whole, magnificent, red and purple
valley hundreds of feet below, shimmering in the blazing sun. I was
on the very edge of a long, thin rocky ledge, just half a step away
from certain death. But I felt his breath close to me and his calm
energy was soothing. 'You're OK . . . You're OK . . . Just breathe,' he
said. I stayed there for what seemed like hours. An eagle soared
above, while warm wind whispered in my hair. Suffering from
vertigo – as I surely did – I could never have imagined doing this.
'Trust,' I thought to myself, 'what an amazing thing it is. I'd like to

experience it more . . .' There were, I decided, more types of blind trust than one. And between the massage table and the Red Rock experience, I knew which one was right for me: I had to listen more to my intuition.

Most years, Sharon threw me a birthday party, and it always had a theme. One year it was the White Trash Party. She served Doritos as hors-d'oeuvre, and white bread hot dogs for the main course. Of course, we drank beer and Coke floats and my tummy never forgave me. Another time it was the 'Come as your favourite sexual fantasy' party. Everyone else was done up in latex and corsets, but I went in a pair of flannel PJs with a teddy bear; after all, I'd spent many months that year working on a large psychological study of people who have an erotic interest in consensual bondage, domination and sadomasochism (BDSM), so I was well ready for something very, very simple. The study showed that members of the BDSM community are not particularly different from the general population, apart from being slightly more intelligent and narcissistic. They are certainly not 'sick' like many people think; in my view, they just enjoy a rather advanced sexual style that's not for everyone.

I was lucky to be alive for my 'Stones' theme party in 1999. Earlier that year I had fallen extremely ill with impacted kidney stones. I was working so hard I had not noticed that my health had deteriorated to the point where I was in a life-threatening situation. I remember being at a meeting in Santa Monica, pleading with a social worker to place a teenage boy with severe mental health problems in an appropriate facility, and thinking, 'I'm unusually hot, and I may faint' but doing nothing about it. I went to my next appointment, where all I could do was lie on the floor – until it finally dawned on me that I was in serious trouble. At that point, I called Cara who drove me to the hospital. She probably saved my life. The kidney stones had to be zapped and removed, my kidneys had to heal, my gall bladder had to be removed, and my whole body had to recover from its crisis; I was in hospital for months. Billy was marvellous. He and Martine took care of the children. But the experience truly scared me. How had I become so dangerously ill without realizing it? I had been taking care of everybody except myself. Was my particular style of . . . narcissism perhaps . . . so acute that I didn't believe such a thing could happen to me?

Interesting. There is a brand of narcissism where one believes one can, with impunity, be all things to all people . . . Had you again internalized parental expectations to the point where you became somewhat delusional?

It certainly seemed that, in becoming a healer, I had completely denied my own needs, which was clearly not healthy, either physically or mentally. Yeah, getting sick was a real wake-up call.

Are you familiar with the concept of the 'creative illness' – a state in which the unconscious mind sometimes triggers physical chaos in order for the psyche to pay attention to something it previously ignored?

Hmm. That certainly rings a few bells.

You had done so well to heal – psychologically. But it seems this lesson – about not over-giving to the detriment of yourself – had to be learned through physical, rather than mental, illness. Hopefully it was your last creative illness – your final 'dark night of the soul' . . .

Ahh yes. I really needed to understand how dangerous self-sacrifice can be. I suppose our culture supports the idea that prioritizing others is a noble, desirable thing – at any rate, always an act of love. But I learned from John Bradshaw and other important writers that it can actually be an act of selfishness, a kind of grandiosity. I'd probably been over-giving to people most of my life in order to feel loveable. That was a tough one. It made me re-examine every relationship in my life – personal and professional. Yet again I had to change.

After I recovered from the illness, I vowed to manage my life better, to achieve a healthier balance between work, family and finding time for myself. I forced myself to start exercising again and began to lose some of the weight I'd piled on through sitting down so much. My birthday 'Stones' party was a tribute to those removed kidney stones. Sharon, of course, came as Sharon Stone, there were several Mick Jaggers, and Billy and I turned up as the Elgin Marbles.

As the twenty-first century dawned I was organizing fireworks and a Scottish ceilidh to be held at Candacraig, our Highland retreat not far from Aberdeen. I absolutely adore Scottish Highland dancing. Ever since we acquired Candacraig we have enjoyed inviting a few people over, pushing aside the furniture, and letting rip with reels like The Gay Gordons and Strip the Willow. I read somewhere that someone who did a study of Scottish dancing found it makes people very happy – or at least it triggers a massive release of endorphins, the 'feel-good' hormones. Well, duh! And if anything helped me reach the *Strictly* finals, it wasn't my baby-years ballet lessons, it was the number of times I've romped through a brisk round of The Dashing White Sergeant while both me and my dance partner were intoxicated on Tomintoul single malt. Let me tell you, staying upright under such conditions, fighting the centrifugal force perpetrated by men who believe the faster they can fling a woman around them the more manly they are – and all that in a long dress and high heels – it's not for the faint-hearted!

For us, most ceilidh dancing took place when family and friends from all over the world managed to gather at Candacraig. The famous and historic Lonach March – a proud display of colour, regalia and pipe music from a band of Highland men and women that always puts a lump in my throat – takes place in August, and so do the Lonach Highland Games. I just love to watch the Scottish dancing competitions, the running races for people of all ages, the 'heavies' tossing cabers and hammers, and the 'hill race' in which competitors bound straight up a steep gradient and back down again (it's a wonder anyone in the area has functional knees).

Attending those wonderfully special Highland events would make anyone loath to leave Scotland, but we could never stay long because Californian schools started early in September. However, one September had a distinctly different flavour from all others. September 11 2001 seemed like the end of innocence. Just prior to that, we'd had the most blessed Indian summer at Candacraig. It was as hot as hot, and hazy, too. I remember playing croquet, having tea, dancing on the lawn in a white dress with lots of pals and thinking, 'This is magical. It's a dream. It's *Brigadoon*.' Two weeks later, and back in the States, the world was in turmoil. Billy called me from New Zealand. 'Wake up, Pamela, and turn on the TV. It's big.' Next weekend the Candacraig mob were huddling together at Eric Idle's place in LA, whispering conspiracy theories and wondering if we should get out of the USA, while a New York-based Candacraig guest, actor Steve Buscemi, was returning to his old job as firefighter – helping out at Ground Zero.

The national – and international – mourning, panic and paranoia that followed the events on September 11 are well documented. I had many feelings about it all, and so did the people I helped in therapy who were from diverse cultural and religious backgrounds. With such fear, chaos and appalling images around us, it was something of a relief to focus on a new personal challenge. When Val Hudson from HarperCollins approached me about writing my husband's biography I told her: 'Don't be ridiculous.' The only popular writings I had published were my scant contributions to the *Not The Nine O'Clock News* books and a weighty tome called *How to be a Complete Bitch*. The thought of penning an entire book by myself – and to have the enormous responsibility of accurately and engagingly telling the precious story of Billy's life – was far too daunting. 'You'll never guess what?' I said to Billy. 'Someone just asked me to write the story of your life – terrible idea, don't you think?' I was shocked when he actually gave the prospect some consideration. 'If you want to do it, go for it! But if you don't, some other prick will and they'll make an arse of it. I'd rather be fucked and burned.'

It was true – there were already several unauthorized and inaccurate books about him. I started thinking, 'If HarperCollins wants to publish a book about Billy, they must believe there's a market for it, so they're probably going to do it no matter what. I'd better think carefully before I give a definite "No".' I knew the real story about Billy's life, I reasoned, and could probably tell it with compassion; but could I do so with the right level of objectivity? Wouldn't it be particularly difficult to maintain appropriate distance at the point when I came into the story? My biggest concern was doing justice to Billy's remarkable and traumatic life. If I did it well I would be protecting him; if not, I could be causing him more pain. It was a huge responsibility.

I really didn't know if I could write a biography – write anything, actually – but, in the end, I said 'yes' and began to talk to Billy about his life in chronological order – not something many married people ever manage to do. It was painful for both of us, and many tears were shed. The writing of *Billy* became an all-consuming task – a far more profound process than simply recording his life. I learned a great deal more about him, and Billy, in turn, gleaned a new sense of his own life, and that seemed to be healing. I did not perform psychotherapy – that would have been inappropriate – but the conversations we had were profound, and often exhausting.

Just prior to the publication date, I was very worried. So was my husband. Would people still accept Billy when they knew about his childhood abuse and trauma? I believed people would respond well to his triumph over that dark past and, naturally, I tried to emphasize that in the book. Thankfully, readers responded with a massive outpouring of support and appreciation – not only for Billy, but for the book itself. 'Wow!' I finally allowed myself to be satisfied. But Book of the Year at the British Book Awards plus millions of copies sold paled in comparison to a happy camper of a husband – job done.

I had become an 'author' – and a successful one – with my first book (I hadn't even known that a person was merely a 'writer' until they were published). It was my third career. *Billy* had been hard to write but, when I was asked to produce a follow up, I agreed to keep focusing on my husband for a bit longer. Honestly, whenever we have a row I feel like reminding him about those three years when I absolutely orbited him. It wasn't easy, although, as an Australian, I could put it in perspective and say it was better than a poke in the eye with a blunt instrument. Yes, sometimes I have to remind myself how lucky I really am.

But what was it like to put your own needs and interests on hold and prioritize writing about him at that point?

Mmm, well I did have a lot of other commitments. And, in 2002, when Billy was about to turn sixty, I planned not one, but two big celebrations for him – one party at Candacraig, plus a trip back to the Fijian island where we'd been married with a gang of friends. *Bravemouth*, which was published a year later, chronicled that celebratory year. But after that I'd had enough. 'I'm sick of writing about you,' I told my husband. 'You're in my head far too much.'

How did he take that?

I think he thought I was joking but, as they say in California, I needed some space. I had really been working much too hard generally – writing, travelling on book tours, seeing patients, teaching, organizing conferences – as well as looking after the family. Something had to give. In Auckland to promote *Bravemouth*, I suddenly had an epiphany. 'I need the sea,' I decided. I'll get a boat and take off into the wide, blue yonder. Well, it was a bit more complicated than that. I had to find a suitable vessel, slowly start closing my practice, and make sure the family would be properly looked after. Regarding the latter, it was pretty good timing. Daisy had just found a place in a wonderful, residential college for young people with special needs, so for the first time in our lives she would no longer require one-on-one care. Amy had developed a passion for mortuary science and was considering a course that would lead her to a career as a funeral director.

Unusual . . . How did you feel about that?

I wondered about it ('Where, oh where did I go wrong?') but actually it's a very good career. She shared some of the course material with me and I found it fascinating – a mixture of medicine, psychology, law and ethnographic anthropology! But it was weird to have your daughter come home and say, 'What I really want is to get my embalming licence.' I've put her on notice to 'improve' my face when I die. 'I want false eyelashes,' I said, 'and a sexy smile.' 'Got that, Mom,' she winced. Have I convinced you yet that we're quite a few steps away from your average family?

Anyway, back in 2002 it was decided that Scarlett – the only one of our kids who had not finished school – would come with me on the boat and do her last year by correspondence course. She had not been enjoying her school, so it was a good plan for her. My other children were happily making their own way in the world – oh, all except Billy, who feared I was abandoning him.

'Come along, too!' I pleaded. During the various voyages that took the best part of the next two years (I wrote about them in *Treasure Islands* and *Murder or Mutiny*) Billy did join me as often as he could. But it wasn't easy for him. Not only was he extremely busy making movies and touring, he had a very unfortunate attitude to maritime matters. 'Boats are like prison,' he complained, 'with the possibility of drowning.' He was relieved when I became a landlubber again.

When Scarlett became our second daughter to attend school in upstate New York, we moved to New York. Daisy was still enjoying her college experience there and we wanted to be closer to her. Cara had settled in Glasgow with her partner, Jonnie, and young son, while Jamie and Amy were enjoying independent lives in LA, so as new empty-nesters Billy and I could see no real reason to stay in California. We found a loft-style apartment in Manhattan and became residents of the city that never sleeps. Well, duh! Not if the constant sirens, over-amped, in-car sound systems and East Village party-goers have anything to do with it. After my maritime adventures were over, I did not immediately return to psychotherapy. I had planned to open a practice in New York at some point but, in the meantime, I accepted offers to do a few British TV shows – notably *Shrink Rap* in which I interviewed well-known people in a deep, psychological fashion. The programmes, which were shown on More4, were well-received and I was proud of them. In particular, I thought my interviews with Joan Rivers, Salman Rushdie, Sharon Osbourne, Stephen Fry, Carrie Fisher and the late Tony Curtis helped tell the truth, not only about who each of them truly was, but also about the state of celebrity generally – that it is traumatic, fails to meet expectations, and is essentially a hollow victory.

Tony Curtis spoke particularly movingly about many things he'd had to overcome in his life – prejudice, ridicule for his lack of formal education, and especially the death of his brother, who was hit by a truck at a very young age. It was hard to believe that a man could reach his eighties still erroneously believing that he had been responsible for a sibling's death, when all he had done was refuse to play with him that one fateful day. I felt so much compassion for him, and wished he'd had the opportunities I'd had to receive help and healing. As Thoreau wrote:

> The mass of men [and women and children] lead lives of quiet desperation.

Billy quoted that line to me well before I understood he was actually telling me something about himself.

In sharp contrast to Billy's jolly, extravagant parties, my own sixtieth birthday celebration in 2009 was a terribly lonely one in a grubby hotel on the seafront in Apia – not the nicest end of Samoa. The island had recently experienced the tragic loss of life in the tsunami that hit the southern beaches of Samoa – including several busy tourist resorts. In a horrid *déjà vu* of the LA earthquake, I had been rudely awakened in my pied-a-terre by a massive shaking that pitched me, whimpering, back and forth on my bed. That earthquake was rated 8.1, so no wonder I cried and screamed and, once more, thought the house would fall on me. I thought that early-morning quake was the end of the problem but, shortly afterwards, I learned about the enormous, freight-train of a wave that took so many lives. I drove down to the beach, saw that people were frantically searching for loved ones, and tried to help. The next few weeks were filled with mourning, funerals, making sandwiches and delivering them to medical teams. I was also asked to help both locals and visitors deal with the loss of family members, property and businesses, by providing grief counselling. Roughly 189 people lost their lives in Samoa, American Samoa and Tonga – and many of them were children.

That kind of crisis counselling is never easy . . .

It's especially hard to help parents through the loss of a child, because you put yourself in their shoes. People who were holding their child's hand one second, then searching for them after the wave swept them away the next tended to blame themselves: 'If only I'd hung on tighter!' But tsunamis can travel at seventy-five miles per hour. There was no way to save them. One father I knew who happened to be on higher ground actually witnessed his wife and daughter being swept away. Just terrible. I am still haunted by the sight of those two sweet bodies embracing each other in one open coffin.

Talking therapy tends to be easier when patients are fully articulate, so for youngsters psychotherapists often use non-verbal methods of helping them to express themselves. When I encouraged the smallest children I worked with – tots who had lost family members – to draw what happened from their perspective, their pictures were utterly heart-wrenching. They depicted themselves as tiny dots in a wild, paper-ripping scribble of a sea that engulfed the whole page. It really gave me a sense of just how overwhelmingly terrifying that wave must have been, annihilating so many villages; the whole nation was in an acute state of mourning.

After my birthday, I left Samoa, and I have not returned. I was both glad and sorry about that. Things had not gone well for me on that island. I had fallen in love with the place from the moment I first set foot on it. It felt like home. In its calm, welcoming villages; by its clear, green water; on its soft sand; in thatched *fales* fanned by cooling sea breezes; by its sweeping harbour, or under its peerless canopy of stars, I felt I could truly be myself. And the people there felt like family ... at first. But eventually I began to feel ... misunderstood ...

Well, that's a familiar feeling for you ...

I know. It was so complicated. I tried to be a good member of my adopted community, to be helpful to children with special needs, to families who had lost almost everything in the tsunami, and to a number of other groups who I felt were deserving of support, but I realized too late that, for most people, my white face carried with it a reminder of colonial oppression and I would never be accepted. I had tried to be culturally aware, but I made mistakes I was unable to fix – notably, my efforts to create a local language TV company utilizing and training local talent failed to thrive. Despite my many wonderful memories, friends and feelings about the place, it was time to leave. Waiting for my flight home to NYC on my birthday, I lay all alone on dirty sheets and, through my tears, watched the cockroaches roam around the floor. Even though I'd chosen to be there, rather than with family and friends, I (irrationally) wanted them close. 'Where's my party?' I sobbed, or rather, 'Where's MY party?' It was pathetic.

Licking my wounds, I returned to New York and almost immediately took off again for the Congo. I've already told you how brutal that was. And the fact that I had felt physically inadequate to protect myself sent me straight back to the gym when I got home, where a lovely but slightly sadistic trainer called Chad began to whip my body into something resembling fitness and health. Boy, it was hard. I felt terribly depressed about the loss of Samoa, and what I'd witnessed in Congolese rural areas. And, as ever, I struggled with my eating habits.

I tried to concentrate on my latest book, a psychological 'how to' called *Head Case*. I worked hard on it for many months, barely venturing out of the apartment . . . Well, I tell a lie. See, my adorable husband has no regard for peace and quiet. As a matter of fact, he doesn't seem happy unless he is surrounded by at least three noise sources. He will turn on the TV in the bedroom, then leave it on while he wanders out to the kitchen. He'll turn on the radio there, then leave it on while he picks up his banjo in the living room and has a good strum. And this is on top of the New York sirens, cars honking and NYPD helicopter noise pollution! So, much of my writing is done in my local Starbucks. Well, frankly, the ebullient NYU students, histrionic dancers from the NY City Ballet company, floridly hallucinating homeless people and amped-up drug pushers are a lot quieter.

Anyway, there I was in New York, trying to finish *Head Case* and every now and then, for a bit of relief in the evening, I'd switch on the TV. It was the season for the American *Dancing with the Stars* and I caught a few episodes. 'Wow!' I said to myself. 'They seem to be having a lot of fun!' I was envious. Not only were the stars enjoying themselves, but they were all losing weight and gaining physical efficacy so fast. Would I ever be fit? Would I ever feel happy again? I was so depressed I couldn't even imagine it.

I decided to seek the help of a famous weight loss doctor who had been recommended by my GP in Los Angeles. It was nighttime when I arrived at his plush Manhattan office – apparently he only sees patients after 5pm. I was ushered into his consulting room and sat waiting for his arrival in a soft armchair facing his desk. I looked around me. It was unusually dark in the room – I presumed that was a strategy to make people relax. Then I noticed something disturbing right in front of me. There was a dinner plate sitting on the desk, filled with . . . oh my Lord, was that . . . human fat? It was definitely fat of some sort – a huge mound of yellowy globular stuff. It had to be human. I was almost cured of over-eating right there and then.

'Pamela?' An apparition seated himself at the desk. Let's call him Dr Cadaver. The man's skin was shiny and white, and his face was weirdly immobile. 'Little too much Botox, perhaps?' I thought to myself. The only other time I'd ever seen that was when I first visited a dermatologist in LA and, with zero expression in his face, he told me he performed his own Botox treatment. Yes, people, he STUCK NEEDLES IN HIS OWN FACE! I ran screaming from that surgery, and I was considering doing the same this night. But Dr Cadaver's whole set-up was strangely mesmerizing. He liked to make motivational tapes for people, and mine was a beauty.

'Pamela . . .!' he boomed slowly into the microphone. 'You've sailed the seven seas. You've raised five children. You've reached the top of your career in three different fields. But you're LOSING . . . to a COOKIE!' It was so shocking, it actually worked. For a while . . .

I sought some proper psychotherapy, but found I couldn't talk with my therapist about the Congo. I still can't. The things I saw there, the stories I heard – I feel I can't burden anyone else with them. The abuse and cruelty – especially the particular style of it – is so extreme that it seems abusive just to discuss it. And then there's the sickening feeling that no one really cares. The Western world worries about Greece and saving tigers, while in that vast, war-ravaged, land-locked country in Africa the unspeakable is occurring and no one seems to give a toss. As a matter of fact, many people have much to gain by keeping things the way they are in the Congo – so it can be exploited for its precious metals and mineral wealth.

In the midst of all this, I got an email from the *Strictly* people. Would I take part in the show in the coming autumn season? My first thought was, 'I'm not a celebrity – why on Earth are they asking me?' But they seemed serious, and I began reasoning with myself that, even though it was entirely contrary to who I was now and could be very risky professionally, what I truly needed at that moment was some lightness in my life, some frivolity. So I continued to talk with the production team, discussing dates and parameters.

It was spring, 2010, Daisy was graduating from college and Billy and I were enormously proud of her. At her graduation ceremony she gave a fantastic, articulate speech, and it was a truly wonderful afternoon. Afterwards, I walked out into the car park, and had my scheduled phone meeting with Moira Ross, the *Strictly* producer. I decided during that conversation that I had nothing to lose but my sadness. 'I love dancing,' I said. 'I'm in.'

'You what!' thundered Billy. 'Pamela, beware. What are you thinking?'

'Well, what's the worst that could happen?' I replied. 'I'll be kicked out after the first week, but it would still be fun for a bit.'

'You'll make a total arse of yourself,' hinted Billy. 'You can't trust those reality show pricks.'

I ignored him and the other people around me who very understandably tried to persuade me that making such a move would be foolish, even dangerous, for my professional reputation. Perhaps I was listening to a deep intuitive sense that it would be OK. 'To be honest,' I confided in Sharon, 'I feel as if I've got very little to lose. I just . . . need something that's all-consuming, amusing, and physically challenging.'

'Of course, darling,' she nodded. 'Go have yourself some fun!'

'Have you had a do-it-yourself lobotomy?' inquired my pal Kathy Lette.

Chapter Fourteen

STRICTLY LOBOTOMIZED

I was still a big fat lump. Not a good way to approach the land of short, spangly mini dresses, cut-out midriffs, and sequined unitards. But I was continuing my gym workouts with Chad, my unrelentingly and savage trainer, so at least I was getting a bit fitter. And there was an Indian dance class taught in my local gym that I'd started to enjoy – Sarina Jain's Masala Bhangra – a combination of traditional, high-energy, north Indian folk dancing with Bollywood-style dance. Frankly, you wouldn't have wanted to witness me attempting those difficult, alien moves, but it was fun and kept my body in motion.

Anyway, just the thought of having to appear on TV in *Strictly Come Dancing* was enough to keep me off the *pain au chocolat*. I began to lose weight. It was actually nice to focus on my body in a positive way again, after so long. I had forgotten how good it makes me feel to bend and sway to music, to be lost in the rhythm. That had been sorely missing from my life, and when it came back I greeted it warmly, enthusiastically – like a precious old friend.

But my first day on *Strictly* was a disaster. It was the day when the entire cast of pro dancers met the celebrities for the first time. First of all, it was very uncomfortable being described as a 'celebrity'. I no longer thought of myself as one, and hadn't done so for many years. We all gathered with the production team in a large room and I absolutely froze. Since I lived in New York, I had no idea who anyone was, well, except for Patsy Kensit, Felicity Kendal and Paul Daniels, each of whom I'd met briefly before. I could only tell the pros from the celebrities by their muscle tone! But everyone else seemed to know each other – or at least they were doing that irksome thing of pretending they did. 'Showbiz personalities', as Billy calls them, create their own fake cocoon of camaraderie, in which it's all very jolly banter and first-name basis, even if you've never met. I simply couldn't – wouldn't – do that any more. I sat in a corner and watched with horror as people executed painfully obvious attempts to command the room's attention. 'Oh my Lord,' I said to myself. 'What have I let myself in for?'

But worse was to come. We began to rehearse for the launch show and, in the middle of the group number, I severely strained my back. I was in agony but, terrified I'd have to leave the show after only one day, I didn't tell anyone. 'Well, that's it!' I chided myself. 'You're going to have to stop already. What an embarrassment! You should have listened to Billy.' At lunchtime, the only way I could relieve that intense back pain was to sit very still in an upright chair. I secretly stuck some ice in the baggie I'd put my liquids in for my flight from New York, and wedged it against my back. I tried to camouflage my slow walk. At the end of the day I went to my hotel, iced the pain again, and tried to stretch out the muscles. I was a mess.

Heaven knows how I managed to continue. It was very stressful and I was tormented by how fit and accomplished – not to mention young – most of the other contestants were. Felicity was roughly my age, but she was fantastically thin, with gorgeous legs. And Kara Tointon was beautiful, thin, young AND a good dancer. Hmmph. As for the pro dancers – I had never seen so many beautiful, taut young bodies together in one room. Karen Bruce choreographed the group number with a lively sense of humour. Since 'the celebs' as – most embarrassingly – we were collectively known, did not know the names of any dance steps yet, she invented hilarious descriptions. 'Noo-noo wipe!' She'd yell when it was time to climb astride one of the boys' knees and do a sweeping back bend while he tried to stop you falling on your arse. 'Well, Pamela,' I chided myself. 'You wanted frivolity – and here it is, in its full, head-spinning glory!'

But there was way more to the show than dancing. I cringed when I was asked to do the promotional videotape segments and panicked about the press interviews. Oh, oh – I hadn't really thought that part of it through. In America I had been cushioned against the vicissitudes of press attention – and no one cared about me anyway – so it was a shock to be catapulted suddenly into the limelight again. Being on *Strictly* was going to mean I'd have to be witty and charming to people I didn't know or trust. Perhaps I should have just started social dancing – did I really have to be going the whole hog?

But, the wardrobe fittings were worth it all! Genius designer Su Judd took one look at me and, ever so kindly, dreamed up some forgiving ensembles. I had the feeling that most cast and crew saw me as someone whose time on *Strictly* would be extremely short-lived but, encouragingly, Su threw together some costume ideas for several weeks ahead, including an outfit for Halloween, which was a ball gown in the shape of a pumpkin. Neither of us could possibly have predicted that, by the end of October, I'd be jiving in a short, sequined mini with flames all around it!

Once again, you were an outsider, experiencing a completely new culture . . .

No kidding. I mean, how often in life generally are you expected to wear a microphone battery pack in your bra! The only way to even yourself up was to pad the other cup and pray you didn't look like Dolly Parton gone wrong. Those costumes looked fabulous but they were always so complicated to get in and out of. Damn! I always seemed to need to pee just before I went on and had to struggle out of the whole thing then back in again before I missed my entrance. And then there was the ubiquitous spray tan; since I'm from a sunny land down under – far, far away from Essex – I'd barely heard of such madness. And spray tans could be hazardous; fellow contestant Scott Maslen failed to contain both of his balls inside the protective paper g-string they give you and ended up with a two-tone sack!

Until the live launch show, none of us knew who our partners were going to be, although there was a lot of speculation, largely based on height. I hoped I'd get Robin Windsor – known as 'Bobby' to his friends. I was partnered with him a bit in the first group number and loved dancing with him. He was kind and accommodating, exactly what I needed. I also thought Anton du Beke would be a hoot, and Vincent Simone was very funny in his cod-seductive, 'Italian stallion' way. Brendon Cole was a New Zealander and very down to earth. I imagined we'd get on. Frankly, they were all adorable. As for James Jordan, I thought he was a serious hunk, with that edge of darkness that always gets me – and everyone said he was a fantastic teacher. But he stayed well away from me in those first days. In any case, I thought he'd be paired with Patsy Kensit. Jammy cow.

When Sir Bruce Forsyth – live on air in our launch show – announced that James was to be my partner, I could do no less than leap into his arms. Literally. My legs wrapped around his waist. Seriously, Pamela? A proper psychologist, a professor? Sexogenarian and mother of five? Was that really a good idea? Not to mention the potential back injury for my partner-to-be. What is WRONG with me?

And that wasn't the worst thing I did to him. When James turned up in New York to train me for two weeks prior to the start of the show, I met him at the airport on crutches. 'I broke my foot,' I lied. James was unimpressed by my practical joke. 'Then why the "f" did I get on the plane?' 'Oh, oh,' I thought. 'So that's how it's going to be.' Our first dance was to be the slow ballroom waltz. We started to train in a Manhattan studio with a large pillar in exactly the right place to seriously obstruct our routine. There is a charming training video of me cracking my head on it and James laughing. He turned out to be a very hard task master, but good fun as well. The two of us began to bond and I could tell he was relieved that I actually knew my left foot from my right. We met up with Billy at lunchtimes. James was a fan of Billy, but my husband had a stern word of warning about my new paramour: 'Pamela, never trust a man who wears such tight pants . . .'

When our first waltz routine was nearly ready, Billy came to watch. He settled in on a wooden bench and James started the music – the romantically lyrical 'If I Ain't Got You' by Alicia Keys. Within thirty seconds my husband started smirking. Next, he was shaking. He tried to cover his mouth with his hands, but pretty soon he was laughing openly and uncontrollably. I think it was the opening that got him, which was rather dramatic – overly so, Billy thought, with hands touching sensuously and soulful looks between us. But when James and I finally performed that waltz in the *Strictly* studio for a live audience – not to mention the fifteen million viewers at home – it went down a treat and earned high praise from the judges. 'You can't win *Strictly Come Dancing* week one,' said Len, 'what you can do is make a fantastic impression on everyone and that's what you've just done.' I was thrilled – actually really moved, almost to tears. No one had ever said such nice things about the way my body moved. In my lovely jade dress, gorgeous hair by Neil and Bryony's best make-up efforts – I felt beautiful for the first time in years. And something personally important happened to me during that waltz. I had been terrified before going out there but when we started, I felt utterly elated. Being in James's arms, whirling around to such romantic music performed by the brilliant David Arch band, transported me so that I forgot about the audience and became lost in the dance. It was utterly magical, ethereal. I couldn't wait for next week and the passion of the salsa – if I made it through to next week, that was.

As you talk about the Strictly *experience, Pamela, you sound alive, optimistic, passionate . . . Dancing connected you with a part of you that you'd lost for years . . .*

Yes. It was enlightening in many ways. But there was also the fact that being in the public eye again was a necessary part of the process – well, if I wanted to keep dancing with James and learning new dances I had to somehow manage to stay in the show – but at this point in my life that was very difficult. I was well aware that I had far fewer fans than any of the other contestants. Well, my career in popular TV had been so many years ago – would anyone even remember? But gradually, people who watched the show at home began to notice and support me. I'm not sure exactly why. Perhaps it was my age, the fact that this wasn't a career move for me – and, of course, James taught me very well so I was able to prove myself as a real contender. It was such a nice feeling to be appreciated. We relied on votes to get us through to the next rounds and I was terribly grateful that they were forthcoming. It was weird – I had an unusual sense that people liked me and wanted me to do well. That was different. And incredibly . . . healing.

One thing that particularly comes to mind about that experience is that it was most fortunate no one had expectations that you would do well – that must have been powerfully helpful . . .

Yes, absolutely. Well, at least that was true at first. But now I realize why it all became so much harder as I went on – suddenly people started expecting me to be good and get high scores every week, which meant it was very painful when I didn't.

How were you managing your anxiety at this point?

Well, it was strange . . . Other contestants were terrified to go out and dance live in front of all those people, and I'm not saying I wasn't just as scared – when that music started at the beginning I'd always feel like throwing up. But, after all the dangers I'd faced in my life thus far – including my most recent experience in the Congo – I was equipped to put it into perspective. 'Pamela,' I would say to myself, 'what's the worst that could happen out there? No one's going to point an AK-47 at you!'

And your partnership was essentially a positive one?

It definitely was in the ways that counted. I suppose I was a little in love with James. At least in lust. Well, he was the catalyst for amazing growth in me – not just into something of a dancer, but from a sad woman into an excited, vital one. I certainly fantasized about him – well, do you blame me? Every devotee of *Strictly* is a little in love with him. But that wasn't easy. Professional dancers are used to physical closeness. They are comfortable with shaking hands with a person one minute, then locking loins the next. But that is extremely challenging for the rest of us, and all *Strictly* 'celebs' struggle with it.

Unearned access to intimate knowledge of another person's body is a discombobulating thing . . .

Yes!

And the process of Strictly *– facing extreme challenges under terrifying conditions together – creates a special type of bond that resembles the 'falling in love' process . . .*

Absolutely! People get very confused about that. No wonder there have been . . . 'incidents'.

Unfortunately, my passion for James was unconsummated. Oh, don't shake your head like that – I'm just telling you like it was. Billy knows I 'liked' him. Just because a person is happily married doesn't mean they don't notice – and occasionally have feelings about – other people. You'd have to be sexually dead otherwise. I know, James has a gorgeous, adored wife to whom I believe he is faithful. But it was hard to deal with the constant physical proximity to such a perfect – not to mention flirtatious – specimen, and it lasted for around six months. For the first time ever, I regretted my high sex drive. 'A shag would be nice,' I complained one lunchtime. The crew gasped, and then guffawed. 'I'll buy you a vibrator,' he grinned. 'What, to add to my collection?' I sniffed. It was good to be able to exchange banter with someone on my own, edgy level.

As a dance partnership, we were good together. James was tough with me – sometimes too much so, I felt at the time, especially when I was exhausted – but I tolerated it and truly appreciated how much I learned from him – and how fast. In turn, he let me know he appreciated my efforts. 'You always give me one hundred per cent,' he would say. That was important to me, that he noticed. And I understood the way he operated. There was so little time to learn each different dance and create a new routine, so treating me with kid gloves would have been an unaffordable luxury. Oh yes, we did well. I'm particularly proud of our coolly passionate rumba, our savage *paso doble*, our cheeky salsa, our brazenly 'showbiz' quickstep and our highly athletic Charleston (my girls Scarlett and Cara turned up in the audience for that, and wondered if they'd have to dash out and administer CPR!). Then there was our Blackpool triumph with our American Smooth – heaven knows how we managed to pull off those lifts. I mean, James was strong but, even after all that dance training, I was definitely no feather!

But people noticed how much weight I was losing. At first I needed major undergarment support, and careful draping of my most unsightly parts – bingo wings, bulging tummy and saggy knees, for example. But gradually I began to notice lovely surprises, like suddenly I was comfortable in a pair of shorts – that hadn't happened for thirty years! I loved my new form. 'Body by James!' I crowed, and adored him all the more for helping me to feel so good about myself. After my salsa (yes, the one where I had a serious teeter after failing to recover properly from a floor spin), the clip appeared on YouTube, with all kinds of comments by men half my age: 'I'm only twenty-six,' said one, 'but I'd shag her!' Oh, yeah! That's what I'm talking about. Silly me for not understanding how the world works before – you throw on a low-cut red dress, twirl and show your legs, and overnight you're a MILF.

But as I said, people really got behind me, and that was incredibly gratifying. I noticed it properly for the first time after James and I performed our Viennese waltz during movie week, to that lovely song 'Unchained Melody' by The Righteous Brothers. It was actually my birthday and Sharon had come over from LA. I ended the number sitting on the floor and, just as the music ended, I came out of my trance and James helped me stand up. Suddenly, I was aware that everyone in the studio audience was on their feet. I looked at the people closest to me and they were looking at me with such sweet, approving smiles, it really got to me. I don't remember at any time in my life being so appreciated . . . so . . . liked.

That felt especially healing?

Yes, very much so. And people still come up to me and say how much they liked me on *Strictly* – it always feels so very nice when that happens. Sometimes they say, 'You should have won!' which is very sweet and supportive of them. Frankly, I was really thrilled just to make the finals. Of course I would have loved to receive the Glitter Ball, but I always thought it highly unlikely. I did, though, really want to do my best for all the people who had voted for me, who were hoping I'd win. In a way, I suppose I became a bit of a poster-child for people over forty, disabusing our society of the notion that people at middle age and beyond can't be vital, athletic, sexy and dance well. Don't get me wrong, it was very hard work. Like many others, I was carrying injuries. I secretly had knee surgery during semi-finals week but after witnessing the incredible stoicism of the pro dancers, I wasn't about to complain. James and I went on to do the *Strictly* tour, and then it was all over. Big let down, but I had to turn my attention to finishing my latest book *Sex Life*.

In just six months I had metamorphosized from a depressed, lumpy, burnt-out woman to a spinning siren cutting a rug with a sexy toy boy. Even my own, brilliant husband seemed more inter-ested in me. 'Eh, Pamsy, any chance you could bring that quickstep costume home?' No wonder there was a huge grin on my face. My experience on *Strictly* was far more than a triumph of weight loss and mood enhancement – although it was certainly nice that, after nearly thirty years together, Billy and I felt a renewed *joie de vivre* in our sex life! – no, more importantly, it reconnected me with all the good feelings I had experienced as a child when I went to ballet lessons and felt that it was my only chance to be truly me. I so much regretted giving it up all those years ago; if only I had kept dancing my entire life, how much happier I might have been. But I tried not to dwell on what might have been. I knew what I had to do now . . . Keeeeeep dancing!

Chapter Fifteen

DOES DANCING LEAD TO SEX?

But that was easier said than done. Now that *Strictly* was over, it was going to be much harder to dance. First of all, no James. Yes, I no longer had a partner, and what a loss that was! Declaring myself to be in love with Argentine tango, I went off to Buenos Aires to study and explore it. *Woman & Home* had commissioned an article about it, and for that I was to have some private lessons and attend as many *milongas* (tango parties) as possible. Oh dear. Little did I know what abject humiliation awaited me. You see, I thought I could do the tango fairly well – after all, James and I had danced a choreographed number to wild applause in the country's main arenas every night of the *Strictly* tour – until I attempted the improvised form. That's the trouble with simply following choreography, it lulls you into a false sense of security and talent. The social versions of the dances I'd learned on *Strictly* – salsa, cha-cha-cha, Argentine tango – turned out to be much, much harder.

With Argentine tango, I really had to start at the beginning – learning how to walk sensually and stealthily, caressing the floor with my feet. I made a start in Buenas Aires, but after I returned to

New York it took many months before I felt confident to move round the dance floor. Then there was the embrace – in Argentina they often dance very, very close, your head on a stranger's cheek – that was hard to get used to. No wonder tango's been called the eight-minute love affair.

They say it takes ten years to become proficient at tango. After nearly a year of pretty intensive lessons with fairly illustrious teachers, I could just about acquit myself reasonably well on the dance floor. But then I had to deal with the business of attending tango evenings and relying on the kindness of strangers. Right from the start, I found the rules of the *milongas* were very hard to follow and, frankly, they upset me. Well, they'd upset any self-respecting woman:

> You must never ask a man to dance. Wait until you're asked. He won't approach your table – smile at him first so he knows you're interested, then if he feels like inviting you to dance, he will jerk his head towards the dance floor. Stand up immediately and join him there. Even if you find you hate dancing with him, you must not excuse yourself until you've danced a whole *tanda* [at least three numbers].

Seriously?

I mean, God forbid men should have to face rejection! Yet women do, all the time. 'Men dance, women sit' is the saying, because there are more women than men at *milongas* and the females who get to dance are not necessarily the best dancers. Yes, believe it or not (!), they are more commonly the youngest and prettiest. Not fair. At the end of a danceless night, a woman will say in Spanish 'I ironed all evening', meaning that she sat all evening without being asked to dance. And me with my rejection issues – horrible!

One night I tested the rules and turned up at a *milonga* – one of the most famous in Buenos Aires – with three young women in their twenties who taught English in the city. All of them were beautiful and none of them could dance one step of tango. One of the girls, a tall, slender Polish beauty called Rula, was particularly gorgeous. She was wearing a very short skirt and a pair of backless, high-heeled wedge shoes – absolutely impossible to dance in. We sat at a table near the dance floor and waited. That very day a male Argentinean friend had been arguing with me about the *milonga* rules: 'Woman who dance well – even if they are older or less attractive – will always have precedence over a young, beautiful girl who cannot dance.' 'Interesting,' I said doubtfully. 'Let's see.'

Within five minutes of our arrival, a man approached our table. 'We can't dance!' chorused the three newcomers. 'But *she* can!' However, the man ignored me and made a beeline for Rula. 'I have never even tried,' she said, smiling. I was smiling, too, but my smile was more of a triumphant, bitter-sweet grin because my theory was being proved, right in front of my eyes. All right, there was seething anger underneath, but let's forget about that for a minute. This guy wouldn't take 'no' for an answer. He persuaded Rula to go with him and actually tried to move her round the dance floor. Now, this is an absolute no-no at a *milonga*. You are not – or at least that's what I had been told – allowed to give lessons on the floor. He was even interrupting the line of dance, for heaven's sake – other people had to navigate around them. Rula couldn't move at all – she was completely stuck – hampered by her footwear and also frozen in fear. I looked around at the crowd – EVERYBODY was watching. The women were absolutely livid – especially the ones who hadn't danced all night. As for the men, they were displaying a mixture of envy and disapproval – although, given half a chance, I suspect each and every one of them would have done the same thing. Then the unthinkable happened – the man realized he was never going to get the girl to dance, so he decided to toy with her instead. For the benefit of onlookers (he was now enjoying the attention), he subtly raised the back of her skirt so everyone could see her skimpy knickers. That's when I intervened. I dashed on to the floor and dragged her away in disgust. I don't speak good Spanish, but I believe what I did manage to spit out at the man was suitably crushing.

All right, my fury was certainly fuelled by the fact that I had done my fair share of ironing. Some nights were better than others. I imagined that *milongas* in New York, LA and London would be run on a more egalitarian basis, but no – male chauvinism is alive and well in every *milonga* worldwide. I eventually got the hang of the *cabeceo* – giving a man I wanted to dance with the right kind of inviting look – even though it made me want to throw up. To be honest, I didn't often see men I really wanted to dance with, possibly because I had been so spoiled by private lessons with some really wonderful dancers, Omar, Giraldo, Ollantray and Leroy. No one at the *milongas* came anywhere near them for skill and charm, so it was particularly horrible to feel relieved and grateful when someone downright unpleasant approached me. I even started feeling guilty whenever I danced because I saw women who were better than me sitting alone for hours. All that cruelty seemed terribly, terribly unnecessary. Even if I was the worst dancer in the world, was it really so hard for people just to be kind and welcoming?

Occasionally, one of the elite 'tango gods' would deign to invite me to dance. When that happened I would be so surprised I'd think he had mistaken me for someone else, or I would assume he'd felt obliged because the person who ran the *milonga* recognized me and insisted. Anyway, the end of my love affair with Argentine tango came one night at a New York *milonga*. Midway through a dance with one of those accomplished, elegant, pony-tailed hotties, he whispered in my ear: 'PamELa [he put the emphasis on the second syllable], would you like to have a sex a with a me?' Not: 'I want to have a sex a with a YOU.' There was a clear assumption that the answer would be a rather desperate: 'Race you to the taxi.' Now, firstly, that broke one of the *milonga* rules, because you're not supposed to talk on the floor. And, secondly, the way he was smirking, he clearly thought I was a sure thing. After all, by now surely I'd have had enough of sitting, ironing, hoping, praying. But, what? Was I supposed to be so grateful I'd got a dance that I'd do anything? Plus, I was pretty sure it would all boil down to a blow job in the cab. Over many years of having all kinds of fabulous sex, I've learned that, unfortunately, the term 'Latin lover' is often a euphemism for 'Worship my willy and make it snappy!' Did you know there's no word for cunnilingus in Spanish? See, I may not be twenty any more, but I do know I'm sexy and I can put my money where my mouth is . . . Or maybe it's the other way round? Yeah, I could have made him scream – if I'd felt like it. 'Listen, you little twerp,' I felt like saying, '*yo te vi nacer*! [That's Spanish for 'I saw you being born!'] You don't know who you're dealing with. I'm a PROFESSOR of sex; if I chose to, I could make you sit up and beg!'

Whew – I'll fall off my high horse in a minute, but seriously, it was the final straw. 'PamELa, would you like to have a sex a with a me?' 'No, thank you,' I replied sweetly, walking back to my table. 'The dance was bad enough.'

So, that's the truth about Argentine tango. Oh, you'll hear all kinds of glowing testimonies about how fabulous it is, how sexy, passionate and all the rest – well, that's only true in very special circumstances. Most of the time, women iron. And feel humiliated. If you want to decrease your self-esteem, take yourself to a *milonga*. Even the nice guys you might have got to know seem to feel obliged to ask you out of pity – the dance version of the 'mercy fuck'. Worst of all, women do not support each other in that environment because they are forced to be in competition with each other. I just couldn't enjoy a dance that made women feel so wretched.

Pamela, I've been listening to your rant as patiently as possible, and I do agree about the social injustice of the situation. However I do have to bring up . . . Well, you are aware that 'ironing' would be a little easier for women who do not have your rejection issues . . . ?

Damn! I knew you'd say that. And it's also the point where Freud and feminism part company. But I'm not going to waste time arguing, because I want to get to the positive part of my post-*Strictly* dance experience:

Thankfully, rescue was at hand in the form of a fabulous dance in which it was perfectly OK – in fact encouraged – for women to invite men to dance. Lambazouk is a Brazilian dance – originally the lambada (remember that famous song?) but it has now morphed into a more contemporary style. It's hot, passionate and thrilling – Dirty Dancing at its finest – as well as a great workout. Best of all, there's only one rule: you walk up to a divine Brazilian man and drag him on to the dance floor. Yippee! Brazilian men actually seem to adore and respect women. They're *kind*. And the women in that scene are nice to each other too. In lambazouk you dance close to your partner, wriggling your hips in a fast figure eight, and follow him closely when he leads you into ten perilous pirouettes, or waves your head round and round in circles until you have no idea where you are. It's the dance equivalent of the date rape drug, but I'm hooked. It's joyful and life-affirming, and what more could you ask for? Does dancing lead to sex? Or is it the other way around? Probably the latter, but only if you do it right. Sex, I mean . . .

God, I love sex. The real thing, I'm talking about, not porn which has replaced religion as the 'opiate of the masses'. I like jive, too, and West Coast swing. For those dances I frequent a little place near Madison Square Garden in Manhattan . . . Although, a young man once led me into a 'death drop' lift there and I broke my tit— Oh, that sounds familiar! Hmmm. Guess I'm almost right back where I started . . .

FORGIVENESS

Forgiveness doesn't come easy, but for the first time in my life, I may be ready. I've tried many times before. In 2003 I knelt in the graveyard in Russell, New Zealand, where my parents' ashes were interred. 'For God's sake, Pamela,' I harangued myself, 'let it go. Just . . . let it go!' But I couldn't. On that occasion I couldn't even locate the elusive pain. Oh, I knew it was there – I'd felt the effects for three decades. Somewhere inside me there had to be understanding. John Bradshaw put it in perspective:

> The love I learned about was bound by duty and obligation . . . I
> suggest that these cultural rules created a deficient form of love,
> and that even with the best intentions our parents often confused
> love with what we now call abuse.

I recognize that the hurt I sustained was not deliberately caused but, unfortunately, insight alone is never enough. More work was required. The first step was to risk connecting viscerally with my deep rage. That was hard until I learned that such a powerful emotion – the one I used to be ashamed of – is actually evidence of the courage and integrity of my inner child. Yes, now that I have fully felt the pain of that rage – its white-hot heat – I may at last be ready to cool off. Oh, please let that be true . . .

Strange that we measure fury and passion in terms of temperature; our emotions do seem to have that effect – 'My blood was boiling'; 'My face felt flushed'; 'Her heart was cold.' Even stranger, my mother spent much of her academic life studying the effects of temperature on the internal organs of small, bewildered beasties. 'Effects of temperature on tadpole hearts *in vitro*' was one of her published scientific papers. (I think that meant she actually removed the hearts, grew them in a Petri dish, and observed what happened when they froze or fried – what an awful job!) Another of her papers was 'Temperature and other environmental effects on ammocoete organs in culture'. When she paired up with my father they wrote 'Locomotory invasion of human cervical epithelium and avian fibroblasts by HeLa cells *in vitro*' and 'Invasive locomotory behaviour between malignant human melanoma cells and normal fibroblasts filmed *in vitro*'. (Well, who knew they were film directors as well?)

I don't understand how any of that work is connected to finding a cure for cancer, but I'm sure there was a substantial relationship. I wonder, did they manage to see the Gestalt of what they were doing, or were they – like many scientists – essentially so focused on minute details they were denied the luxury of the bigger picture? I dunno. I dunno. I must say, it's hard to get my head around what it must be like to spend many of your waking hours (for that's what they did) waiting for a tadpole's heart to melt. Perhaps that's why their own hearts seemed so . . . frozen?

My first therapist, Lu, called me a deprived child. That shocked me at first, but now I accept it as the truth. Outwardly, I have presented myself as a confident, powerful woman, but deep down it was a different story. With few signs of love or appreciation – even encouraging words – within the family, I did what all human beings do in such a situation – I grew up feeling deeply insecure, unworthy and full of rage, and I sought validation from others. It is a precarious and futile way to live one's life, and it can only lead to further profound disappointment.

In the past, I was always able to feel empathy for others, but not for myself. My need to feel understood, adored and loved – the right of every child, which was denied me – spurred me to find places in the world where I could, at least temporarily, achieve a sense of belonging. Initially, these were the public arenas of my career in show business, places over-populated by people imbued with longing, just like me. It wasn't until I embarked on my psychology degree that I began to have a first inkling of just how damaged I really was. But that took a long time to sink in. I was so alien to myself that I didn't even know that I didn't know who I was. Things I read – Alice Miller's wonderful book *The Drama of the Gifted Child*, for example – spoke deeply to me; yet at the same time my conscious mind was insisting, 'That can't possibly me?'

Worst of all, I must have unconsciously repeated some of the mistakes of my parents in my own parenting style; oh, I hugged and encouraged my children, and I told them that I loved them but, like my mother, I was . . . very busy. I just hope they can forgive me if I seemed . . . preoccupied. But isn't that the challenge we working women always face? All right, we give lip service to the appropriateness of 'having it all', but show me a working mother and I'll show you a guilt-ridden soul. Yes, recently I have actually come to reframe my mother's busyness as the challenges of a highly intelligent and capable woman trying to make her way in the essentially male scientific world. She was doing her Ph.D. when she had me, for God's sake. Back then, how many women did that? Would I have preferred a Valium-popping Stepford wife of a mother? Wouldn't I then just have internalized an acute sense of longing – of a different nature? And Dad – he was the product of a large, pioneering, multi-racial family, who undoubtedly had a less-than-satisfying portion of whatever was in the love-and-affection pot and never learned to express his feelings the right way. Yes, as my first psychology professor, Dr Joy Turek told me: 'It's not a matter of whether or not you're going to fuck up your children; it's a matter of *how*.'

On that cheery note, I'll say thank you for staying with me. I suppose it hasn't been easy. And if I've triggered thoughts about your own life, your own pain, I'm glad. In many ways, that was the point of it all. But I want you to feel hopeful, so here's the essential truth about raising children: if a child feels that she is loved for who she truly is – rather than for who her parents want her to be – she will be happy and feel safe in the world. Can you do that for your kids? OK, then. Thank you. I feel good now. Don't forget, will you . . . ?

In the evening of life, we will be judged on love alone.
Saint John of the Cross

Strange, my other, therapist's voice is quiet now. We are one. It's a relief she's stopped talking, analyzing. Just like my mother . . . Ahh . . . Are they one? Now that I no longer sense her expectations of me – that inner push, push, push I inflicted on myself – I can finally breathe . . .

But let's you and I revisit Brazil for a short while, walk calmly along the beach in Porto Seguro. The tourists are gone just now. The thump, thump, thump of the loud speakers are absent for a bit. You can even hear the breeze ruffling the palm fronds. It's low tide, and someone's out there, picking up sea-urchins. Hey, there's a shack selling *açaí*, that Amazonian energy berry, and am I just imagining it or is the sand dotted with large, round craters, the impressions left by scores of women with gigantic Brazilian bums – *bom dudas* they call them – proud manifestations of the fact that, for all the women in the world, body image is shaped by culture. The wind picks up and we break into a scamper. My thighs are flapping, my tummy is bouncing, but I no longer care.

And other important things have happened while we've been together – I've told you who I am. And you've formed your own opinion, which is your right to do. I wish I could honestly say that whatever it is, it's OK, that I don't mind ... But, well, I do, so be nice. What's more important, though, is how do I now see myself? Well what I always needed to see myself as – a survivor. And I've finally become a proud woman who has learned to value – far above all her achievements – her ability to be more at peace with herself. It's taken a long time, but ahhhh – I'm here. What is WRONG with me? At last I know the answer – hah! I never thought I'd say this but the answer is – nothing too terrible!

So, now, let's talk about you ... Who exactly are you? Yes, you ... I'm listening ...

Who are you?

Progress Notes – Dr P. Connolly

Patient has made a good recovery. In recounting, reliving and re-assessing her life – including previous trauma, illness and past treatment – there has been a positive shift in her self-perception. All too often, healing from childhood trauma, anxiety disorders, stress, eating disorders – in fact any kind of psychological challenge – can be a frustrating process of 'two steps forward, three steps back'. Fortunately, the patient has summoned the perseverance to continue the painful process of self-examination, and it seems to have paid off. She understands the role of risk-taking, extensive physical self-improvement, over-eating and compulsive care-taking in her life, and has learned how to manage them.

It has been healing for her to tell her story; after listening to others for so many years, the patient herself needed to feel fully heard.

She now self-identifies as a survivor, rather than a victim. This is a breakthrough.

However, although the patient does have considerable perspective on her parents' own circumstances, and can intellectually explain their abandoning actions – including what she experienced as a lack of love and understanding – she regrets that she has so far been unable to 'forgive' them. I say, 'forgiveness' is overrated. In fact, her continuing anger towards her parents is an unconscious means of staying connected with them. One day she will realize this and let go of her fury. That will be her moment to move on.

In the meantime, her rage serves certain useful purposes, such as fuelling her passion for adventure – which is, after all, essentially life-affirming. And it has facilitated the escaping of many yowling cats from an extremely large bag on which is inscribed 'The Varnished Untruth'. In view of this veritable plague of feline creatures, perhaps she should have called it (in reference to the quote on page 3) 'World Split Open'.

But perhaps not . . . I still hear a faint meowing . . .

Case closed . . . for now.

GRATITUDE

I'm grateful to all the women in my life. After experiencing my mother's coldness and envy, it took me time to learn to feel safe with women generally. But my girlfriends, especially Sharon, of course, but also Trudy, Michelle, Aly, Kathy, Tania, Sarah, Jo, Lizzie and many others, including Lu – my healer, mentor and guru – have taught me the things my mother was unable to teach – especially how to be a woman. And, just as importantly, they've helped me take myself less seriously. My daughters have shown me how wonderful it is to give and receive affection. And Martine, who has now worked for our family for twenty-six years, has been the best mummy a grown woman could ever have. As for Nanna and Auntie Sally – without them I might never have been able to feel loved or safe in the world.

I am grateful to all the men in my life – the goodies and the baddies – I have learned from each and every one. Andre, Paul, Steve, Dennis, Phil, Terry – as well as every one of my gay friends – have taught me that there are wonderful, kind and nurturing men in the world. As far as my lovers are concerned, yes, there have been many. I haven't used real names for the few I've mentioned in this book, because I think they would prefer to be anonymous, and I would certainly like them to respect my privacy, too. But the most profound learning in my life has often occurred via my lovers. Perhaps I only truly learn in the presence of someone with whom I share intimacy; for therein lies safety and ultimate acceptance. OK, eroticism is thrilling and powerfully life-affirming, but embraces are sweeter – and more healing. Thank you. Thank you. Thank you.

I was very lucky to meet Billy. He's been a rock, a sanctuary in my life, although many people – including me, early on – have imagined it was the other way around. But he has provided me with longed-for consistency of affection, and the closest thing to uncon-ditional love you can get past the age of five. Oh, he's also upsetting and infuriating sometimes, and a terrible curmudgeon. When he's on stage he talks about me behind my back – God knows what people know about me that I'm unaware of. And one day I really am going to throw that banjo out the window, I swear. But did you know he's now a visual artist as well as everything else he excels at? He does absolutely brilliant drawings. Proper scary stuff, actually; as dark as all good art should be. He thinks I analyse them, but I really don't . . . Well, not all the time . . .

As for my children – what wise creatures they are, all five of them. I asked each for 'bad Mom' highlights – expressly for your reading pleasure – and Scarlett, for one, sent quite a comprehen-sive list:

1. **Your habit of landing the plane from your airline seat, arms outstretched.** (Yes, I used to pretend I was flying the plane. Even when the girls were old enough to know I wasn't really controlling it from my seat, I still kept it up – to their . . . amusement? Horror? Mixture of both?)
2. **You showing up in curly green elf shoes to pick us up**

from school on St Patrick's Day. (Got that. See page 267.)

3. **You introducing yourself to my first college roommate as me when I was getting another box from outside. Needless to say, she was very confused.** (Don't even remember that. But a good wheeze, eh?)

4. **Your hope that my lack of boyfriends in high school was due to lesbianism. P.S. I'm sorry I disappointed you.** (Hah! Hah! Very true!)

5. **You and me getting chased down a very skinny path by a ram around the edge of the Grand Canyon when we were on that road trip – I think we were wearing the army helmets Neil purchased for us at the time.** (Oh yes! Neil MacLean is Billy's cousin, a hilarious man who lives in LA. And that ram really was vicious. But more of a mountain goat, methinks? Perhaps it feared we were a small army invading its territory?)

6. **You requesting that I do a hip hop number to Outkast's 'Rosa Parks' for Grandma when she was in the hospital, which I did.** (Now that's just plain weird. Did I really?)

7. **I needed a last-minute costume for my friend's birthday when I was about ten and you dressed me in all your clothes as Carol Channing, even though I had NO clue who she was. I was a huge hit with all my friends' parents, however . . .** (A thoughtful and creative parental response, I say.)

8. **You used to say I looked like the Gerber [baby food brand] baby, and for one of my birthdays you got me an enormous Gerber baby cake – VERY disturbing.** (Now, what's wrong with that? Don't make me use my CAPS LOCK to whip your ass!)

I also have plenty of lovely Mom stories. However, I assume that's not the angle you're going for . . . That list is much longer. Xxx (Awww! Love you, too!)

Yes, as I told you before, my children think I'm ridiculous, and they're quite right. I'd love to be a fly on the wall when they discuss me, to observe the eye-rolling complaints. They're old enough and smart enough now to second-guess me, and some may even try to parent me from time to time. I won't object. You can look after me, if needs be; just don't ever treat me like an old lady. I'll race you to the beach.

My Stairs

Just in case you're wondering, I do know I'm blessed, so please stop thinking I'm a spoiled, ungrateful bitch. Wherever I am in the world, there are seven stairs. Somewhere, anywhere. It doesn't matter – I find them. And I climb up and down in gratitude:

Up

1st stair	*Thanks for the love I receive and give*
2nd stair	*Thanks for my health and the health of my family*
3rd stair	*Thanks for the food, clothing, shelter – and many other gifts – my family and I receive*
4th stair	*Thanks for my friends – their love and support*
5th stair	*Thanks for all the fun and laughter in my life*
6th stair	*Thanks for my ability to grow and learn*
7th stair	*Thanks for my ability to be grateful*

Down

7th stair	*I let go of my anger*
6th stair	*I let go of my bitterness*
5th stair	*I let go of my hatred*
4th stair	*I let go of my envy*
3rd stair	*I let go of my distrust*
2nd stair	*I let go of my longing*
1st stair	*I let go of my pain*

THANK YOUS

Several kind people read the manuscript and offered suggestions that I mostly ignored, notably: 'Did you really have to make it all about you?' (Billy); 'Wish you could tell the real story. It'd make *Fifty Shades of Grey* look like *The Little Mermaid*' (Kathy Lette); 'The part of Sharon needs expansion' (Sharon). They had idiosyncratic reactions to various items, such as the masseur story: 'Take it out!' (Billy); 'No one's going to believe you didn't shag him' (Kathy); and 'You mean he didn't . . . ? Damn! I paid him $250 to get you off' (Sharon).

Fortunately, Carly Cook provided proper, helpful suggestions – as well as wonderful support – while Jo Roberts-Miller gave me sterner, detailed notes to stop me getting cocky. And Trevor Leighton made me look much prettier on the cover than I do in real life (and I mean MUCH!) – turn up at a book signing for a closer look; you'll soon see what I mean.

Right from the start, Kerr MacRae showed very kind enthusiasm for this book, and without him I would not have had the gumption to write it. He also dances a mean Scottish reel, which in itself makes him a superior human being. My agent Ed Victor took time out of his busy life to look after my interests. Thank you, Ed. No one likes to be interrupted when they're lying in a rosemary bath being hand-fed Bündnerfleisch by Nigella Lawson.

And I suppose I should thank my parents for being dead so I could complain about them. Hah!

Oh, stop it. Did I ever say I was nice?